ADVANCED FLY-FISHING TECHNIQUES

SECOND EDITION

The Lyons Press is an imprint of The Globe Pequot Press

Printed in the United States of America

10 9 8 7 6 5 4 3 2 1

Library of Congress Cataloging-in-Publication data is available on file.

Kreh, Lefty.
    Advanced fly-fishing techniques : expert advice from a master angler / Lefty Kreh ; illustrations by Mark Susinno.—2nd ed.
            p. cm.
Includes bibliographical references and index.
    ISBN 1-58574-338-0 (alk. paper)
  1. Fly fishing. I. Title
    SH456 .K74 2002
    799.1′2—dc21

2002003568

This book is dedicated to
Ev, my wife,
who for more than fifty years
has been the best friend who ever happened to me.

CONTENTS

INTRODUCTION

Why is it that a few anglers in a region always seem able to catch more fish than their friends? Throughout the world a small group of fishermen seem to have all the success. While they don't always catch a lot of fish, they rarely fail. And even when their catch is rather slight, other fishermen undoubtedly do worse. Some people would have you think that it's luck. But it's much more than that.

It's really a combination of things. The successful few know how to tie knots that are strong. They understand equipment, and they have the best tackle they can afford. More importantly, they know how to take care of it. For instance, consider the proper care of drags on reels. Almost all drags are composed of one or more soft and hard washers. When the adjustment nut is tightened to restrain an escaping fish, the softer washers are under tension. When the day's fishing is complete, the adjustment nut should be backed off, relieving pressure on the softer washers. But many fishermen disregard this simple maintenance step. And for days, weeks, and longer, the adjustment nut is under tension, slowly squeezing the life from the softer washers. This turns them into hard ones. Then when a fish tries to escape, the washers that are no longer resilient will release in jerks, not smoothly. This breaks the line, and the fish escapes.

Those few successful anglers also know how to cast. In fly fishing this is one of the most important facets of the game. These anglers have also accumulated a thorough knowledge of the various fish species and their habitats.

This book is an effort to outline the steps that it takes to become an advanced fly fisherman. An in-depth discussion of tackle should give most anglers a better understanding of the gear, and how to use it in different situations. I deal with casting in a new and different manner. No more of this nine- to one-o'clock stuff that people have been using for more than two centuries. Instead, I present a different concept that allows the angler to fish one day with a light 3-weight line for sipping trout, and a few days later to confidently and easily handle a 12-weight tarpon rod.

How to find fish, how to make the approach, and the proper lines and flies for various conditions are all addressed in detail. The superb drawings of Mark Susinno clearly illustrate these concepts. It is my hope and belief that, not only will this book bring you more pleasure from the sport, but you'll become a better all-around fly fisherman.

Tight lines, but not too tight!

LEFTY KREH

One

TACKLE

Most people select their fly-fishing tackle improperly. They start with the wrong premise. Usually they decide on a rod to buy, then a line to match it, then the reel they prefer, and finally the flies they will need for the fishing. Actually, the flies should be selected first. They determine whether or not you will be catching fish. For example, you could have a perfectly matched steelhead outfit that throws a heavy No. 4 fly across a big river. But that outfit would be nearly useless when casting small dry flies. And the perfectly matched light dry-fly outfit would be ineffective when casting to or fighting a sixty-pound tarpon.

First you should select the proper flies that will catch the fish in the environment you will be fishing. Chapter 5 in this book gets quite heavily into all types of flies, for all fish, from a smutting trout to a hungry sailfish. So for now please accept that it is the fly that should be chosen first and then the rest of the outfit.

Lines

Once the assortment of flies is determined, the next thing you need to select will be the line that will properly transport them. The major difference between fly fishing, spinning, and plug casting is that with the last two types of tackle, the lure is the weight that drags the line from the reel to the target. Flies are nearly weightless. Take a dry fly in your hand and try to throw it any distance—you can't! You need something to haul it to the target. That weight is a fly line—which can be likened to an unrolling sinker. Just before the stop on the backcast and the forward cast, the line is straight. On the stop, the line begins unrolling, transporting your fly to the target. While we say we cast a fly line, actually, we unroll it.

I think most fishermen know that there are four basic types of fly lines: level taper, double-taper, weight-forward, and shooting taper. To make things a little more complex, within these four tapers there are many variations. For example, the Cortland Line Company produces more than 350 different fly lines. Scientific Anglers equals or exceeds that number. Fortunately you won't have too much of a chore deciding which lines you'll need once you define the kind of fishing that you'll be doing.

Lines are given numbers from 1-weight to 15-weight, with the most commonly used lines ranging from 3 to 12. Approximately the first thirty feet of the line is weighed, and of course this must be matched to the rod for optimum casting. Most anglers have several different outfits, and each outfit will need a different weight of line to match each rod. Manufacturers usually furnish small labels that can be attached to the reel spool, indicating the line's weight or number. But these often fall off, or you may switch the line to another spool. There is a simple method of marking fly lines so that at a glance you know what line is on the spool—and its taper.

All you need for most lines is a black permanent marking pen. With a new line you will make identifying marks about a foot beyond the nail knot where the leader is connected. For the example, we will use a No. 8 line. Make a mark that indicates whether it is a 5 or a 1. A wide black mark that encircles the entire line—say ¾ inch in width—indicates a 5, and a 1 is indicated by a small ring around the line, no wider than ¼ inch. Thus an 8-weight line would require one wide mark and three narrow ones—5 plus 3.

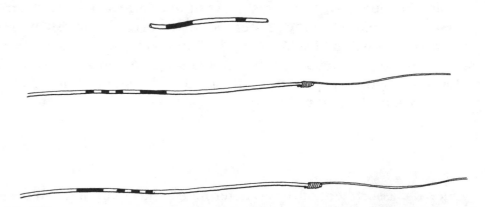

Most fly fishermen own a number of lines. Each has a designated weight, from 1 to 15. There is an easy way to mark the lines for identification with a permanent marking pen. Make a 1-inch ring around the line to represent 5 and a small ring to represent 1. Thus the markings at the top of the drawing represent a 6-weight line. Since weight-forward lines, as the name implies, have their weight concentrated at the forward end, I make a 1-inch mark nearest the leader, and the smaller marks behind this. Thus the line in the middle is an 8-weight, weight-forward. For a double-taper line, which has its weight concentrated in the middle, I make the small marks toward the leader and the larger one in back. The bottom illustration thus represents an 8-weight, double-taper line. Using this system will enable you to identify the weights and tapers of multiple lines at a glance.

To determine the taper is also easy. If the line is a weight-forward 8, place the wide black mark up front, closest to the nail knot, and the smaller marks to the rear. For a double-taper 8, I would place the three small marks forward and the big mark to the rear.

On dark lines where a permanent marker wouldn't show, you can cut small sections of shrink tubing (available from electrical supply houses), slip them on the line, and hold the line in boiling water for about fifteen seconds. They will be permanently fixed on the line, and they don't affect the line or its performance.

Let's first look at the tapers, and the advantages—and disadvantages—they possess.

Here the author demonstrates a long cast. Long casts are often necessary on big waters and with spooky fish. Note that the line flows straight to the target, with no sag.

Level Taper This is a line that is uniform in diameter throughout its length. It is the least expensive of all lines. The major disadvantage of this line is that it is difficult to shoot line with it. And because there is no diminishing of the taper at the front end, it tends to splash down to the surface near the fly heavily—often frightening fish.

There are two places where a level line works well. For the fly fisherman who casts a specific length of line or roll casts for short distances over and over, this line is excellent. For example, many anglers in the South who maintain the same distance from the shore and bug for bass will use a level line. It works well and costs considerably less than tapered lines.

The other situation where it is used frequently is when fishing a shooting taper, which most anglers call a shooting head. The shooting head is held outside the rod guides on the cast. Attached to the head is a much thinner, level line, which allows the heavier head to drag more line toward the target. This thinner line is called a shooting line. Very thin monofilament was first used for this purpose, but it has generally been replaced by the level shooting line. Most manufacturers make several diameters of level shooting line, ranging from about .027 to .038. The .027 has a breaking strength of about fifteen pounds, and being thinner, it is often used on lighter outfits where large fish are not being caught. For saltwater use and where strong fish may be encountered, distance is sacrificed a bit on the cast by using the thicker but stronger lines that can test as much as thirty pounds or more.

Double Taper This is a level line where both ends taper to a much thinner diameter. They taper identically on either end. Before modern fly lines were developed, double-taper lines had a finer end than a weight-forward and were often used for dry-fly fishing because they gave a slighter, more delicate presentation. But today a conventional double-taper and a conventional weight-forward have essentially the same taper.

The major advantage of the double-taper is that, being thinner at each end, the line casts easier than a weight-forward on a roll cast. During the roll cast the heavier line in the back more easily lifts the lighter line in front of it, so most anglers are able to roll cast farther. Another advantage of double-tapers is that mending line (lifting some of the line off the water and throwing a bow with it) can be accomplished easier with the heavier midsection of the double-taper. One other advantage to using double-tapers is economic. Since each end tapers identically, when one end becomes worn, you can reverse the line on the reel and use the other end. The major disadvantage of a double-taper is that it is difficult to shoot much line on the final forward cast. The heavy belly section resists being pulled through the guides toward the target.

Weight-forward This has become the most popular of all fly lines. It has a front section that tapers to a relatively fine end; behind this taper is a larger-diameter line that runs for about one-quarter to one-third the length of the entire line. This is commonly referred to as the head. Then there is a rear taper that ends with a long rear section—a rather thin level line. This thinner portion is often called the running line. The concept is that if the heavier head is held outside the guides on the cast, it can easily drag much of the thinner running line when released toward the target. Thus, you can retrieve fairly close, pick up the fly, make a cast, and shoot line a considerable distance. The weight-forward is the workhorse of all lines, and for almost all fishing situations is the single best all-around line.

The major disadvantage of a weight-forward is that because the head is heavier than the running line, most anglers find that they have difficulty making the thinner running line pick up and unroll the heavier head toward the target on a standard roll cast. It is also more difficult to mend on a long cast with the thinner rear portion of a weight-forward.

Shooting Taper or Shooting Head This is a line with a heavy front section (most commercial shooting tapers are about thirty feet long) that is attached, usually with a loop, to a considerably thinner line. This thinner line is usually called the shooting line, which is really a rather thin, level fly line. There are a number of diameters of shooting lines, ranging from approximately .027 to .038. While many anglers prefer to loop different heads to the shooting line, I prefer to connect mine differently. Loops, unless skillfully made, tend to hang in the guides. Most heads are constructed with a loop at the rear of the line. The shooting line is knotted or looped to this. This can be an advantage. The angler can carry a variety of shooting heads and can quickly change heads to suit existing fishing conditions.

To connect any shooting line but monofilament, I splice the head to the shooting line with a five-inch section of hollow line called Cortland Braided Mono Running Line in fifty-pound test. Insert the shooting line halfway inside the braided line. Then whip-finish or nail knot the very end exiting the braid. Repeat the process by inserting the shooting head into the other half of the braided line until the shooting line touches the head. Whip-finish the end of the braid. Then coat *only* the whip-finished area to keep the ends from coming apart. I prefer Pliobond, a rubber-based glue. The braid acts like a Chinese finger trap and will grip the head/shooting line securely. But if you glue all of the braid you will lose the Chinese finger tension and have a weak connection. This connection allows the line to flow smoothly in and out of the guides, much like a weight-forward fly line.

A major disadvantage of the shooting head is that it is nearly impossible to extend much more than a few feet of the shooting line outside the guides while false-casting. This thin line is so weak that when the tip is stopped on the cast, the line won't unroll and carry the heavier head. Instead, it collapses. If you are retrieving a fly and you see an opportunity to make another cast, you can't simply lift a lot of the shooting line and the head from the water and make your backcast. Instead, you have to re-trieve back to near the head, then make your cast.

The major advantage of a shooting head is that the angler can cast far-ther than with any other fly line. This allows for searching a great deal more water with the fly.

Shooting heads are made with every kind of fly line, including floaters, intermediates, fast sinkers, and even lead-core trolling line.

The shooting line is usually a specially made line sold by Scientific An-glers, Rio, Airflo, or Cortland. Many anglers are now using braided leader butt material in about twenty-five- to thirty-pound test. What makes a poor shooting line is monofilament—of any kind—although many people use it. Mono has several disadvantages: If you lay it in a boat or on the beach, during the cast it tends to blow all over the place. Because mono is so light, when you make a backcast and release the swift-moving head, it is traveling so fast that it often lifts all of the monofilament at your feet in a single motion, jamming it against the guides in a big snarl. Level shoot-ing lines and braided leader butt material rarely tangle on the shoot.

However, monofilament shooting line offers fewer troubles if it is kept wet. When dry, it tends to stick together, creating problems. By using a sponge and wetting down a boat deck where the line is lying, or keeping the line wet, the angler vastly reduces the problems associated with monofilament. A Line Tamer (a commercial product you strip line into while fishing) will help greatly with monofilament, especially if you place a small amount of water in the bottom. The best size monofilament for heavier lines (7-weight or larger) is twenty-five- to forty-pound test, with thirty-pound a good compromise. For fly lines lighter than 7-weight, twenty-pound monofilament works well. Special monofilament shooting lines that have less coil memory are made by various manufacturers and are recommended.

A major advantage of using monofilament shooting lines is that they are much thinner and have considerably less resistance in the water. When you need to get a fly (such as a lead-core head on the saltwater reefs, or a fast-sinking head to freshwater trout, or stripers well below the surface of a lake), monofilament will allow the line to sink much deeper in a shorter period of time. Monofilament, because it is so thin, is also hard to hold in your hands and will often cut your flesh when fighting truly big fish.

Types of Fly Lines

For many years, only floating lines were made. These were lines with a braided core that formed the shape of the line. Lines are no longer made that way. Modern lines also have small hollow glass balls imbedded in the outer coating that help support the line on the surface.

Slow-sinking lines, medium-fast-sinking lines, fast-sinking lines, and lines that really bomb toward the bottom have been developed. Tungsten dust is usually imbedded in the coating and determines the sink rate.

In the late 1960s Shakespeare introduced a line that was ahead of its time—made from all monofilament. A coating of clear monofilament was constructed on a solid monofilament line. Such a line offers low visibility to the fish. This line was relatively stiff and slick, and you could cast farther with it. Because the core was weak, anglers finally rejected the line. Modern manufacturers have solved that problem and gone a step further. They are using a braided core over which a monofilament coating is constructed. This results in a strong line that has reduced memory and shoots very well.

Monofilament not only casts better but also is less visible to fish. This is especially helpful when the angler is casting to a school of tarpon, where the line may spook the fish. If an over-cast is made with a conventional line, generally the tarpon will flee if the line moves through them. But on numerous occasions I have seen the fish ignore a monofilament line. Since the line is clear, shorter leaders can also be used, increasing the angler's ability to make a good presentation to tarpon—especially in the wind.

Most monofilament lines sink rather fast. They descend somewhere between what is called an intermediate or slow-sinking line and a fast-sinking line. Since many fish, when swimming through the water column, rarely will drop down to take a fly (but will rise to one), the angler has to time his cast so that the line lands and the fly sinks to the fish's depth, but not below it.

Remember, if you tie a Conventional Nail Knot on most monofilament lines, it will probably slip off during a fight with a large fish. The knot will strip the coating from the core and slide free, losing your fish. One of the easiest ways to connect backing and Leader to a monofilament fly line is to make a Whipped Loop. (See chapter 7.)

Most anglers, when casting a weight-forward line, have a particular length of line outside the rod tip that they can easily pick up to make the backcast. Picking up too much usually results in a poor backcast; picking up too little means extra false-casting may be needed. With a monofilament fly line, it is difficult to determine when you have the correct amount of line outside the rod tip for a backcast.

You can use a nail knot to help you solve this problem and to catch more fish. I suggest using eight- or ten-pound test monofilament for this purpose. You need to install the nail knot on the line so tightly that it nearly buries itself in the line. Then clip both ends short and smooth.

It is often advantageous to have a nail knot located at some point on the fly line. For example, different casters prefer to have different lengths of line outside the tip-top to pick up for the backcast. Also, when fishing at night, you often cannot see the line well, if at all. Strategically placed nail knots allow you to tell by feel where you are on the fly line.

To determine where to put the nail knot, go to a lawn, or better yet to a pond or stream, carrying with you a permanent marking pen. By making a number of backcasts, you can determine what is the best length of line for your pickup. Make a mark with a permanent marker, and install a nail knot at this point. Now all you have to do is concentrate on fishing and retrieving line. When stripping in line you will feel the nail knot—and know that it's time to make a backcast.

You can do the same thing when roll-casting. Install a knot where it is best for you to make a good cast. If you fish at night for trout in one or two pools from a specific position, establish during daylight how much line you need outside the rod tip to drop the fly exactly where you want when standing in position in the stream. Then install a nail knot. Now you can cast accurately in the dark.

For most anglers, a weight-forward floating line will suit the largest variety of fishing situations. A floating line offers a number of advantages. The most important is that it remains on or close to the surface, allowing the angler to easily lift the line from the water for a backcast. Because it floats, you can fish your flies in very shallow water, reducing the chances of the fly snagging on the bottom. If you need to fish in water as deep as six or seven feet, and there is not too much current, you can employ a floating line effectively if you lengthen your leader to ten or twelve feet and use weighted flies.

A disadvantage to a floating line occurs when fishing waters where the surface is cluttered with floating grass or weeds. During the retrieve, any grass that lies under the floating line is "funneled" down to the leader and fly, spoiling the presentation. When this occurs, a slow- or fast-sinking line is recommended. If the line falls over a piece of grass, the line tends to sink, and unless it is caught in the direct middle of the grass, the vegetation will slip off as the line goes beneath the surface. Another disadvantage of floating line that is not generally recognized appears when you are retrieving an underwater fly and there is a chop on the surface. Here, your fly is swimming quite differently than you may think. Each undulation of the waves causes the floating line to undulate. It would be similar to you holding one end of a rope that lay on the floor and then rocking your hand up and down. The other end would jump all over the place. In choppy water the angler loses some retrieve control.

Floating lines are also often more difficult to cast into the wind, because they are larger in diameter and also are more buoyant against the air. When you are forced to cast constantly into the wind, a slow- or fast-sinking line will often allow you to cast easier and farther.

Steelhead anglers know that the fish will hold at a certain depth in a river. Offer the fly too high above them and they refuse it. Use a line that sinks too quickly and the fly will snag on the bottom. There are floating, slow-sinking (sometimes called intermediate), fast-sinking, and extra-fast-sinking lines; all of these lines can be used under different conditions. Selecting a line that works at a specific depth is critical to steelhead success.

One of the keys to catching giant tarpon is to wait long enough so that you can clearly see the fish and the fly when it is presented. This means rarely casting to a tarpon that is more than forty feet from the boat. Special tarpon taper lines have been developed; these have a short front taper and head, allowing the angler to get into action with a minimum of line outside the rod tip. Similarly tapered lines are available for bonefish. But unlike tarpon fishing, angling for bonefish often requires long-distance casts. It is well to remember that any weight-forward line where the head is very short (such as saltwater tapers, bug tapers, and tarpon and bonefish tapers) when casting acts much like a shooting head, making it more difficult to deliver a good, long cast. During false casting the thinner running line behind the heavy head does not unroll as well as the thicker running line on a conventional weight-forward taper. If you are a better caster, I suggest fishing for bonefish and bass with a standard weight-forward line.

A special fly line—one that is extremely useful in tarpon fishing and has great application when fishing anywhere that the angler doesn't want the fish to see the forward end of the line—is one with a clear monofilament tip attached to a standard weight-forward floating line. The clear section is about fifteen feet in length. Add a leader to this and you have more than twenty feet of clear line and leader that allows the angler to present the fly to the fish and reduces the chances of spooking the fish.

Usually, a sinking-tip line has approximately the first ten feet that sinks, and the remainder of the line floats. You can modify this line for certain kinds of fishing; the modifications will greatly enhance your success. By cutting the first five feet from the forward end (you now have only five feet that sinks), you can do things with this line that you can't with any other. Because the sinking tip is now much shorter, you can make better backcasts under overhanging limbs. This allows you to place your fly in areas where other anglers can't, unless they have modified the line. Another neat trick that can be performed with this line is to attach a popping bug or deer-hair bug (one that floats) to a leader about eight feet in length. If you make a cast and begin retrieving as soon as the bug hits the water, the sinking front of the line does not have an opportunity to pull the bug beneath the surface, so you can retrieve as you would with a floating line. But if you pause, the weighted sink tip pulls the bug slowly below the surface. The longer you wait, the deeper the bug descends. Start retrieving and the bug begins to swim upward, finally breaking the surface and popping and gurgling on top as the retrieve continues. This often draws strikes because the bug works the surface noisily, then swims below, pops up, and repeats the whole procedure.

There is a major advantage to a weighted line over a floating one when retrieving underwater flies, especially streamers. A full-sinking line tends to pull the fly at a constant depth throughout the retrieve. A floating line tends to lift the fly every time the angler draws it tight. Between stripping motions, the fly tends to descend a little. This means that it is much more difficult with a floating line to get a fly down and swim it at a desired depth.

Floating fly lines will ride on the surface as long as they are clean. When their surfaces get clogged with dirt, this causes them to sink. Many anglers add a cleaner, but often this cleaner is a greasy material that floats the line for a short time, then, because it is greasy, collects more dirt. Soon it becomes even more difficult to make the line float. The proper treatment to make a line float is to clean it properly. With older fly lines the best cleaning treatment was to use Bon Ami or a mild scouring powder on a soft cloth. This removes everything from the surface. But many modern fly lines contain a thin, slick lubricant that makes them slide through the guides easier, giving you more distance on the shoot. Bon Ami or other coarse scouring substances will actually polish this coating from the line, detracting from its performance. *Never use detergent, for it will remove some of the valuable lubricant from the line.* To properly clean a modern fly line, immerse the line in warm water that has a mild liquid soap (*not detergent*) in it. Gently wash the line with a sponge or an old piece of terry cloth. It is vital to good line performance, however, to rid the line of all that soap after you have removed the dirt. Rinsing the line in cold water and drawing it through a damp cloth a number of times removes the soap.

Reels

There are several different kinds of fly reels. The automatic style, rarely produced today, was really not suitable for most fly fishing. Another type has gears that, with one turn of the reel handle, cause the spool to revolve several times. Gears are often weak in such reels, and some fly fishermen feel it gives an unfair advantage to the angler. Fortunately, such reels have lost favor among most fishermen.

The two basic reel designs commonly used today in salt water are the slip-clutch (sometimes referred to as anti-reverse) and the direct-drive. With either model the spool will make one complete revolution when the spool handle makes one full turn. From a design standpoint, generally a direct-drive reel has stronger gears and is better suited to fighting very large fish. A slip-clutch reel means that even if the fish is pulling line from the reel in an escape attempt, the angler can continue to turn the reel handle, although no line will be recovered. The flaw in this design is that many times the angler wastes energy turning the reel and retrieving no line.

The direct-drive reel is considered by many experts to be the best choice for fighting larger fish, especially in salt water. With a direct-drive you know exactly when you are recovering or losing line. If you are turning the handle, you are putting line on the spool. Many accomplished anglers feel that this is an important point. They don't waste any energy, and they know exactly how much line they are getting back from the fish. The disadvantage to a direct-drive is that if you hold onto the crank when the fish is running, you can easily break the leader. And there is another important consideration for those who work with their hands, such as musicians and surgeons. With a direct-drive reel, any time the fish pulls line from the spool, the reel handle is going to revolve. Failure to let go of the handle means the leader will break. If you do let go, and that whirling handle strikes the fingers, they can be badly bruised—or even broken. Just about everyone who has used a direct-drive reel and fought a fast-running fish has been rapped severely on the knuckles when the fish flees. I feel that all direct-drive reels should have only one handle. It's easy to locate during the battle—and it cuts in half the number of times your fingers will get banged if you fail to let go in time.

The shape of the reel handle is important. I believe that a direct-drive handle should differ from a slip-clutch handle. With a direct-drive reel, the angler must release the handle instantly if a fish surges away, taking line. The quicker the handle is released, the less chance of breaking the leader or having the whirling handle strike the fingers. And the smaller the handle, the less likely you are to be struck by it. For that reason I feel that direct-drive reel handles should be smaller than most of them are, and that they should be tapered so that the smaller end is away from the reel. This allows the angler to get rid of it easily. The handle should be no longer than one inch. Admittedly, this makes it a little more difficult to grasp the handle when cranking in line—but I feel that the benefits outweigh this disadvantage.

Slip-clutch reels are very popular. First, they are more forgiving and easier to use with little experience. If the angler continues to crank on the handle when a fish is pulling line from the spool, the only harm done is that the angler is working for nothing. Second, there is no worry about cranking against the surging fish and breaking the leader or bruising the fingers. For slip-clutch reels, I favor handles that are larger and easier to grip. The best handles are perhaps those that are slightly flattened and scored or roughed, allowing you to firmly grip them.

Actually, anyone skilled with both kinds of tackle can fish as well with a direct-drive as with a slip-clutch. Proper fish-fighting technique requires that you pump large fish by raising the rod and reeling in only as you drop the rod tip toward the fish. The best fish-fighters control the line not only with the drag, but also with the fingers of the hand holding the rod. The fingers trap the line against the rod blank during the upward pump with the rod. Then the fingers relax as the rod is lowered, and the released line is spooled on the reel. It makes little difference whether you use a direct-drive or slip-clutch if you know how to control the finger that traps the line.

Another misconception began with trout fishermen: which hand you should reel with when fighting a fish. Many trout fishermen will cast with their right hand and reel with their left. They do this because they don't have to change hands when fighting a fish. That's fine for trout, where reeling in line is generally a small effort. But when a steelhead runs off 150 feet of line, or a bonefish or offshore saltwater species takes twice that amount of line or more, the situation drastically changes. First, during the heated run, you have plenty of time to switch the rod to the other hand—that is not the problem. Your "reel" problem is that you are going to have to recover all that line—and often very quickly. While a few anglers who have for many years used their off hand to crank a fly reel may do well, the average person will perform a great deal more efficiently if he does this with the hand he works best with. That means that a right-hander will do best to reel with the right hand. Part of the problem is that a fly reel handle revolves in a very small, tight circle, and this makes it difficult to retrieve at high speed. The average right-hander who uses the right hand to recover line with a spinning reel is turning the handle over a larger diameter—something much easier to do than with a fly reel. When you turn the handle on a spinning reel, the spool revolves four to five times—not so with a fly reel.

The drag on a fly reel is rather important. No satisfactory reel used in fresh water will have such a light drag (or click tension) that it overspins and backlashes when line is pulled quickly from the spool. The drags that have certainly stood the test of time in salt water on hard-fighting fish are those with a cork ring (often impregnated with some other material) that is pressed against the inner face of the spool during the battle. Reels that have a series of washers contained in a small cavity within the reel tend to build up heat in the cavity, and the smaller washers often erode faster in the heat of battle. That is not to say that other types of washers are poor performers. But experience certainly has proven that the cork washer works extremely well over long periods of time. What is important, regardless of the type of drag used, is the rate of adjustment. Any drag that goes from off to full force in a short motion (by either turning a small adjustment knob or flipping a lever) is liable to get the angler in trouble. When distracted by a fighting fish, the angler can easily establish too much drag and break his leader. Good drag adjustment nuts or levers allow you to move through a relatively long span from off to full drag. Another important factor to consider on any fly reel is that the drag works only when the angler is recovering line. There are a few fly reels where the drag resistance used to fight the fish is on all the time. This means that the angler must overcome this force when he is reeling in line.

Nearly all fly reels have a drag composed of one or more soft and hard washers. Such a drag works well only so long as the soft washer or washers remain soft. Should they harden, the drag will be erratic and the leader will probably break during a fight. It is extremely important to release any drag tension at the end of each day's fighting. *A drag with the nut left screwed down for long periods of time slowly squeezes the life out of a soft washer. In time it will harden, and the drag will be ruined.* Actually, any reel—from a delicate fly reel through spinning, plug casting, and offshore trolling models—should be stored with the drag relaxed to protect those soft washers.

If the reel you have has no drag washer—only a clicker—you may be able to modify it slightly to get a really good drag. With reels such as the rather inexpensive Pflueger Medalist, you can do some work on the reel to give you an excellent drag. Remove the spool and cut a section from the backplate that you can easily slip the end of your finger through. Smooth the edges and paint the plate. Reinstall the spool. When a fish wants to run, you can restrain it by simply applying pressure against the inner face of the spool through the hole you have cut. In fact, you can put on so much pressure that the leader can snap—so take it easy! The spool, as on the Medalist, may have a series of holes in it, and you'd think this would hurt the fingertip when using it for drag pressure. But it really doesn't.

Here's another neat trick that results in a fine drag with a rim-control reel. Cut from an old belt (styled for men) a piece of leather that resembles a paddle. The leather paddle should be about the size of a penny—no larger. The handle for the paddle should be about a half inch. Lash the handle to one of the braces between the two reel side plates in such a manner that the paddle itself sits over the rim portion that you would normally push your fingers against to restrain a fish. Now, instead of using fingertip pressure, you can press against this small leather paddle. If the fingertips or palm is used on a rim-control reel that is revolving as line peels off the spool, the skin, which is damp at the start of the run, will dry

You can make an excellent drag for a rim-control reel by lashing to a cross brace a leather tab from an old belt, shaped as shown here. This will allow you to exert pressure on a fast-running fish without burning your fingers.

under friction. This can change the drag ratio. But the leather allows a constant, smooth drag.

Spool width on fly reels is something that should be considered, too. The wider the spool, the more troubles can accumulate for the angler, especially if a large fish is hooked. As line is recovered, it must be wound in a level manner. Too often during the heat of battle this is forgotten: Line piles up on one side of the spool, and then begins slipping to the other side. This often results in the line jamming in the spool and the leader parting. Narrow spools eliminate this problem. Trout fishermen who fish small streams and move from pool to pool to cast their offerings do a lot of reeling, although they may not realize it. Each time they leave one pool to walk to another, they wind in the line. Yet many trout fishermen prefer very tiny reels, with spool diameters of less than 2½ inches. Such small spools demand that you turn many revolutions to recover any line. Fly lines tend to take the position in which they are stored. Thus line pulled from a reel with a small spool comes off in tight little coils that interfere with fishing unless removed. I prefer trout reels with a spool diameter of at least 3½ inches: If the spool is narrow, it can have a large diameter and still be as light as a tiny, wide-spool model.

Reel Care

Fly reels need very little care, but that small amount means the difference between one that will give years of service and one that fails—often during a fight. If reels have only a spring click that acts as a drag, then you need only place a small amount of grease on the spring to ensure that it will last a long time. But if there are any soft drag washers, you need to back the drag off at day's end. If the drag is a cork-type washer, almost all reel manufacturers have their own special lubricant, which they will supply upon request. Place a small amount of the lubricant on your fingertip and rub it well across the surface of the soft washer. Remove any excess with a dry fingertip. You don't want to add too much of the lubricant—just apply a smooth, thin film. Treated in this way once a year, such a drag will remain in good condition for years, even under hard fishing.

The shaft of any reel should be lubricated with a thin film of grease. Oil is okay on freshwater models, but under a series of hard runs, I've seen the oil disappear. Thin grease holds up better. The reel handle may get dirt or grit inside the shaft and won't spin. Remove the handle, grease the shaft lightly, and reinstall.

The greatest concern about how to care for reels is among saltwater anglers. Almost all manufacturers tell you to use a warm water spray or warm water on a sponge to wipe off the reels. Cold water doesn't take all the salt away. Use warm water mixed with a bit of liquid soap. Use an old toothbrush to clean any areas that you can't easily wash. The two places where salt will collect are the reel foot and wherever there are screws—which includes the handle.

Actually, many freshwater reels, if cared for after every trip as described earlier, will usually last a long time in fresh water. I have several Hardy reels that have seen service in salt water for more than twenty-five years. The finish is a bit marred, but the reels still work perfectly.

Rods

Selecting the proper rod for your kind of fishing will mean the difference between endless days of enjoyment and endless frustration—and often broken tackle. Buying a more expensive rod will not make you a better caster—only learning to cast will do that. But there are good reasons why the top manufacturers' products cost more. Simply put, some rods will outperform others designed for the same purpose—if the angler is skilled enough to utilize the better rods.

There are basically three categories of fly rods: those used for trout fishing; those used to cast flies a longer distance or buck the wind; and those that are mostly fish-fighting tools. Most rods fall in the first two categories.

Most fly rods that trout fishermen use will range from seven feet, six inches to nine feet in length. A few people advocate very short rods, those from five to six and a half feet in length. However, almost no rods this short are manufactured today, simply because anglers have found them to be inefficient. They certainly are not more sporting, because the shorter the rod, the more leverage can be applied against the fish during a fight. Boat rods for tough-fighting billfish and tuna are always short, and no experienced offshore angler would consider fighting a powerful tuna or marlin with a long rod. Short rods do work well where fishing is done in what I call "tunnels." These are very small streams where brush overhangs the streams so that your casting is severely restricted. However, if on a small stream you occasionally run into such a situation, you can reduce the rod's length by simply sliding the casting hand up near the butt guide and placing the butt section behind your back; as soon as the cast is finished, slip the hand back on the rod handle to fish out the retrieve.

If you fish dry flies on small streams that are fairly open, a seven and a half to eight-foot rod is a great tool—although a nine-footer serves well, too. The shorter rods will allow you to tuck a cast more easily back under an overhanging branch. But if you are going to use dry flies, streamers, and nymphs, a nine-foot rod will be much more efficient. The longer lever allows you to roll-cast easier and to manipulate the line and fly much better than a shorter one. There are very few cases where a rod longer than nine feet will be a better tool for the trout fisherman who uses dry flies or fishes small streams.

The trout rod should be delicate, but a little on the soft side (not too stiff and powerful), and throw a line from size 1 to 6. Too many people, when selecting a trout rod, take it out and test it by trying to throw seventy-five feet of line. This tool will be used to make average casts from twelve to forty feet, and you want the fly landing gently on the surface. Some of the modern fast-action-tip rods can handle the entire fly line on the cast—but they are so quick that I feel they do not make ideal trout rods.

The second category of rods is designed mainly to transport flies over long distances. Such fishing situations include driving bonefish flies into a breeze, throwing a wind-resistant popping bug across a lake, propelling a steelhead fly well away from you, fishing the shallows in salt water, or fishing for Atlantic salmon. This rod will handle a line from size 7 through 11. Such lines have the weight to drag a heavy or bulky fly a long distance. Frequently the angler will want to cast forty to seventy-five feet—or longer.

Fish-fighting rods are designed primarily for fighting big fish such as tarpon, amberjack, sailfish, tuna, and other husky adversaries. Near the end of the battle these fish must be physically hauled to the surface, and a

WRONG WAY: "High-sticking" a fly rod, as Larry Kreh demonstrates here, is one of the easiest ways to break it. With a large fish on the line, only the fragile tip is bent, and it is likely to snap. Also, high-sticking applies very little pressure to the fish.

RIGHT WAY: Instead, hold the rod low, and keep your hand near the grip. This allows you to use the strong butt of the rod to exert maximum pressure to tire and lift a big fish.

rod with the backbone to do the job is needed. For many years we had rods that would do this, but they were so stiff and powerful that they were very poor casting tools. Today a number of manufacturers make graphite fly rods that are strong enough to defeat literally any fish we would likely take on a fly, and yet the tips are supple enough so that they cast very well. These rods usually handle lines from size 11 through 15. Such rods often have a fighting grip made of cork between the rod handle and the butt or stripper guide. However, I don't recommend this. While it certainly is a comfort to hold onto this cork grip when fighting a fish for an hour or more, it is not needed to use the full power of the rod when battling the fish. The entire rod below this grip is not bending; thus, the most powerful portion of the rod is not being utilized. Instead, gripping the rod as close to the conventional handle as possible allows full use of the entire rod and will defeat the fish faster.

Handles on fly rods are important. The correct shape can make the difference between having fun, being uncomfortable, and maybe even getting blisters. Most trout fishermen prefer the cigar shape. It is also the most popular with most manufacturers. The half-wells is a handle that swells at the upper end—and a full-wells swells the same at each end. Half- and full-wells grips are almost always preferred by experienced anglers who use rods that throw line sizes 7 through 13. The half-wells with the swelling at the upper end of the handle is really all you need. The swelling at the forward end of the handle gives the thumb something to push against at the end of the forward cast—which many people find desirable. The cigar-shaped handle gives no support to the thumb during the cast and even tends to drift away from it at the end of the forward cast. Most trout fishermen don't really need the thumb support, since the casting is usually short-range. The major reason manufacturers make the cigar shape is that on the rack in the store, the tapering cigar handle is a pleasing design. It sells better. If you would like to replace a cigar shape with a half- or full-wells handle, any competent local rod builder can do it for you. Cork is still the best material anyone has come up with for handles.

Rod guides have a lot to do with how well you cast, how far you cast, and often whether you land a fish or not. It's a good basic rule to know that for every foot of fly rod, there should be one guide (not counting the tip-top), although there can be one more guide per foot. For example, an eight-foot rod should have eight guides and a tip-top, and a nine-footer should carry nine guides. If there are more than that, the guides will sometimes tend to overweight the rod tip, and with fewer than that the line is not well supported between the guides and tends to sag.

The largest guide, the one closest to the handle, is called a butt or stripping guide. This is the most critical guide on the rod when you shoot line on the cast. Line, on the shoot, does not flow smoothly through the butt

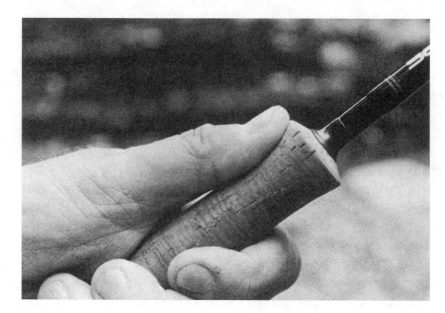

The half-wells grip shown here is superior for 7-weight and larger fly rods. The thumb rests on the upswelling at the forward end of the grip, allowing you to exert firm pressure to cast long distances with heavy fly lines.

guide. Instead, it comes toward the guide in undulating waves. On a high-speed shoot the line tends to overlap the guide and then fold back before flowing through. Small guides act like a funnel, with a small hole that throttles the line and restricts the casting distance. I'm totally convinced that the smallest butt guide on a light trout rod (throwing lines from size 1 to 6) should be a 12 mm, and a 16 mm would be better. It is also important to know that once the line has entered the butt guide, it is traveling almost dead straight through all the other guides. So only the butt guide needs to be larger than normal. When trout fishing, the angler often shoots a small amount of line. But he is forced to do this with only a small

The cigar-shaped grip shown here is seen mostly on lighter rods for 1- through 6-weight lines. It is popular because it is esthetically pleasing, but it is not so practical because the handle tends to move away from the thumb on the forward cast. But since light rods are usually cast only short distances, this is not a serious handicap.

amount of fly line and the leader outside the rod tip. This makes it difficult to shoot much line, since the small amount outside the tip is being asked to pull the heavier tapered line through. For that reason, a larger than normal butt guide is desirable.

When using line weights from 7 through 13, the angler often desires to throw a long distance. This means considerable line must be shot through the butt guide to reach the target. For that reason, I feel that the absolute minimum size butt guide is 16 mm. A 20 or 24 mm is even better. The problem is that such guides look too large in relation to the rest of the rod—so anglers are slow to accept this idea. But if you try it, you'll be able to shoot longer distances.

The butt or stripping guide is usually a ceramic ring, as is the next guide on the lower portion of the rod. The rod tip generally is stainless or chrome-plated, as are the light wire snake guides. Again, if the snake guides are too small, they will choke the line, restricting the ability to shoot line. While it is pleasing to see a rod whose guides taper in size as they near the tip, in actual practice, all snake guides should be as large as possible, so long as they don't overweight the tip. Another advantage of having large guides—and the largest possible opening in the tip-top as well is that if a knot appears in the line or backing when a fish makes a run, there is a better chance of the knot passing through. Some fly fishermen install single-foot ceramic guides on their rod tips, believing that they will increase distance when shooting line. My tests show that you actually get less distance when using these guides. Supporting that is the fact that tournament fly casters, who actually measure all casts, tried and rejected them. These guides have much more surface and create more friction than snake guides. And because they weigh so much more, they tend to overload many light rod tips, creating undulating waves in the line during the cast, which reduces distance.

Leaders

For the angler, the leader is, hopefully, the invisible connection between the fly line and the fly. Fly leaders have three purposes: 1) They reduce impact on the water, so that the fly settles softly. If the fly were attached to the line, it would crash to the surface, alarming many fish. 2) The leader allows the fly to have natural movement during the retrieve. 3) It has to be strong enough to restrain the fish, but weak enough to give it a sporting chance to escape.

There are several different leader designs. The simplest are level leaders, which are a single section of nylon monofilament connecting the line to the fly. Tapered leaders are those where each section of monofilament from the line to the leader diminishes in size. Tapered leaders are the most commonly used.

The third kind is generally used in salt water but also is constructed to catch such toothy freshwater fish as northern pike and musky. These leaders have a short section of heavy monofilament or thin wire attached immediately in front of the fly, often called a shock or bite tippet. It prevents the fish from either abrading through or severing the leader with sharp teeth during the battle.

Level leaders are frequently used to advantage in two areas: with sinking lines and flies, or when bass fishing in heavy aquatic vegetation. Many experienced anglers use a very short single piece of monofilament when fishing sinking lines. Unless the waters are very clear, fish are rarely leader shy underwater, and the short length of leader attached to a sinking line allows the angler to fish the fly deeper in the water column. The length ranges from one to four feet. There is no reason to taper a leader this short, and so a single strand is attached to the fly line and fly.

Fish are not leader shy in vegetation, either. And knotted tapered leaders will cause problems, as the knots tangle in the floating vegetation. A straight piece of monofilament testing between fifteen and twenty pounds turns over bass flies well and allows you to pull the fly from any grass it may snag.

Tapered leaders are used where the splashdown of the fly line may frighten the fish and you want to turn the fly over well. Attaching a piece of monofilament slightly smaller than the fly line to it, and then using pro-

Shorter leaders, like the 12-inch leader used for this bluegill, are usually the most effective choice with sinking fly lines. A short leader allows the fly to go deeper, and helps you to keep in touch with the sunken fly.

gressively shorter lengths of monofilament until you reach the tippet (the thinnest, weakest part of the leader, which is attached to the fly), you can construct a leader that allows you to turn over the fly, even in a fairly stiff breeze, and set it down without alarming the fish.

There are all sorts of formulas for building leaders, and many suggest that you need a ruler and a micrometer. All that is really not necessary. Except for dry-fly leaders, the following method of making a tapered leader works very well for bonefish, bass, steelhead, trout, and saltwater shallows, as well as almost anywhere else.

What is important is to make the butt section half the length of a tapered leader. For example, a ten-foot leader would have a five-foot butt section. A fly line unrolls to the target, and so must the leader. What is needed in a tapered leader is enough *flexible weight* so that the energy that unrolls the fly line will continue to unroll the leader. For rods throwing an 8-weight line or heavier, I urge you to use fifty-pound test monofilament for the butt section. For rods throwing line weights 6 and 7, you could use forty-pound test mono. Just remember, this formula is for all tapered leaders except dry-fly leaders. What monofilament you use to build the leader is important. Be sure that it is all the same brand. Don't mix different companies' monofilaments. *The best monofilament is the premium-grade spinning line from a reputable company.*

Here is an example of how to build a basic bass or saltwater leader. Remember, you don't have to be exact; if you are a few inches off in any of the lengths, don't worry about it—so long as the butt section is half as long as the total leader.

For a fly line 8-weight or larger: A butt section of five feet of fifty-pound test, connected to about eighteen inches of forty-pound test monofilament. Attach to the forty-pound about twelve inches of thirty-pound test, then add a foot of twenty-five-pound test, six inches of twenty-pound, and a tippet of eighteen inches. You might be astounded by how well you can turn over a big fly into the wind with such a tapered leader.

For most trout fishermen, tapered leaders for dry-fly work are best purchased. For years, I constructed all my dry-fly leaders. But I have not fished a commercial dry-fly leader from seven to twelve-and-a-half feet in the past several years that didn't perform very well. While some people may prefer to use a micrometer and make their own, the answer for most anglers is simply to buy what they need.

Shock leaders are those with a shock or bite tippet tied between the end of the tapered leader and the fly. These should be constructed with special knots so that all connections are stronger than the monofilament used to build the leader. The Bimini Twist is recommended for building leaders where all knots are stronger than the tippet section. See chapter 7 for more information on how to tie the connections.

Two

Modern Fly Casting

Tradition is a fine thing, and it's the part of fly fishing that many people revere the most. Yet at times, tradition stands in the way of obtaining more pleasure or increased skill levels from our sport. Several hundred years ago in England and other parts of Europe, anglers began fishing with flies. These were small wet flies, and they were fished on narrow streams. The equipment of the time consisted of a wooden rod (often more than twelve feet long) to which was attached a very short, braided line of strands from the tail of a horse.

Casting distance was just across a small stream. A casting technique that used this antiquated equipment was developed. The rod was brought from about the nine o'clock position to about one o'clock. Stopped sharply, it threw the line, only a few feet in length, behind the angler. Then the rod was returned sharply to nine o'clock, completing the cast. It worked fine, and so trout fishermen began to write about and adopt the nine o'clock to one o'clock method. It became a part of tradition.

Today most instructors still teach this method. Yet we no longer use a wooden rod, a short horsehair line, or gut leaders. We also don't fish just for trout in small streams. To be successful, the modern angler must be able to cast distances considered impossible two hundred years ago. The flies are often larger and more wind-resistant, and we fish not only tiny streams but large rivers, and even the oceans of the world.

But people are still using a method developed for what is now considered a totally antiquated type of equipment and under a vastly different set of fishing conditions.

Almost all fly fishermen should and could cast better. *I believe the nine to one o'clock instructional method is why we have so many poor fly casters today.* It should be obvious that we need to consider another method of casting—a modern way. But tradition remains strong, and anyone who offers something different from the clock face method is often criticized and even ridiculed.

Over the past forty years I have been teaching fly casting professionally. In the beginning, I taught the universal method: Start at nine o'clock, sweep the rod upward, make a power stroke, and stop at about one o'clock. Then sweep the rod forward to eleven o'clock and make another power stroke. I soon learned that with this method, only the strongest men could throw a long line or get any distance under difficult conditions. A strong man may be able to false-cast sixty feet of fly line. But a small woman does not have the strength to cast the same way. What is needed is a method that accommodates the physical characteristics of all fly fishermen. Gradually it dawned on me that the method was inefficient. It was also evident that few women or children enjoyed the sport, except for fishing where small flies were thrown a short distance.

My favorite form of fly fishing in my early years in the sport was to catch smallmouth bass from large rivers, such as the Susquehanna and Potomac, where long casts and retrieves produced many more strikes. A subtle change came over my casting. I began bringing the rod back farther on the cast, and things went smoother and easier. Casting was easier, even at a distance. The best way to learn anything is to teach it. Over the years I realized that four basic principles apply to any cast made with a fly rod. These are not my principles. They are basic physics that apply to the first person to pick up a rod and someone who will begin casting a hundred years from now. Regardless of anyone's casting style, we are bound to these four principles. They are the base on which every cast is built. Understanding these principles allows an angler to become a better caster. Understanding them also permits the caster to critique his efforts and to improve them. When something goes wrong, one or more of the principles were violated.

What is also wonderful about this method is that power strokes are eliminated. Muscle no longer is required. A woman of 110 pounds with slim wrists can cast nearly as far as a muscular 200-pound man. But the method flies in the face of tradition, and for that reason, many people who have spent a great deal of time learning the "old way" will have difficulty accepting this. What is so rewarding to me is that most people who have never fly fished (and have no preconceived notions about the sport) become accomplished casters in two or three lessons. Best of all, they are not working at it, and they can critique their own efforts.

Principles of Casting

According to the dictionary, a principle is a "fundamental truth, law, doctrine, or motivating force, upon which others are based." Here are the four cardinal principles of fly casting, on which every cast is based. *It's important to realize that they apply to whatever method or style of casting is used.* This means a frail person has to obey the same principles as a 250-pound man.

1. **You cannot make any cast until you get the end of the line moving on either your back- or forward cast.** So you don't frighten the fish, it is *wise also to lift all the line from the surface (but not the leader) before you make the backcast.*

2. **Once the line end is moving, the only way to load the rod is to move your casting hand at an ever-increasing speed and then bring it to a sudden stop.** The sudden stop is usually called a power stroke. Applying power often spoils the cast. Instead of calling it a power stroke, I prefer to call the final, sudden stop a speed-up-and-stop. The faster you speed up and stop at the end of the cast, the faster the line will travel. The size of the loop is determined by how far the rod tip moves during the speed-up-and-stop. The tip travels in a gentle arc, and the longer the speed-up-and-stop stroke, the larger the loop.

3. **The line will go in the direction in which the rod tip speeds up and stops.** If on the backcast the tip stops while it is going up, a straight backcast occurs, which is what you want. But if the tip stops going back and down, a sag occurs and it must be removed before you can make another cast. With almost all forward casts, the rod tip should speed up and stop parallel to the water or slightly climbing.

4. **The longer the distance the rod travels on the back and forward casting strokes, the less effort is required for the cast.** The rod is a lever (an expensive one, but a lever). If the rod is brought back with the thumb pointing up, the body will only allow it to bend just in front of the shoulder. That is why people bend or twist their wrists, which results in line flowing directly away from the target. It is important that you unroll the line directly away from and back to the target for the most efficiency. To take the rod and hand as far back as you can reach, without elevating the elbow, *you must use only the forearm and not bend the wrist.* Use of a full arm will cause the rod tip to travel in a small arc, causing a loss of energy. With the thumb in the proper position, tilt the bottom of the reel inward, so that the side plate is at a 45-degree angle. Make a side

Here the author demonstrates that the line always travels in the direction in which the rod tip speeds up and stops. In a cast as flat as this one, virtually all the energy of the cast is directed straight ahead at the target.

LEFTY'S METHOD OF FLY CASTING: These drawings show the proper stroke for a strong backcast. Rotate the rod hand about 45 degrees away from the body, as shown. Use only the forearm! If you use the full arm the backcast will be faulty. Keep your hand at a 45-degree angle as it moves up, straight back, and away from the target. Try not to bend the wrist.

LEFTY'S METHOD OF FLY CASTING: These drawings show the proper stroke for a strong forward cast. As soon as the backcast ends, the rod hand starts coming forward. The forward cast begins with the rod at a 45-degree angle away from the body, but as the rod moves forward, the hand comes around in an oval. When the shoulders are back where they were at the beginning of the backcast, the rod should be vertical, and the thumb pointing up and directly behind the rod handle from the target. At this point, make a very brief acceleration in the direction of the target (with no wrist movement). This, combined with a quick stop, will form a tight, fast-moving loop. As soon as the rod is stopped, drop the tip "just a frog's hair." Tilt your thumb toward the water just enough to know you have moved the tip. Too much downward movement will cause the loop to open up too much.

A long-billed hat prevents you from seeing the fly line in flight and detracts from ultimate accuracy.

Here Norm Bartlett wears a shorter hat brim like that on a baseball cap. This allows him to follow the fly line in flight and obtain better accuracy.

cast using only the forearm. You can now move the rod directly away from the target, and the fly line will follow.

Casting Techniques

You don't really cast a fly, although we say we do. When you cast a line, the rod tip stops on a stroke, and the line unrolls. To be most efficient, the more the line unrolls directly away from and back to the target, the less energy is wasted, and the easier casting becomes. Here are **three aids to casting** (they are not principles and you can violate them) that certainly will make you a more efficient caster:

1. If you are right-handed, the right foot should be positioned to the rear and the left foot slightly forward. Left-handers should do the opposite. This allows the body to move back and forth.
2. Before you make the backcast, the *thumb should be positioned behind the rod handle from the target, and the wrist should not be twisted through the back and forward cast.* This accomplishes two things: Energy in the cast is better transmitted backward and forward. You can move the forearm, sideways, vertically, or any way you wish, so long as you don't twist the wrist. Twisting the wrist causes the line not to travel straight back and forth, and will waste energy.
3. *The elbow should not be elevated on the cast.* Imagine you have walked up to a shelf that is the same height as your elbow. Place your elbow on the shelf. Imagine that during the entire back and forward cast, the elbow never leaves the shelf. The angle of the backcast is determined by the direction the rod is moving when it stops. Raise the elbow off the shelf and you will create problems in the cast.

Let's examine the average angler's cast and what might happen to defeat their efforts. Most fishermen start their backcast with the rod tip well above the waist. There is a sag in the line between the rod tip and the water, and there is some slack on the surface. The rod is brought up to make the backcast, but no cast can be made until the end of the line is moved. This occurs with most fishermen as the rod reaches a near vertical position. A sudden power stroke is made by snapping backward with the wrist. The lower part of the fly rod stops, but the tip dips down and back behind the angler. The line is going to go in the direction that the rod tip stops. *Because the tip went back and down, the line does the same, and although the fly may be well above the angler on the backcast, a deep sag (slack) results in the line.* The angler cannot make a forward cast until he or she gets the end of the line moving. For most anglers, much of the forward motion is wasted in removing the slack from the line. Then another wrist snap (power stroke) is made to propel the line forward. As the lower portion of the rod stops quickly, the rod tip again dips down and throws part of the line toward the water, resulting in a large, inefficient loop. With this method, the rod contributes very little to the cast, and a great deal of unnecessary effort has to be expended.

Let's examine how a cast is made using the modern method. For most situations, we should start with the rod tip below the waist. Remember, the longer the rod moves through the stroke, the more it helps the angler make the cast. Once all slack has been removed, raise the rod rather quickly, without ripping it upward. Watch the end of the fly line. After it is lifted from the water, the backcast can be made.

Here is another area where the modern technique differs drastically. *Remember, the line is going in the direction in which the rod accelerates and the tip stops, so it is vital that the final portion of the backcast make the tip stop slightly upward and back—never downward.* If little or no wrist is used, and the backcast is made with the forearm (not the whole arm), the chances of a good cast are dramatically improved. The size of the loop is determined by the distance that the tip accelerates at the end of the cast. Bending the wrist tends to increase the acceleration distance, producing larger loops. Once the end of the line is away from the surface, you can make the backcast. The cast is now made with a smooth and gradual acceleration, and at the end of the cast, you make a sudden and rapid acceleration of the forearm only in the direction you want the fly to go, coupled with a very quick stop! This will send the line straight upward and backward behind you. The shorter the acceleration, the tighter the loop. It is the distance you speed up and stop that determines the loop's size.

Once the backcast starts, there is two-step operation. The rod hand begins to accelerate (moving ever faster), and at the very end of the cast, over an incredibly short distance, it speeds up dramatically, then stops! The distance you move the hand to the rear before you accelerate and stop on the backcast is determined by how far you want to cast. For short casts of less than thirty feet, the rod hand need move to the rear only a short distance. But if you want to make a very long cast (maybe eighty or more feet), the rod hand should move far enough to the rear that the arm is almost straight, *but the elbow stays on the imaginary shelf!* Remember, the more help you need on a cast, the farther to the rear you move the arm, so that the rod can travel through a longer stroke.

It is when you want to end the backcast with the hand well behind the body that the modern method again differs from the traditional way. The rod can now move through a long stroke. While this is helpful for distance, the ability to take the rod way back and low to the water's surface will allow you to make a number of different casts that would be impossible if you brought the rod up and stopped it vertically.

When you are ready for the forward cast, you can come forward sideways, angled, or vertically, and so long as you position the rod by moving the forearm and not twisting the wrist, you'll make a great cast. If you go from a side backcast to a vertical forward cast, the rod hand will travel in a slight oval on the back and forward casts. See the drawings for a more detailed explanation.

To make the forward cast, begin a smooth acceleration, and at the very end of the cast, make a very short speed-up-and-stop so that the rod tip goes in the direction you want the cast to go. Remember, the tighter the loop, the shorter you have to make the acceleration (or the

If you make a short speed-up-and-stop of the rod tip straight ahead, you will develop a nice, tight loop like this one.

speed-up-and-stop) at the end of the cast. Don't drop the rod tip immediately. The bottom of the unrolling loop is connected to the rod tip. And to prevent a tailing loop (the leader tangling at the end of the forward cast), I'll explain later that you need do only two things to forever eliminate the problem.

Direction of the Cast

Most fly fishermen must be confused about the angle at which they should direct the forward cast. Some instructors teach that you should throw directly at the target; others say the cast should be directed about eye level, while some instructors really don't define the direction. Yet the angle at which the forward cast is directed is critical to successful fishing. In fly fishing, there is no one casting angle that is correct all the time. You need to consider what you are trying to do: where you want the fly to go; what you want to do with the line while it is in flight; the direction of the line and fly; the kind of fly you are casting; whether the line is a sinking or a floating type; and how the fish will take your offering. While this may sound complicated, it really isn't.

It is also vital to understand that some types of casts cannot be made unless the cast is directed at a specific angle. Thus it becomes imperative to understand the importance of knowing when to throw a cast down toward the water, at eye level, or at a slightly climbing angle.

For the average cast, you will probably do best to direct the cast at about eye level. Perhaps 80 percent of your casts should be thrown in this direction for optimum fishing results. There are a number of advantages to throwing the fly and line at eye level. One of the most important is that at the end of such a cast, the line's energy is expended straight ahead, and when the line completes its forward motion, it falls softly to the surface. Another major reason for making most casts at eye level is that the line, traveling well above the surface, can be trapped at command in the line hand. This stops forward progress and permits the angler to accurately stop the fly so that it falls gently on the water.

Downward Cast

There are rare times when throwing the line in a slanting downward angle—directly toward the target—is advantageous. Of the three directions in which you can make the cast, the downward angle should be used the least. A major reason for throwing a line down and straight at the target is that it allows the caster to drive the fly under overhanging bushes, boat docks, bridges, or other obstructions. By throwing a high-speed cast, the fly or popping bug can be "rifled" back under the brush or trees.

Another time when this cast is good is when you want to attract the attention of a fish. Many jungle species lie well back under floating vegetation, as do bass that may be hiding back in the lily pads. What is needed is a hard "plop" of the fly or bug—the sound draws the attention of the fish, which moves out from the cover to see what has fallen to the surface. One of my all-time favorite terrestrial flies for trout is the deer-hair ant. This fly plunks down to the surface with what often is an attractive sound to nearby trout. This is one of those rare times when a decidedly hard splashdown of the fly or bug is required. These are the two major situations where a sharply slanted downward cast is desirable.

When you are throwing into the wind, a major problem comes at the end of the cast, when the breeze blows the fly back toward the caster—reducing distance, spoiling accuracy, and allowing unwanted slack to accumulate in the forward end of the line. To deliver the fly to the target with no slack in the line, throw the cast at a downward angle with enough force so that it speeds to the target. As soon as the loop unrolls, the fly is thrown into the water—thus no blowback of the line or leader occurs. This same technique works when there is a strong side wind. You can't shoot line on this cast. Throw directly downward at the target, and the moment the rod stops (the direction of the cast has been determined), lay all of the line in the water so it can't blow sideways.

Disadvantages: The reason you don't usually want to throw a slanting downward cast is that it causes the fly or bug to turn over fast, and that hard splashdown in most situations will cause the fish to be alerted—or alarmed. If there is a general rule to fly presentation, it is that you should offer the lure so that it doesn't alarm the fish or put it on guard. The more naturally a fly approaches the fish, the more likely the fish is to take it. The more disturbance that is caused on the cast, the less likely the fish is to take the lure—excepting the few times when a noisy presentation is required. Another problem with the down-slanted cast is that unless it is perfectly thrown (which is rare), the belly of the line strikes the water first. The rest of the line can then only unroll toward the target. The problem is that if the fly is to land on target, the cast must be perfectly thrown—for once it is committed, it can go only in that direction.

Climbing Cast

A cast that is directed above eye level is very useful and absolutely necessary in some cases. For distance casting, the fly should be directed this way. If you shoot a bullet from a rifle, the moment the projectile leaves the barrel, it is falling; only its swiftness of flight determines how far it will go before it falls to the earth. The same thing occurs with a fly line. A fly line travels forward as the loop unrolls. When the loop unrolls or the line straightens, the whole line and fly fall to the water. To delay the impact with the water on any part of the line, the cast should be made at an angle of climb that allows the loop to unroll as far as the cast will go. Even if you have enough energy in the cast to throw the line a hundred feet, if the cast is directed at a target sixty feet away, it will travel only sixty feet. When casting fast-sinking fly lines, aim them at a slightly higher angle, for these weighted lines fall faster. If you cast a fast-sinking line just above eye level, distance is often compromised.

There are many casts that require you to do something to improve the fishing situation after the rod's forward motion is stopped and the line is in flight toward the target. For example: A **reach cast** is one where the angler throws across a wide current flow (tidal or river). If the line is directed straight from the angler to the fly, the swift current will push on the mid-portion of the line on the surface and cause it to bow. Once the bow in the line is downstream of the fly, there is a snap-the-whip effect, greatly speeding up the fly's drift, and spoiling any drag-free drift. Fish rarely take such an offering. A reach cast allows you to place the line upstream of the fly. Drag doesn't occur until the mid-portion of the line is pushed downstream from it. But you cannot make a reach cast if you throw at a downward angle, or even at eye level. What is necessary is a high, slow cast. Then, while the line is unrolling toward the target area, the slow speed of the line and its height above the water allow the angler time to lay the rod and line over in an upstream direction. A fast eye-level or downward cast will place the line in the water before the rod has moved very far.

Another place where a high cast is necessary is when completing a **tuck cast.** This is a technique by which a weighted nymph or streamer is thrown out and the leader and fly are "tucked," or folded, back under the line. The fly then sinks deeper, while the portion of line upstream from it drifts back toward the angler. It is simply impossible to throw a tuck cast unless the line is directed at a high-enough angle so that there is room for the fly to sweep back under the line and fall to the surface. Even an eye-level cast will not allow the fly enough space to tuck back under.

Another situation where a climbing cast is advantageous is when you want to put slack in the forward end of the cast, so that the leader falls in soft waves, giving a drag-free float. This is called a **pile or stack cast,** a stutter, a puddle, and a half dozen other names (it gets a new name every few years). By throwing a climbing cast, the line is fully extended, and as it falls to the water, the front end collects in slack waves. The higher the angles of flight, the greater the number of curves, especially at the leader end. This is a very effective cast that is employed by many good dry fly fishermen.

Wind is the enemy of the fly caster—so many think. But it can also be your friend. You can use the wind to help you make longer casts if it is blowing from behind you. Throw a low backcast, then come forward with a much higher climbing angle than normal. The wind will catch the line, and when this is done properly, you'll be able to throw more line than you can buy.

Climbing casts do have disadvantages, however. The major problem with throwing a fly at too high a climbing angle is that once the loop un- rolls and the line is fully extended, it will fall with too much slack in the front of the line and leader. Also, throwing high into a wind will cause the line to be blown back a considerable distance, thus shortening the cast. There are a few isolated situations where a **side cast,** with the line traveling parallel to the water, is best. Where there are overhanging ob- structions, such as boat docks, trees along the shoreline, and bridges, and you want to get the fly well back under the obstruction, a properly thrown side cast will deliver the fly farther back under than would a de- scending vertical cast. Also, when you want to throw a wide curve to the left or right, a larger curve can be thrown with a side cast than with any other method.

While perhaps the best direction to throw the fly on most casts is at eye level, to fish effectively you will have to adjust your casting angle to accommodate the existing situation.

Roll Cast

When there is little or no room behind the angler to throw the back- cast, a roll cast is often used. Most casters do not do this well. Perhaps it is because they don't apply the four basic principles. The average angler's roll cast is made by bringing the rod back to just past a vertical position, then snapping forward and downward with the rod tip. What results is that the forward end of the line falls in a cluttered mess. Of all casts made by fly fishermen, I think the roll cast is performed most poorly.

When roll-casting, the forward cast is made just as you would make any normal forward cast. Only the backcast is performed differently. With a floating line the backcast is made by bringing the rod slowly back, sliding the line back and in contact with the surface. Don't lift it in the air. For very short casts of less than twenty feet, the rod can be stopped at a near vertical position. But when longer casts are to be made, use the fourth principle—and allow the rod to drift well behind you. The farther you need to roll-cast, the farther back you should tilt the rod. *On a very long roll cast, the rod will be positioned way back and nearly parallel with the water.*

Even though a normal backcast is not possible, the rod must still have some resistance to pull against in order to load and throw the forward cast. That resistance is obtained by allowing the line being brought back to come to a stop—even if only for an instant. As soon as it stops, surface tension grips it, giving the rod something to pull against. A major mistake made by many roll casters when using a floating line is that the line is not allowed to stop, so there is nothing for the rod to pull against on the forward cast. As soon as the stop is made, a normal forward cast should be made. Move the rod forward in a smooth, ever faster sweep, with a quick speed-up-and-stop in the direction you want the cast to go—usually at eye level. If you make a long speed-up-and-stop, or bend the wrist more than just a little, the line will unroll in a large loop, and slack will accumulate at the forward end of the cast.

To summarize a proper roll cast: You need to do four things. Slide the line slowly back, keeping it in contact with the surface. The farther you need to cast, the farther back you bring the rod. Allow the rod and line to stop, then sweep forward, making a conventional forward cast. Follow these simple rules and you'll be able to make easy roll casts and improve your fish-catching.

Roll Pickup Cast

If you are using a sinking line, you still make the forward cast the same as just described. The backcast is made a bit differently, however. It is impossible to lift twenty or more feet of sinking line from the water to make a backcast. The line must be raised to the surface first. This is accomplished by making a roll cast. Remember that the line is going to go in the direction that the rod tip stops. To make what is called a roll pickup, bring line in until about twenty feet remains outside the rod tip. Raise the rod up and back, lifting more line from the water. Then make a roll cast—accelerating forward *and upward* on the stop. This will cause the line still underwater to roll upward in front of you. As soon as all the line has left the water, make a conventional backcast.

You can use the roll pickup cast to lift a popping bug from the surface. Many poppers, when a normal backcast is made, dive underwater and make a loud, whooshing sound that often alerts or frightens fish. To eliminate this problem, make a roll pickup cast, and when the bug is lifted silently from the surface, make your backcast. The same cast can be used to lift a dry fly from the water to prevent alerting a trout when a backcast has to be made.

This is an inefficient way to begin a roll cast. The rod is held vertically and the line often sags behind the angler.

This is an inefficient way to execute a roll cast, thrusting the rod tip forward and down. The loop is large and sloppy.

The end result of a poor roll cast. Since the size of the loop is the distance you speed up and stop the rod tip, and the line goes in the direction in which the tip stops, it travels in a large, circular loop and falls in a tangled mess.

An efficient roll cast. Position the rod as far back as conditions allow. Note that the rod hand should be held low to help form a small, tight loop.

An efficient roll cast. Keep the rod hand low and on the same plane as it travels straight forward. The arrows show the hand positions at the start and end of the cast.

The result of a good, efficient roll cast. Try to make this a normal forward cast with the tip stopping straight ahead, and the cast will travel fast and far.

A side roll cast will allow the angler to penetrate under overhanging branches, where other casts would not allow him to reach. The rod and line are brought back in a normal manner, and after the rod and line are stopped, the rod is dropped to the side and low to the water before the roll cast is made. What is critical to making this cast properly is to understand that the line is going to go in the direction in which you accelerate and stop the rod tip. That means that during the acceleration the rod must travel parallel to the water. To further explain: If you start the speed-up-and-stop at the end of the cast with the tip two feet from the surface, the rod must stop two feet from the surface!

Let's examine a few casting situations to see how well the principles work. If you are fishing due north and a fish rises to the east, the conventional method requires you to make two or three false casts so that the backcast can be positioned approximately 180 degrees from the target. This makes it easy to then throw at the target. Using the four principles, you can make a single backcast and drop the fly on target. Keeping the rod tip low, you move the rod from due north until the tip points at the target—or due east. Don't stop (if you do, the line stops moving and you can't make a good cast)—then make a backcast due west (180 degrees from the target). The line will roll back to the west, allowing you to cast eastward to the target in a single fluid motion. This same technique can be used when you are fishing flowing water. You make a cast, the current sweeps the fly downstream, and now you want to return to the original position. Simply keep the rod tip low and move it upstream until it points at the target. Then make a backcast in the opposite direction, come forward, and drop the fly on target.

Casting into the Wind

Wind is an enemy when it blows in your face. But there are some ways of getting around the problem. A mistake made by many fly fishermen is that when they need to throw into the teeth of the wind, they will use a line one size heavier than the rod calls for. If they are casting an 8-weight rod, they put on a 9-weight line. But that is just the opposite of what they should be doing. Instead, if they are a reasonably good caster, they should use a 7-weight line. Using an 8-weight rod and switching to a 9-weight line means that you will be casting a heavier, more air-resistant line. Even more important, you won't be able to throw as tight a loop—something you really need to do when penetrating the wind. The reason is that a line one size heavier will cause the rod to bend deeper on the back- and forward cast, creating bigger loops. This means that you are throwing more of your energy around a circle instead of at the target. Instead, if you are a decent caster, put a 7-weight line on an 8-weight rod and *extend the line to about forty feet, or a little more. This will give you sufficient weight outside the rod tip to load the rod just as if you had an 8-weight with thirty feet outside the tip.* And you will also be casting a thinner line with less air resistance. Another plus is that you are holding a lot more line in the air when false-casting, so you won't have to shoot as much line through the guides. By using a weight-forward line one size smaller than what the rod calls for, and extending a bit more line during false-casting, you'll find that you can cast much better into the wind.

Casting with the Wind on your Rod-Hand Side

Many anglers have a problem when the wind is on the same side as the hand holding the rod. I'll describe how a right-hander would do it, but left-handers can follow the directions and make the proper correction for their casts, too. The problem is that—on either the backcast or, more likely, the forward cast—the wind will blow the line, leader, and fly toward you, possibly sticking you with the hook. Many people use a backhand cast or some other cast that restricts natural movements. It would be best to make the cast under these conditions so that you are using normal and fluid casting motions—and that is possible. If you are right-handed and the wind is blowing from the right, lower the rod, remove the slack, and then make a backcast that is a sidearm type to your right. This will carry the fly line well upwind of you. As soon as you come forward, the fly is going to drift to the right—and we depend upon that when making the recommended cast. So bring the rod forward so that the rod tip is tilted slightly over your left shoulder, and the line will pass downwind of you on your left side.

Common Casting Errors

There are a few basic faults that create problems for fly casters. Fortunately, most of them are simple to eliminate. The number one fault—holding the rod tip too high—is when starting the backcast. This results in making a backcast too late, causing deep slack that will have to be removed with forward rod motion before the line can be driven forward.

Another common fault is elevating the elbow while casting. This is very tiring, and it tightens all the muscles in the rod hand. Worse, unless the angler is very skilled, tailing loops often result with long casts. A tailing loop occurs anytime the rod tip stops in a straight direction (remember principle 3—the line will go in the direction the rod tip stops). A straight line is not necessarily parallel with the water. One of the quickest ways to get a tailing loop on a longer cast is to stop the rod in the vertical position and then come forward, making a speed-up-and-stop. The rod tip travels in a straight line.

All tailing loops are caused by the rod tip stopping in a straight line. A loop has a top and bottom. When both are on the same plane (the line goes in the direction you stop), and if the tip stops going straight ahead, you will get a tangle or tailing loop. The critical mission throughout the cast is to keep the top of the loop on the top, and the bottom of the loop on the bottom. Most anglers get a tailing loop because they raise the elbow on the backcast, and as the rod hand moves forward, the elbow and rod hand travel downward. On the speed-up-and-stop, the tip travels downward in a straight line. This causes the line from behind to crash into the line in front of it. To maintain the loop on top throughout the forward cast and eliminate all tailing loops, you need do only two things. But to make it easier to do them, it is best to keep the rod hand as low as you can at the end of the backcast. Here are the two simple things you need to do:

1. **The rod hand must stay at the same height from the beginning to the end of the forward cast.** If the hand drops, the tip stops in a straight line and a tailing loop results.
2. **Turn the thumb down slightly at the end of the speed-up. If done correctly, the thumb should be parallel with the water.** The bottom of a loop is at the rod tip. By coming forward in a straight path and turning the thumb down, you make sure that the top of the loop stays on top, and the bottom dips below it as the thumb turns to the correct position. If the thumb points upward when the rod stops, the tip does not get a chance to duck under the top of the line, and a tailing loop results.

A major fault of many anglers is lowering the rod tip as soon as the speed-up-and-stop is made. This simply widens the loop and reduces distance.

A fault of many powerful men is that they cast too hard. This causes the rod to vibrate up and down, putting shock waves in the line. Look at the rod tip at the end of either cast. It should come to a dead stop. If you see up-and-down waves running through the line, or the rod tip is oscillating perceptibly, you are using too much power.

The Double Haul

Next to mastering the proper casting stroke, the double haul is the most important tool a fly caster can learn. It permits you to throw a longer line, cast against the wind, and present heavier flies and lines with less effort. Once you master the double haul, you can use it to some degree on nearly every cast. Before discussing my concept of the proper double haul, I must explain a few facts of fly casting.

A. You don't cast a fly line as you would a lure. Instead, you *unroll* a fly line. Once the line unrolls or straightens, it begins to fall. The line obtains distance by unrolling. When it is completely unrolled, it will go no farther.

B. All casting strokes are divided into two parts; a relatively long motion in which the rod is gradually accelerated, ending with a much faster and shorter speed-up-and-stop of the tip. The speed-up-and-stop is often referred to as a power stroke. Of course, isn't a power stroke; it is a speed stroke.

C. The shorter the distance the rod tip travels during the speed-up-and-stop, the tighter the loop will be. The faster the rod tip accelerates during the speed-up-and-stop, and the more abruptly it stops, the faster the line will travel.

The first portion of any back or forward cast is a relatively long sweeping of the rod. This causes the rod to flex or load. If at the end of the sweep you release the line in your hand, it will travel only a short distance. If at the end of that sweep, you complete the second portion of the cast—a brief, fast, speed-up-and-stop of the rod tip—and then release it, the line will go a considerable distance. **Without that brief speed-up-and-stop of the rod tip, a very poor cast results.** *And, the shorter and faster the tip moves during that speed-up-and-stop, the farther the line will unroll.* Remember this, because it will help make you a better double hauler.

If we compare the double haul to the rod motion, almost every fly fisherman could improve his or her haul. **What we really want to do to make the most effective double haul is to mirror the action of the rod.**

Most fishermen haul on the line continuously throughout the backcast and again throughout the forward cast. This has exactly the same effect on the cast as if the rod were sweeping back and forth (like a windshield wiper), *without employing the speed-up-and-stop of the tip.*

Like the rod stroke, the most efficient haul consists of two parts. There is a relatively long pulling on the line (to mirror the first movement of the cast). When the rod speeds up and stops, the hauling hand should also speed up and stop, mirroring the rod's action.

The speed-up-and-stop of the rod tip and the greatly accelerated second portion of the haul should be simultaneous. The long pull on the line helps bend or load the rod. **If the speed-up-and-stop of the tip and the greatly accelerated second phase of the haul start and stop at the same time, line speed is dramatically increased.**

Why don't you make a long, continuous pull, as so many people advocate and do? There are four reasons: 1) Anglers who make a long, continuous pull on the line often end up on the forward cast with the line snagged behind the rod handle. 2) If a long haul is made, you need to make another haul on the forward cast. Unless everything is just right as you bring the line hand up, slack enters the cast and must be removed before a forward cast can begin. 3) The distance that the rod tip moves during the speed-up-and-stop determines loop size. If you make a short speed-up-and-stop with the rod hand and continue to haul, *the tip flexes farther through the stroke, and a larger loop results.* 4) The faster you stop a rod tip, the greater the line speed. If you make a short speed-up-and-stop, but keep hauling on the line, *the tip doesn't stop.*

If you mirror the rod's stroke during the haul, a much more efficient cast will result. If you pull on the line throughout the long part of the casting stroke, you will load the rod deeper. Now that the rod is really loaded, if you coordinate the second part of the haul and the speed-up-and-stop simultaneously, tip speed is greatly accelerated, and greater line speed and distance are achieved.

Three

SEEING FISH

Being able to see fish is often an asset in catching them, and when you are pursuing some species, it is vital to success. One of the first keys to remember is that most of the time, fish really don't look like themselves in the water. A smallmouth bass—with its mottled coloring—is very difficult to see. A brown trout—even a big one—lying on a gravel bar is nearly invisible until it moves. Most of the time you should not be looking for something that looks like a bass or trout. When you are looking for trout that are nymphing, an open mouth, a flash off the body, or a movement of the tail can help you locate the fish. In flowing water the surface is often ruffled, making it tough to see. But if you stare at a certain spot, the surface often smooths briefly, allowing you a clear window to look through.

Many fish have silvery sides, such as tarpon, permit, and bonefish. Over the eons these fish developed their highly reflective sides for a very important reason. They act like a mirror. When you look at bonefish, tarpon, or permit, you aren't going to see the fish most of the time. Instead, the fish will reflect the environment over which it is swimming. This may sound impossible, until you first see a six-foot tarpon cruising along over dark green grass and then realize that you didn't notice it until it was within a few yards of the boat. Had that same tarpon been swimming over a white bottom, you would have noticed it a hundred yards away. While the silvery sides reflected the light-colored bottom, the dark back would be a giveaway. Unfortunately, permit and bonefish have very little on them that is not silver—making them harder to see. Bonefish have a faintly blue tail, and permit have a dark edge along the back and tail which can give them away. Often bonefish or permit are easier to locate if you look for the shadow under the fish—if the bottom is light-colored. Many times the shadow will be darker and more visible than the fish.

There are number of indicators that a trout may have taken your nymph. One of the best is seeing the white inside of the trout's mouth. The tiny flash of white in this photo is enough to show that the fish has sucked in the fly and it's time to strike.

One of the most important factors in seeing fish is to recognize how the sun's angle can help or hinder you. Sun produces glare, and any time the sun is in front of you, glare becomes a problem. The more directly in front of you the sun is, the worse the problem.

To spot fish in water less than a foot deep, look at the surface. Here a distinct ripple reveals a school of bonefish cruising through the shallows. Any time you see a wave or ripple that appears to be going against the current, it's likely caused by moving fish.

Casting to a cruising bonefish, as Sam Talarico is doing here, is one of the most difficult feats in fly fishing.

Sun glare reduction. Whenever possible, keep the sun behind you, or at least to one side. In this way glare is reduced to a minimum. Light is polarized at 88 degrees from the sun. So if you can get the sun directly to your right or left, there is an area of water in front of you devoid of glare. It is the same effect as looking through polarizing glasses—even if you aren't using any. When you are fishing shallow waters and poling directly toward a bright cloud on the horizon, it is almost wasted motion if you are trying to see under the water. The white cloud, reflecting on the surface, makes it nearly impossible to see anything underwater. The wise angler will always plan his approach so that he uses the light to his advantage. This may mean wading to the other bank or moving the boat in a different direction to get the best light conditions.

Peering into shadowed areas or looking against a dark background, such as a high bank or trees, will also reduce glare. When moving slowly along a lake shoreline, or prowling a trout stream on a bright day, you may have noticed that where there is shade, you can clearly see the bottom and any fish in the water. Again, planning your approach to take advantage of this condition can often mean more hook-ups.

Many anglers, especially younger ones, wear no hat when fishing. You can conduct an interesting experiment that proves the value of using one. Stand on an elevated streambank or lakeshore, and look into the water while wearing no hat. You will see a certain amount of bottom. Then put on a hat with a light-colored underbrim—you'll immediately see more of the bottom. Now exchange that hat for one with a dark underbrim, and you may be surprised at how much more of the bottom you can see. The bright glare of the sun causes you to squint when no hat is worn. This reduces your vision. A light underbrim reflects back to the eyes some of the glare reflected off the water—again vision is reduced. The dark underbrim will enable you to see the bottom—and any fish—much better. A simple way to blacken a hat brim is to paint it with liquid shoe polish. Be sure to let it dry for twenty-four hours before wearing (something in shoe polish makes my eyes water unless it is aired well before use).

It doesn't take many trips for even a novice angler to realize that polarized sunglasses are a necessary tool when searching for fish. They also protect the eyes while casting, as they greatly reduce glare. In some fishing situations they are simply useful, while in others they are as essential as your fishing tackle.

There are all sorts of sunglasses. Fortunately, manufacturers are now aware that anglers need polarized sunglasses, and they are easily available. The most commonly used and least expensive are those with soft plastic lenses. These soon scratch and become nearly useless. Over a period of years, the average angler who wears these will buy many pairs. Much more economical are those made of hardened plastic or glass. With minimal care, these glasses will last for several seasons of hard use. If you have good distance vision but have trouble seeing things close up, you can save money by purchasing polarized glasses with a small magnifying glass in the lower portion of each lens. You can also buy an inexpensive pair of small magnifiers that you can stick on the inside bottom of the glasses. People who wear prescription glasses have two choices. They can buy clip-ons, which are temporarily attached to their regular prescription glasses. I've tried every type I can get my hands on, and none are really satisfactory to me. The best answer, and it's a bit expensive, is to buy a pair of prescription polarized sunglasses. With any glasses you purchase, if possible, buy the scratchproof type—they will remain free of scratches so much longer, and the extra investment is relatively small.

Polarizing glasses come in several shades or tints, and there is no single tint best for all fishing situations. The most popular for fishing is some sort of tan. This color seems to build contrast and makes fish easier to see under a variety of conditions. Some offshore skippers claim they can spot fish better with the blue-gray tinted type, but I find the tan still best here, too. If you fish trout streams, where you often are in shade or not too bright sunlight, a slightly yellow tan is good. This yellow really builds contrast, and on overcast days on saltwater flats, I find these invaluable. However, these yellow-tinted lenses are not recommended for bright sunny days on light-colored flats—too much eyestrain. In fact, on white sand flats, such as those on Christmas Island, I find that even the tan color is too bright, and my eyes tire quickly. On such brilliant flats I prefer the dark blue-gray lenses.

The manufacturer has to construct the polarized lenses for the fisherman's most likely viewing angle. There are occasions when not enough glare has been removed. Sometimes you can remove extra glare by tilting your head slightly to one side or the other. It's a neat trick and worth knowing.

Just about every angler has found that glasses will fall off the face and sink quickly if they are not somehow attached to the head. Usually a strap or other device that goes about the neck and is attached to the side frames prevents them from being lost. The problem I have found with most of these devices is that they allow the glasses to slide down on the nose when I sweat. You can purchase some devices that have a built-in tensioner that keeps the frames tight against the head. Many women object to them because they pull against their hair, and I find that the constant tension sometimes gives me a headache. There are a host of gadgets to hold your glasses. I came up with an inexpensive solution that allows you to adjust the glasses as tight or loose as you prefer—and they will never move, once you adjust them. Best of all, there is no tension. Use two pieces of Velcro and attach one to either side of the frame with a piece of string. I use old fly line. Position the glasses where you want them, then mate the male and female Velcro and they'll stay there!

If you use polarizing glasses where the stream is shaded, you have little need for side shades. But if you fish open areas, such as many western rivers and certainly salt water, glare that comes in from the side reflects on the inside of the glasses. This can create problems seeing fish. You can make your own side shades or buy them from a number of commercial firms.

The surface of the water can often help you locate or see fish. It isn't necessary, sometimes, to actually see the fish—so long as surface disturbance reveals their location. For example, redfish, bonefish, trout, pike, or any good-size fish swimming in less than a foot of water will produce a perceptible wake. This can be seen under calm conditions for a long way. But remember that the fish is moving, and the wake will be trailing along behind it. To successfully offer your fly, you must throw far enough in front. There are many other surface indicators of fish. An offshore skipper will frequently see billfish either free-jumping or basking. No one seems to know why they do it, but sailfish especially will suddenly leap into the air once or even several times. A leaping sailfish can be seen from a long distance. Basking billfish often will appear to be sleeping just under the surface. Generally the dorsal, and often the tail fin, will be sticking out of the water. Other fish will do this, too. Cobia and tripletail, for example, love to hang around markers, and on slack tides (high or low) they will rise and lie just under the surface—clearly visible.

Enter a quiet basin early in the morning, and you will often see tarpon that are laid up and resting. They lie motionless with a part of their dorsal or tail above the surface. I've seen permit do the same thing, and I suspect there are many other fish that will. Twice I've spotted northern pike lying alongside a log with the tail and dorsal fin sticking several inches above the surface. Snook, seatrout, and barracuda on a grass-covered flat will often lie over a white sand hole. They will lie there motionless, ambushing any hapless baitfish that wanders by. If you know the habits of the fish you are searching for, such fish can be seen from a long distance. Almost any fish that is located under calm conditions will be extremely easy to frighten. That means that any approach and presentation must be done with the utmost care.

One of the most exciting of all surface indicators is **tailing fish.** The fish will stand on its head, or at least tilt at an angle, so that while it is rooting out a morsel of food, the tail is above the surface, waving a come-hither to the fisherman. I think that tailing fish offer some of the most exciting visual treats in fishing. In salt water, bonefish, permit, and redfish are frequently seen tailing. Mutton snapper will sometimes come to the flats and tail. The boxfish, which no one pursues with a fly rod, also tails on the flats. Many inexperienced bonefishermen have stalked a boxfish,

One of the best ways to locate tarpon is to see thcm roll as they breathe in air.

thinking it was a bone. But it has a different appearance. The little, vibrating tail sets up a peculiar spray of water much like a small pump. Once recognized, a boxfish will rarely fool you.

But some freshwater fish will tail, too. I have frequently located a good trout because it was tailing. In lakes and in some streams that are rich in aquatic growth, trout will tilt downward and run their head into the weeds, shaking them in an effort to dislodge nymphs, sow bugs, scuds, and freshwater shrimp. They ram headfirst into the weeds, wiggle their bodies back and forth to loosen the food, and then back downcurrent to eat whatever tumbles free of the vegetation. When they are dislodging the insects, they frequently will tip the tail or dorsal fin above the surface.

In both fresh and salt water, when being chased by a predator fish, be it a bass or a barracuda, minnows will leap above the surface in an attempt to escape. Any angler who sees baitfish leaping frantically above the water and can get a streamer fly in front of them is almost guaranteed a strike. The fish are in a feeding mood and will strike most any properly presented offering. Small silver sprays of minnows are often seen on bonefish flats. These little showers are often tough to see, but an experienced angler looks for them. I believe that bonefish feed on them. But they do give away the presence of a bonefish, so that you have a better chance of seeing it.

A sudden swirl on the water, no matter how little, was made by something below. That's a good excuse to investigate. Saltwater flats fishermen often refer to **nervous water**—though you can see nervous water offshore, too. What they are saying is that the surface has a different and minute rippling to it. Minnows, for example, or baitfish offshore, will create myriad tiny ripples that are distinct from the area surrounding the nervous water. This same phenomenon happens on lakes, especially big ones like the Great Lakes. Any time a wave pattern looks different from the other waves around it, you probably have either baitfish or predator fish in that area. That is worth investigating.

Another surface indicator of fish is where two masses of water with different temperatures collide. This causes an upwelling of the warmer water striking the cooler water. Such **currents** do two things: They often produce a temperature that results in productive fishing. And the upwelling can carry a lot of baitfish to the surface. This, of course, attracts predator species. Many times when the two bodies of water collide, there will be a difference in the colors of the water, such as where the Gulf Stream meets the inshore water. This is so markedly different that the water changes from the deep purple of the Gulf Stream to the pale green of inshore water in a matter of inches. But in many lakes (particularly the Great Lakes), the meeting of these two bodies of water of different temperatures is indicated by a single fine ripple or line. To the knowing angler, this is the hottest spot in the area to fish.

Of course the most recognizable surface disturbance made by a fish is the **ring created when a trout rises to a dry fly.** A trout, rising and sucking insects from the surface, is for many fly fishermen the greatest of all thrills. This ring is one of the quickest ways to locate a trout. However, take a close look. Often what appears to be a rising trout is not one taking insects from the surface. A trout sucking in insects that are drifting on top will frequently leave an air bubble. If you watch a trout take a half dozen flies and there is never an air bubble, it's a good bet that the fish is not taking them off the top. Instead, the trout is following, up through the water column, aquatic insects that are emerging. The insects have lived for a long time on the streambed. Now they are drifting or swimming to the surface, where they will open their wings and fly away to mate and die. Trout feeding on these emergers often appear to be feeding on floating flies—but they aren't. They are hurrying after insects traveling upward in the water column. Frequently the trout near the surface captures the insect. The trout then turns to descend to catch another one. During that downward turn, the body of the trout will often break the surface. The observant trout fisherman will note that if no bubbles ever appear, it is likely that the fish is taking nymphs or emergers below, and the angler will not try to tempt the fish with a dry fly.

Bubbles can also tip off the knowing angler. Tarpon breathe both underwater and above. One of the quickest ways to locate tarpon is to see them rolling. The head rises above the surface and moves forward slightly, and then the front of the body comes barely out as the fish breathes air, and it tips downward and disappears. These are called rolling tarpon; seeing them roll is a good method of locating them. When you are traveling areas such as creeks and small bays where tarpon have been rolling, you may not see the fish. But you can often tell they are there by seeing a series of bubbles floating on the surface. Many times when a tarpon rolls and breathes, the expelled air (in the form of bubbles) will remain on the surface for several minutes—a tip-off for sure. Another place where bubbles can give you a lead on a fish is where a snook or other fish has crashed against the shoreline or under overhanging brush while chasing bait. Such a foray will often leave considerable bubbles that are easily detected, if the angler knows what to look for.

If **vegetation** grows right to the surface, the movements of fish can often be detected. This is especially true with northern pike and bass, which seem to enjoy cruising among concentrations of lily pads and similar water weeds.

Another indicator used to locate fish in shallow water is **mud.** If the water is clear and fish begin feeding on the bottom, they will stir up a lot of mud in an effort to dislodge food that is hidden in the soft bottom. Bonefish create such muds with great frequency. In the Bahamas, for example, as well as the Yucatan area, I have seen muds as large as a football field. These were created by hundreds of bonefish nosing around in the

Small puffs of mud indicate that a bonefish has been rooting out food. Large mud streaks like this one show where a ray has been thrashing the bottom. Other species often follow working rays, so you should always try a cast at muds like this.

bottom. The same thing occurs when seatrout or weakfish burrow in the bottom to get at shrimp, crabs, and other food morsels. Generally the tide will dissipate the mud. To be sure that you are offering your fly where the fish are actively rooting in the bottom, determine the tidal current's direction and move to the upstream end. Locate the brightest mud. This indicates the freshest and most recently disturbed bottom. Mud disturbed where fish have already moved on will be less intense and is not worth fishing.

Solitary bonefish will also create miniature muds, which can be invaluable in locating them. The larger fish can create a muddy spot as big as a dinner plate, which once seen is easily detectable. Usually the fish will tilt its head downward and close to the bottom, sensing a morsel buried just below. The bonefish will hover over the prey and then suck in both the prey and the small amount of bottom covering it. The silt and loose material pass through the gills, creating a puff of mud while the bonefish swallows its prey. An observant angler will see a tiny, thin cloud of indistinct mud. This says a bonefish has sucked a hole in the bottom, but some time ago. Looking around, you locate another dense mud cloud. Following this can often lead to a feeding fish as you chase from a denser mud cloud to one even more recently made.

Another mud indicator is seen when a **ray is working in the shallows.** Stingrays, leopard rays, and other rays will swim along, then decide that prey is hidden below. To frighten the prey out of hiding, the ray will hover just above the bottom and flap its powerful wings violently up and down. Shrimp, crabs, small fish, and other prey species will panic and attempt to flee. The ray, although slow-moving, will gather in many of these escaping victims. But because the ray is slow-moving, many fish that are much quicker are keen to move in and capitalize on the situation. As the ray pounds the bottom, the faster fish will hover either above or tight against the ray, waiting for prey to attempt to escape. The swifter fish quickly grabs the escapees. Since these predator fish are in a feeding mood, the angler can also capitalize on the situation. If you see a streak of mud in the shallows, move in and be sure to carefully approach the streak where the mud is the brightest or densest—that is where the ray will be working. Cast a popping bug or streamer fly directly in front of the ray and retrieve it. If there is a predator fish in the area, you will get a hookup.

Fish will follow rays even when they are not actively pounding the bottom. The fish will swim along very close to a ray for two reasons. One reason is that they anticipate that the ray will soon be pounding the bottom. The other reason is that a bulky object like a ray is likely to frighten many prey species just by its approach, giving the swifter fish an opportunity to feed. This is quite similar to the cattle egret, which walks alongside cattle and feeds on the insects that are frightened by its hooves.

Fish will follow rays in deep water, too. The largest cobia I ever saw (easily more than 100 pounds) was following a huge manta ray at least ten feet wide in air-clear waters off the northeast coast of Australia. Cobia and tripletail are frequently seen swimming with a ray, even well offshore.

Another surface indicator that many people use to score with is **floating debris.** Dolphin (not bottlenose porpoise) in offshore waters are famous for this, but many other species in the open sea are attracted to floating objects such as trees, logs, boards, and barrels. **Weedlines** are also great attractors. The line of weeds closest to the shoreline is usually not productive. This is often called "bay grass" and is comprised mainly of stringy shallow-water grasses that have drifted seaward and clumped together. True seaweeds, such as Sargasso weed, are a haven for many small fish. The baby fish of many species are born in the open sea and have few places to hide and grow up. These weeds offer that haven. It's enlightening to dive just a few feet beneath the surface and peer upward under a bunch of floating Sargasso weed. All sorts of tiny fish live there. On calm days the angler can slowly cruise in the boat alongside floating weedlines and locate all sorts of predator species that are also cruising and looking. Even schools of fish such as bar jacks and dolphin can frequently be seen investigating these weedlines.

Oil is another surface tip-off to some species of fish. Bluefish, for example, will often attack menhaden and other species of baitfish that are rich in oil content. If hungry blues are feeding well beneath the surface on such oily prey species, an actual oil slick will form. It is often faint, but easily detectable to the knowing angler. Even when you can't see the oil, the surface where the oil lies will often be calmer than the surrounding area.

Color can also tell the angler where the fish are. A pod of tarpon, even if they aren't rolling, when approaching over light-colored bottom will appear as a dark blue mass that is much different from the bottom color around them. This is also true of large schools of bluefish, tuna, and other species. Channel bass are reddish-brown in color when they enter shallow bays, as they do each spring along the Outer Banks of North Carolina or in the Mosquito Lagoon in Florida, and are easily seen. A large school is easily seen as a big copper-colored area.

Water depth is another factor that must be considered when you are trying to locate fish. If the water is less than a foot deep, you should look in an entirely different manner than if the depth is greater. Fish worth catching that are moving in water less than twelve inches deep will produce visible wakes or ripples on the surface that indicate their presence and the direction they are swimming. Thus the angler should be looking at the surface for indicators.

But when fish are deeper than one foot in the water column, you need to look for them very differently. Instead of staring at the surface, you must train yourself to look at the bottom only. At first this may sound foolish, but it is perhaps the most important factor in locating fish more than a foot below the surface. To demonstrate this, let me cite an example. If you were looking at a car being driven past you on the street, you would, of course, see the car clearly. What you might not see is someone standing on the pavement beyond the car, simply because you were concentrating on the car. But if you were looking at a person, and a car drove between you and that person, you would surely notice the car. The car interrupted your vision. If you stare intently at the bottom and any fish swims over that bottom (between you and what you are looking at), the fish interrupts your vision and you notice it. I can't emphasize too strongly how important it is to learn to look at the bottom when the water is deeper than a foot.

The angler who approaches an **eddy in a stream** often never sees fish that are there. There is a myth that all fish face upstream—not true! What fish normally do is face into the current. There is a distinct difference between upstream and into the current. Most fish in a body of water will be facing upstream. But if there is an eddy along the shoreline, the fish will be facing into the current. If you are going to locate fish, you need to realize this. Approaching an eddy, fish may be facing downstream, if they are holding in the eddy close to shore. Others may be facing toward the near or far shore—depending upon their location in the eddy.

The fly fisherman who fishes **salt water,** other than shallow flats, may use many **other indicators to help locate fish.** The sea is a vast place, and the key to locating fish is to realize that you will find them where their food source is. Fortunately you have cooperative assistants many times. These are **birds.** Any good bluefisherman or striper chaser knows that birds are the best way to locate schools of fish. Of course, birds tip off anglers around the world to all sorts of schools of feeding fish. The fish will drive the schools of bait to the surface. The incredible eyesight of gulls, terns, and other species means that they will quickly locate the feeding area. With good binoculars, you can cruise and search for flocks of birds. Not all birds will be on fish. But if they are diving quickly down to the surface, and then swirling back upward, then diving again, you are in luck. Either such birds are grabbing baitfish that are near the surface trying to escape the predators, or the baitfish have been chopped to bits and the pieces are floating and available to the sharp-eyed birds. Birds that are circling above the surface but rarely diving quickly below are also good indicators. They probably have located either a school of bait or a school of fish moving along in search of bait. If it is the former, the birds are hovering, hoping a school of predator fish will come along and start things rolling. Many times you will find a large concentration of birds just sitting on the water. The same situation exists here. The birds know either predators or bait are below, and they are waiting for the carnage to start.

In the warmer seas of the world, the frigate bird is a prized indicator, usually of a single or several large fish. With a seven-foot wingspan, and the lightest bones of any bird for their size, they go to sea and stay aloft for as much as a week. They have no oily feathers, so if they fall into the sea, they may drown. But they soar over the open waters searching for baitfish. With their long, hooked bill they can dive down and pluck small fish that are just under the surface. They earned their name from the fast-sailing frigate ships that were able to overtake slower sailing ships and steal their gold and other goods. The frigate, while airborne, will often harass another bird that has captured a small fish. It frequently forces the other bird to drop its catch, so the frigate can dive and steal it. If there is bait or predators around, they will see them long before anglers will. And if a frigate bird dives suddenly for the surface, push the throttle to the wall and race to the spot—there will be either baitfish or predator fish at the scene. Frigates are one of the best ways to locate billfish and large bull dolphin.

When running offshore, and inshore for that matter, many skippers are looking off in the distance in hopes of seeing their quarry. I can't tell you how many times I have been with an experienced guide or charter captain, and they were looking in front of and around the boat as it sped along. They frequently located fish that we would never have noticed.

Splashes are also good indicators that fish are feeding on bait at the surface. Tuna and bonito, for example, often are located first by the little white splashes of water that they make as they chase bait to the surface. Some fish make a specific type of splash, and with some experience, you can even tell what kind of fish is feeding there. King mackerel and several other species will sweep up from down deep and take a baitfish at the surface. The swift upward chase often carries these fish many yards above the surface, and they resemble a launched rocket. I've seen large mackerel clear the water at least twenty feet in an arcing leap. Many small species,

The frigate bird is one of the best indicators of big fish on the open ocean in the warmer seas of the world. If you see a frigate bird circling low, or diving at the surface, race to the scene—there's almost surely a large fish there.

Bright, big splashes like these, either inshore or offshore, are a sure sign that some predatory species is forcing baitfish to the surface. Always get to breaking fish like these as fast as possible.

such as queenfish and mackerel, will leap a few feet above the surface as they chase bait.

Fish are creatures of the edges, just as many other animals are. Deer, for example, feed mostly along the edges of the forest. Groundhogs nibble grass close to cover, a fox hunts the hedgerows—an edge. Many species seem to feed along the edges.

If there are two currents of different speeds, the fish seem to gravitate to the edge where they meet. Anglers often refer to places where **two currents are joined as a seam**—a good word. The fish will lie along the slower-moving current, only inches from the faster water. This allows them to rest, yet they can dart out and quickly grab any morsels that are transported by on the swifter current. Many steelhead anglers make the mistake of walking to the base of a riffle and starting to cast across and downstream. But they often miss the best spot in the pool. The place where the water tumbles down through the rapids has a quieter edge where it enters the head of the pool, and often this is only yards from the bank. A prime holding area for steelhead is where the swifter currents of the riffle or rapids join the quieter water. In a river, if you had only one kind of water to fish, working the seams with your offerings would deliver more fish than testing any other water types.

Shade makes another kind of edge. Fish will lie just inside of the edge of the shade, in ambush, waiting for prey to come to them. The edge created by temperature changes in large lakes or the sea congregates baitfish, thus drawing predators to the area. Two different water temperatures will form an edge that invites predators. A rip on the sea is simply two converging currents, and such an edge is a prime place to inspect with your fly. When fishing, look for any kind of edge and probe it with your fly.

Scientists have conducted many surveys to determine who catches fish. In a number of different angling situations, it has been determined that about 10 to 20 percent of the anglers catch most of the fish. That means that most of the fishermen catch very few. One of the major factors in why some fly fishermen catch many more fish than most is that they know what to look for, and how to locate, the fish they seek.

Four

APPROACH AND PRESENTATION

Successfully catching fish with a fly rod begins before you leave home and ends when the fish is either landed or released. Those 10 to 20 percent of anglers who consistently score do so because they have mastered certain techniques. Any fish that is alerted to danger or is suspicious is going to be more difficult to catch. There are a number of factors that should be considered when you are after a fish. First, you need to be concealed from the fish, if possible. If there is even a hint of your presence, the quarry will be more difficult to deceive. It follows that when you approach any fish, whether you are wading, stalking from shore, or in a boat, if you can get near it without giving it even a hint of your presence, you better your chances of success. Use patience; don't rush. Take time to figure out your approach, what fly is needed, and how you'll present it to the fish. Remember, the first cast is always the most important one, and every succeeding cast tends to decrease your chances.

Once you have approached close enough to make a presentation, other factors take over. The angle at which you approach, and the direction in which you cast and retrieve the fly, are vital to success. Of course, the type of fly you use is also critical. When the cast is made, how the line lands on the surface, and the impact of the fly—all are important.

Finally, the fly must come to the fish in a natural manner. Even novice dry-fly fishermen know that drag will spoil their chances. But there are other factors, such as how the fly drifts or is brought to the fish, that cause the fish to strike or turn away.

When the fish accepts your offering, there are right and wrong methods of setting the hook. Once the hook is set, the angler needs to know

WRONG: Standing up like this will likely alert the trout to your presence.

how to fight the fish so that the battle is won but the fish isn't totally exhausted. Finally, if the fish is to be released, there are proper methods of doing this, and handling mistakes that may result in a gallant fish dying needlessly.

The approach, what flies to use, where and how to cast, use of the proper fly line and leader, the correct retrieve—and finally, hooking, fighting, and landing the fish are all vital knowledge for successful fly fishing. To make things a little more complex, the environment where the fish is caught (lake, stream, saltwater flats, open sea) will create special problems.

RIGHT: Here, Amy Cerrelli demonstrates the correct approach, keeping herself low and concealed behind the brush.

Approach

The clothing and equipment you wear mean a great deal in terms of how close you can get to fish. In England a number of years ago I fished with John Goddard, one of Europe's most famous angling writers and perhaps the best trout fisherman I ever fished with. He taught me a lesson that has resulted in my catching more fish. Our first day was to be on the Wilderness section of the famous chalkstream, the Kennet. Arriving there, we opened the boot (car trunk) and pulled out our tackle. Rods were rigged and then I put on my fly vest.

"I'm not sure that you should wear that. Have you anything else?" John asked.

"What's wrong with it?" I asked.

"It's the wrong color and I'm afraid it will frighten the fish," John answered almost apologetically. "This is the color I use," he said, pulling out of the car a medium green one. Mine was a bright khaki color, similar to most vests used in the United States.

Having no other vest with me, I fished that day with mine. John had a spare at home that I wore the rest of my week. On several occasions I switched jackets, and I became aware that trout would seem to sense me quicker when I was wearing the khaki one. The country and streamsides of England are a rich, lush natural green. My khaki vest was so bright by comparison that I felt it did alert many trout.

When I came home, I realized that all my vests were the same khaki color. Using green Rit dye, I tinted a summer mesh and a standard jacket green for eastern US streams, which are usually in wooded areas. Out west, where much of the habitat is light tan or brown, I use the khaki jackets. I now use several colors of jackets and also wear clothing that blends with the local environment. I am certain that doing this has increased my ability to sneak up on fish.

Many years ago I decided to paint my Grumman aluminum canoe. I did so because I had been fishing with two friends who were in another, similar model on a small pond of the Eastern Shore of Maryland. The sun was low in the sky, just peeking over the trees. One angler was fly casting in the front; the other paddled him along the shoreline. As the angler moved his arm back and forth to make his cast, the canoe rocked in unison with his motion. Each time the canoe tilted back, a bright flash of light bounced off it. It reminded me somewhat of a channel marker light in the dark, giving off periodic flashes of light to alert boaters of danger. I felt that the bright side of the canoe was doing the same thing for the fish. Since that time all of my boats and canoes have a dull coat of paint. I feel that the popular bass boats with a metallic finish can also sometimes alert fish. And any boat with bright, reflective sides that is in shallow water, attempting to sneak up on fish, can at times frighten fish or at least alert them to the angler's presence.

Trout fishermen often give away their presence to the fish by the equipment they are wearing. The yo-yo hanging on the fly-fishing vest that attaches to the hemostats or line clippers is often plated with chrome, giving off flashes of light. Some fly boxes that you wear on the chest are also bright aluminum—not a good idea. I recently fished with a fellow who wore a bright yellow hat on a meadow stream in Pennsylvania. From 100 yards away you could see his every movement—I'm sure that trout near him could, too.

Here John Zajano demonstrates excellent approach technique. He is free of bright objects such as dangling hemostats. Wearing a camouflage shirt and olive hat, and crouching behind a rock, he has a good chance of hooking a trout.

Many anglers, particularly young ones, never wear a hat. Nearly all older and more experienced anglers always do. There are good reasons for wearing a hat, and the design of that hat is also important. If you are hatless and you are studying something in bright light, the first thing you do is place your hand above your eyes. That's because you know that shading the eyes will let you see better. Think about it; it is almost an instinctive motion to shade the eyes when you want to see well. Yet many anglers will go hatless, even when they are seeking fish that they are more likely

Fish—especially larger ones—seek shade. Here Dave Whitlock casts into the water shaded by a boat dock. This is a favorite spot for bass in deepwater lakes.

to catch if they can locate them before making the cast. If you would like to conduct an interesting experiment in how to better see fish, try this sometime. Stand on an elevated streambank and look at the bottom in clear water, and you will see a certain portion of it. Then put on a hat with a bright underbrim and you'll see more of the bottom. Replace that hat with one that has a dark underbrim, and you'll see still more bottom. The sun's bright glare, when you are not wearing a hat, restricts your vision. A hat with a white underbrim helps, but glare reflected back from the water's surface makes it difficult to see well. A hat with a dark underbrim immeasurably increases your ability to see.

Experienced anglers know that, when wearing polarizing glasses, adding side shades prevents glare from entering from behind the lens. This is especially true on saltwater flats. The more you can shade the eyes, the better you can see. Shade offers another advantage, too. The angler standing in the shade when casting to a fish along a stream will be less visible to fish than one in bright sunlight. So when planning an approach, locate shady spots from which you can cast—it'll pay off. Fish also seek shade. They have no eyelids, and bright sunlight must be hurtful to them, for they seem to avoid it when they can. Given a choice, almost all fish will rest, or even seek an ambush spot, in the shade. The shady side of a stream will produce more fish if both sides are somewhat similar. Even small amounts of shade can be productive. A single channel marker post or buoy, old stump, eroding bridge piling, or rock offers shade, and fish are attracted to such structures. One professional bass fisherman told me that on a bright sunny day, if there is a bass in open water near a single small, upright stick, the fish would be resting with one of its eyes in the shade of that small stick. I believe it, too. Any shade-producing structure should be approached and fished. Docks are keen places to catch bass; even moored boats pay off. A channel holding fish in fresh or salt water, if it has steep sides, will usually have more fish on its shady side. When approaching any fishing situation, always look for shade—it is a useful tool in figuring out where the fish may be.

There are some good anglers who hesitate to use brightly finished fly rods—especially for trout. It's true that you can often see the rod giving off flashes of light as it swishes back and forth during casting. But I can't honestly say that a shiny rod ever lost me a fish.

Rubber-soled waders and hip boots are treacherous, and where needed, felt soles are certainly recommended. In some areas even felts are not enough, and some type of soft, aluminum cleats are worn either on a special shoe or imbedded into the sole. But these metal cleats do make a grating noise when you wade over rocks. Unless they are absolutely necessary, I don't use them; I use felt soles instead. For safety and the ability to wade quieter in deeper, swift water, a wading staff is recommended. Most have a metal tip on them. I recommend that the tip be placed against the bottom as quietly as possible. My favorite sole for wading shoes is not felt or cleats, but the material that is used on the soles of mountain climbers' shoes. It makes little noise when wading and is a tough rubber-like material.

The basic approach to the fishing spot is also important. All sorts of factors should be considered. When trout fishing, you need to know if there is room for a backcast. You need to establish where the fish may be lying in the pool. You will want to know if they are nymphing or taking dry flies. If you are lucky enough to hook the fish, how will you fight and land it? Such factors will decide how you can approach the pool.

In a bass fishing situation some of the same questions will have to be answered. Many years ago I was offered a job in Florida. I lived in Maryland and fished the Potomac River for smallmouth bass—still my favorite form of freshwater fishing. During the last early fall month that I lived in Maryland, I determined to get in as many trips for smallmouths as I could. In that month I caught twenty-nine bass larger than three pounds. In this region that would be considered a significant accomplishment. Most of these bass were taken on a fly rod. A number of them were more than four pounds. What was amazing was that I caught almost all of these trophy bass from about ten very specific locations, even though I was fishing miles of the river. What was even more interesting was that in almost all of these hot spots, I determined that the big fish took the fly or lure only when it approached from a certain direction. That meant that it was important to get into the right position, make the correct cast, and then bring the lure or fly back in a very specific manner. When that was accomplished, the bass would strike.

When you approach a stream for trout, if you are a novice you may have no idea just where you should retrieve the fly, be it a nymph, streamer, or dry. If you are fishing a stream that you have never tested before, you may not know the best places to fish. In a trout pool the food lies mainly among the rocks and smaller stones in the riffles. We often refer to this portion of a trout stream as the grocery shelf. It is where the nymphs, small minnows, crayfish, hellgrammites, and many other types of organisms live. These are the food supply for the trout living in the deeper water below the riffles. Such food is often washed downstream by the current. Mayflies, in the process of emerging or laying their eggs, float on the surface and drift into these pools, where hungry trout are looking for them.

Understanding this, the angler should then realize that the insects don't just drift through the pool in a random manner. In almost every pool there are several major currents that flow faster than most of the other water passing downstream. These currents are well defined, if you know where to look for them. I call them food highways, for they are the areas of the pool that will carry the bulk of insects drifting through it. Fortunately these are easy to locate. The water rushing over the rocks in the riffles creates tiny air bubbles that collect into lines of foam. The bulk of the foam lines will be carried (just as the insects are) through the mini-currents or food highways of the pool. So when you approach a pool, study it carefully. You will find that these food highways are clearly indicated by the foam lines. These are the most productive places to fish and should be thoroughly searched with your flies. I am not referring to foam that collects in a static state along the shoreline, but flowing lines of foam.

When working a field, bird dogs seeking quail will begin on the downwind side of the field, moving into the wind that hopefully will carry to them the scent of the birds. Bonefish act in the same manner most of the time. They usually will move up on a flat on the downcurrent side and work into the current, sniffing out shrimp, crabs, and other prey. This tells you the likely direction the fish will be swimming.

Giant tarpon, when in the shallows, prefer to roam in waters from six to twelve feet deep. That's the first place to seek them. But they also like to follow underwater walls or banks. In tarpon country, locate water of

WRONG: The shape of a rock in the current determines where you should cast. Here the current is moving from left to right. Because this rock slopes into the current, no fish will hold upstream of the rock where it would have to flight the flow. Therefore you should not cast to the upstream side as the author is doing here.

that depth that has a drop-off and you stand a good chance of finding these prized gamefish.

Lighted bridges at night in the tropics, especially in Florida, lure in baitfish, attracted to the glare of the lights. This in turn brings in snook and tarpon. To locate these two species, carefully examine the water just inside the shadow created by the structure. The fish will always be holding on the uptide side of the bridge, pouncing on any prey being swept along.

RIGHT: The back of the rock, on the downstream side, will offer quiet water where the fish can easily hold position out of the flow. This is where you should cast.

When you are searching for many kinds of fish, a pair of binoculars can be invaluable. Offshore skippers have used them for years. They aid in seeing distant birds, checking debris to see if fish are near it, and seeing free-jumping fish or bait being chased to the surface. They can also be handy to check for bonefish muds and to locate tailing redfish, permit, and bonefish.

Binoculars are most useful to freshwater trout fishermen, particularly if the angler is working a smaller stream. A surprising number of larger trout quickly become aware of an approaching angler. Often a larger fish will be lying out in the open, and as the footfalls of the angler are sensed through vibration, or the fish sees the angler's movement, it eases silently under a rock or moves to cover. Many large brown trout, for example, will ease out from an undercut bank, searching for any food that may come their way. If the angler stands back and uses binoculars to check out the pool, there is a good chance that the fish in the open, or that big brown along the bank, will be located, and a proper approach and presentation can be made. When trout fishing, I use a pair of 4-power glasses that are ample for what I need. Such glasses should be small enough to fit in a fly vest or jacket so that you can carry them easily. For most saltwater work I prefer at least an 8-power, and I am really enthusiastic about the new types that are auto-focus—saves me time adjusting them.

When approaching any potential fishing situation, always move as silently as you can. Climbing down a steep bank often means knocking loose rocks and debris that may alert the fish. Instead, look for a place where you can approach the water without creating any disturbance. I once fished Silver Creek, in Idaho, and was deceiving a few of its wary trout when another angler came along. He climbed to the top of the fence, leaped to the ground, and approached a good pool upstream from me.

Jim Finn is using field glasses to help him locate trout. But binoculars can be helpful for spotting fish in many situations, in both fresh and salt water.

Moments before his arrival there had been at least seven fish rising there. The rises stopped, and the angler, although making a cautious approach and a good cast, caught nothing. I'm convinced that when he leaped from the fence to the meadow along the stream, the loud impact when his feet hit the ground was communicated to the fish in the nearby pool.

Many times on lakes and large rivers, as well as saltwater flats, I have seen boatmen roar into the area at full bore, then chop the throttle, pick up a rod, and start casting. Usually they caught nothing. As the swift-moving, heavy boat lost its momentum, it sank into the water, shoving a big wave ahead of it that washed up on the shore. The boatman could not have made a better announcement to the fish below that he had arrived. Electric motors certainly help an angler get into position more silently than noisy outboards. But in my experience, I have watched many fish in both fresh and salt water as an electric motor nears them. While they don't flee, they do seem to be aware that an unnatural element is in their environment. And I think they become a bit harder to catch. That is not to say that electric motors won't let you catch fish, but I do believe that the less you use one, especially in calm water, the better your chances. Whenever you can, choose to pole a boat, rather than using an electric motor for approaching fish. Paddling is also recommended when possible.

In addition to a silent approach, the angler should avoid a visible approach. A common fault among many trout fishermen is to come to the stream and stand on a high bank, or a gravel bar. To any fish in that pool, the angler must look like a skyscraper. It would be much better to use the brush along the stream to hide in while observing the pool. It is very important to keep your body as low as possible when approaching a pool. The same thing is true when wading for bonefish. If the fish approaches you, kneel down. I have caught a number of bonefish with both knees resting on the flat, just to keep my profile low. If you are on the bow of a boat that nears a bonefish, tarpon, or permit, and it gets too close, kneel or bend low. It has been said many times that the best trout fishermen on small streams will wear out the knees of their hip boots before they do the soles. If you fish small streams, you know that kneeling, crawling, and keeping low are key to catching many fish.

Tides

Understanding the tides and how they affect fishing is critical to saltwater fly fishing success. Even if you are fishing with a guide, an understanding of tides will help you better plan a trip. For example, there are some places where a spring tide is best—while at other places a neap tide is the best one to fish.

The tide is the rise and fall of the sea, caused mainly by the relationship of the moon and sun to the earth. It is important for fishermen to understand how tides affect fish and fishing success. Rising water allows predator fish to swim and feed in areas they can't get to when the tide is lower. On falling tides, as portions of the sea or bay bottoms are drained, the predators' foods are concentrated.

There is another reason why tides are extremely important, and it is not generally realized. Once it is understood, however, the angler can often make decisions based on that understanding. *In salt water, baitfish, crabs, and other prey that predator fish feed upon don't usually have a specific home, as many prey species do in fresh water.* For example, in fresh water, minnows, crayfish, and nymphs tend to remain in the pool where they were born. When a flood comes, bringing a rush of water, these creatures attempt to stay in their home pool. They will hide under or behind rocks, seek shelter under a streambank, or make other efforts to stay there. They fight being swept away from their home.

But saltwater prey species in most cases have no special home. They simply go where the currents take them. To swim against the tide would be wasted energy and foolish—so they allow the tide to carry them hither and yon. Realizing this facet of sea life can help you make many decisions about where and when you should fish.

First, a basic understanding of how tides work in most parts of the world is vital. In most of the world's seas (there are some exceptions), you can figure that roughly every six hours there is a high tide, followed approximately six hours later by a low tide, followed six hours later by another high tide, and six hours later by a low tide. In other words, approximately every twenty-four hours there will be two high and two low tides. It is also important to understand that during one week, the tides will not come up very much, nor will they fall very low. The following week they will rise a considerable distance and fall a great deal. This routine is repeated over and over, so that one week you'll see the water rise only slightly and fall very little, followed by a week with a lot of water on high tides and much of the bottom exposed on the low tides.

One other factor is also important, and that is that tides are roughly one hour later each day. What this means to fishermen is that roughly every two weeks, the tides repeat themselves, but there will be a slight variation in how high and how low they rise and fall. How does this information help the angler? If you were on Blue Bottle Bank at 10:00 A.M. on a Saturday morning and fish were pouring through, feeding on bait being carried by the tide, you would not want to return there the following week at that time—for the tides would be reversed. But if you returned exactly two weeks later at 10:00 A.M., the tides would be identical, unless there was a major weather factor that might influence the flow of water.

These anglers are working an incoming tide for bonefish. In most areas this is the best tidal phase to fish for these elusive speedsters.

If you found fish feeding well at 4:00 P.M. today, you may not find them at 4:00 P.M. tomorrow. But if you would return at 5:00 P.M. (tides are roughly one hour later each day), there is a good chance that the fish would repeat their performance.

How can you tell when there are extra low and high tides, or tides that don't rise and fall too much? One simple way is to look at the moon or a calendar showing moon phases. If the moon is in a quarter phase, there will be little rise and fall of tide. But if there is no moon or there is a bright full moon, you will find that tides will rise and fall considerably. Incidentally, tides that rise very high and fall very low are called spring tides. A good way to remember this is that they spring up and spring down. Tides where there is a minor rise and fall in the water are called neap tides. The word is spelled neap—but almost every person familiar with tides calls them "nip" tides.

If you want to know where to fish in an area, whether it is a redfish flat, the surf, or a shallow bay, go there on a spring low tide. At such a tidal phase more of the bottom will be exposed than at any other time. You will see where there are troughs or depressions close to the surf edge, and where you can put a fly in a place that fish would be lurking at higher tides. Oyster bars, reefs, a half-buried sunken boat, or other debris on the bottom are easily seen at the very lowest stages of the tides. On a spring tide the higher water may hide these places. Such information can save you hours of testing waters that will not be as productive.

Bonefish, permit, and other species feed on all tidal phases, but in many places they prefer to feed on an incoming tide. You may want to determine when there will be an incoming tide early in the morning, as light brings good visibility, rather than going a week later when the tides will be falling in the morning. There are some fishing locations where you would not want to be early in the morning on a spring high tide, for the surrounding flats are often flooded, and those flats may be choked with mangrove shoots—something that will cut a leader and sometimes a fly line when you are battling a fish. In these areas, neap tide phases would be better to fish. Spring tide weeks are also better when you want to seek permit, for many flats do not have enough water on them in neap tide weeks to allow this species to maneuver well on them. A permit needs at least a foot more water than a bonefish to move around well on flats. Tarpon fishing is almost always better on spring tides. These fish seem to like a lot of moving water.

Even if you don't know much about tides, when you plan to book a guide, ask him about the tides and when he feels would be the best time for you to fish with him. The more you know about tides, the better an angler you will become.

Presentation

If you have finally located and approached your quarry, now you must make a proper presentation. There is more to presenting a fly than simply casting it to the fish. It is vital to understand several points when offering a fish your fly. First, if the fish has even a hint that an angler is nearby, getting it to accept your fly becomes more difficult. So it's important to make as careful, silent, and unseen an approach as possible. Second, whenever a fish approaches the fly, or the fly approaches the fish, this approach should be as natural as possible. All its life the fish has seen prey act in a certain way as it is attacked, or the prey approached the predator fish in a particular way. Anything that differs from the natural act may alert or alarm the fish, reducing your chances. These two principles should be always paramount in the angler's mind as he offers his fly to any fish. Understanding and considering these principles as you look for fish, approach them, and then make your presentation are vital to consistent success.

We have already covered locating and approaching the fish. The second principle (that a fly must approach in a natural manner) is something that even many experienced anglers fail to appreciate. Because of that failure, success often eludes them.

Let's look at a natural situation, with a fish facing into the current, looking for food. The prey comes drifting toward the predator in the current. As it nears the fish, it suddenly is aware of the danger, so it darts off to the side, and hopefully to safety. The fish sees the prey as it approaches and as it bolts away. The predator surges forward and grabs it. All of this is a natural situation.

Let's take several examples of how anglers often fail to appreciate this and thereby lose an opportunity to hook a fish. Wading against the current, the angler sees a nice fish holding upstream from him. Positioning himself below and to the side of the fish so that he doesn't have to throw his fly line directly over the fish, he makes a cast. The streamer fly lands far enough upstream from the fish so that it doesn't alarm it. Allowing the fly to sink to the fish's level, the angler makes a retrieve. The fly comes directly at the fish, which suddenly sees its approach. As the small fly gets nearer, the fish moves forward to strike. But the tiny fly doesn't flee at the sight of the predator. Instead it continues to come directly toward the fish. Suddenly the fish realizes instinctively that something is wrong (it's

Captain Flip Pallot works his client into position so the fly can be presented upcurrent of the fish. This results in a more natural and successful approach.

never happened before), so it flees until it can assess the situation. An opportunity for the angler has been lost.

Let's look at another situation that often occurs. It happens a great deal when sight-fishing from a boat. For the purpose of illustration, let's assume that the angler is proceeding due north. A fish is seen approximately west of the angler, holding in the current or tide. A cast is made well in front of the fish in approximately a northwesterly direction, and the fly lands well beyond the fish. As the retrieve begins, the current, sweeping south, carries the fly toward the fish, even though the fly is also being brought back toward the angler on the retrieve. As it nears the fish, the fly is actually even with or slightly downstream of it. The retrieve continues, causing the fly to come directly at the fish or, worse, to approach it from slightly downstream as the current sweeps the fly farther south. To the fish, something that resembles prey is attacking it, and so the game is lost again.

One more example: The angler sights a fish directly in front of him and casts directly over the fish. Even if the fish was not spooked by the line or

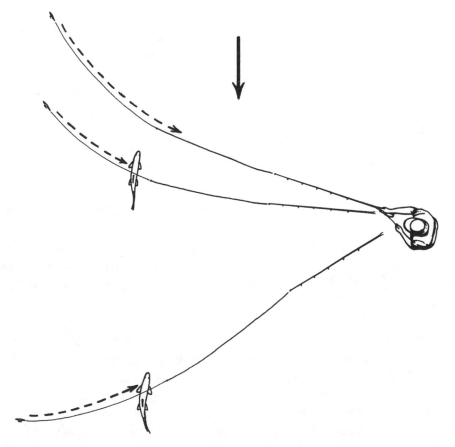

Any fly cast across a fish's back or retrieved so that it comes up behind the fish will likely frighten it. Throw the fly far enough ahead so that it passes in front of the fish and you will probably draw a strike.

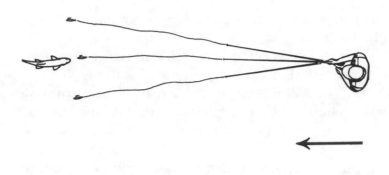

If a fish is heading directly toward you, or directly away, it is best to throw the fly so that it lands slightly to one side of the fish. On the retrieve it will appear to be trying to escape.

The lower drawing shows a fish heading away—the worst possible scenario. *Never* cast over the fish—this is bound to frighten it. Instead, cast ahead and to one side, and try to make the fly appear as if it is trying to get away.

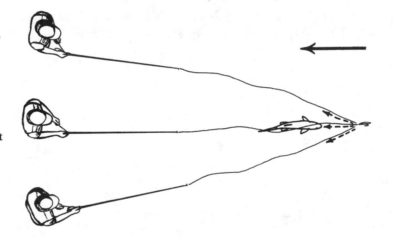

leader falling on top of it, the chances of success are radically reduced. The angler will be forced, from this position, to retrieve the offering directly at the fish. There are some cases when nothing else is possible—so you take a chance. But if there is any way that the angler can get off to one side and offer the fly so that it doesn't come at the fish in an attack position, hookups are far more likely to occur.

Here is another basic problem of presentation that often ends in defeat. Somehow the angler gets very close—less then twenty-five feet away—to a fish before it is seen. This could be an angler wading and suddenly seeing a bonefish, a trout, or many other species holding just in front of him. The fish is facing the angler, but as yet it has not seen the fisherman. The normal reaction, if you are offering an underwater fly, is to crouch, make a cast, and try to get the fish to follow and hit the fly before it sees you. Usually that doesn't happen.

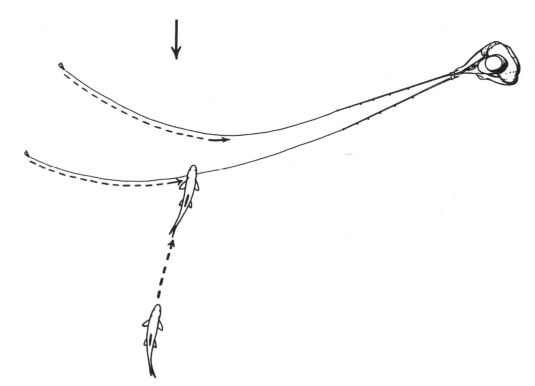

Even good fishermen make the mistake of allowing the fly to appear as if it is "attacking" the fish. The dark arrow at the top indicates the current flow. You may see a fish cruising against the current and throw the fly ahead of it. But if you do not throw it far enough ahead, the fly will come toward the fish as if attacking it, something prey species simply don't do! This will likely spook the fish. Instead, make sure to throw the fly far enough ahead so that on the retrieve it will pass in front of the cruising fish and appear to be trying to escape. This tactic is likely to draw a strike.

What needs to be evaluated here is what we are trying to do, other than get a hookup. We need to realize that the fish will follow the fly for some distance before it grabs it. Once this is understood, the angler can accommodate the situation by making a different cast. As is shown in the drawing, the angler makes a curve cast to the right or left (whichever he does easily). The fly lands to one side and in front of the fish. The leader and forward part of the line are in a big curve on the water. As the retrieve starts, the fly swims at right angles to the fish, but well in front of it. The fish moves in to inspect the offering. The fly passes by the fish and continues on (at right angles to the fish and angler) until the curve is lost and the fly begins coming back toward the caster. With the curve cast the fish may follow a fly ten to twelve feet without getting any closer to the angler. Such a cast under these conditions means an infinitely better chance of drawing a strike from a fish that's too close.

Another basic principle of presentation and retrieve is the angle of the rod. It is recommended for some nymph fishing that the rod be held fairly high, with the tip often above the head of the angler. But for almost every situation where you are stripping in line to manipulate an underwater fly, the rod tip should be kept very low, always below the belt. When bass bugging, retrieving a streamer, bringing in a bonefish fly, or anytime you retrieve an underwater fly, the rod tip should be very close to the water, or with the tip actually an inch or two under it. This is a basic rule that

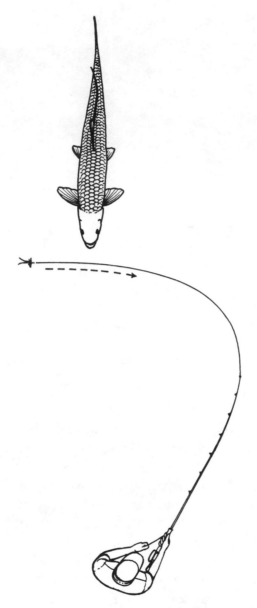

If you suddenly spot a fish very close, your natural reaction is to make a quick cast at the fish and retrieve the fly. But this will draw the fish even closer to you as it follows the fly, and often it will see you and get spooked. Instead, throw a curve cast in front of the fish. As you retrieve, the fly will travel several feet directly in front of the fish before turning and heading toward you. This trick may earn a strike from a fish you would otherwise have frightened away.

will get you more fish. The fly is retrieved with the line hand and the rod pointing at the fly.

Here's why: With the tip at the surface or slightly beneath it during a retrieve, no slack occurs, and even slight nibblings at the fly can be detected. Because no slack occurs, the fish will often hook itself; this certainly makes it easier for the angler to strike more effectively. Bass buggers and those who fish streamers have been guilty for years of using the rod to manipulate the bug or fly. The cast is made. The angler flips the rod tip up and down, which activates the bug or fly. As the rod tip drops

WRONG: King Montgomery demonstrates that by flipping the rod tip up and down to manipulate the fly, you will create slack that makes it difficult to keep in touch with the fly, feel a strike, and set the hook when you get a hit.

each time, slack falls into the line. If a fish hits when this slack has accumulated—and this often happens—the strike is often missed.

Another problem occurs when fishing a popping bug. The purpose of stripping the line and then pausing before making another pull on the line is to allow your fly or bug to stop briefly, hopefully exciting the quarry. But when a rod is held high, as most anglers do, or the tip is used to manipulate the fly, little or no pause ever occurs with your offering. Tie on a popping bug and cast it out on the water, and you'll be better able to see what I mean. Flip the rod tip up and down, activating the popping

RIGHT: Instead, keep the rod tip low and pointed at the fly, and manipulate the fly with your line hand. This way the line remains taut, you can better control the fly and detect strikes, and you will greatly increase your chances of a hookup.

bug, but keep the rod tip above the level of your waist or belt. Watch the bug; it will keep moving for an extended period after the rod tip has stopped moving. When the rod flips up, the line is pulled taut, dragging the bug nearer. As the rod stops but is held a few feet from the surface, a sag occurs in the line between the rod tip and the surface. This gradual sagging of the line continues to drag the line toward the angler. But if the rod tip is held at or slightly under the surface, each pause during the stripping routine guarantees that the fly or bug also stops moving.

Another basic rule of retrieve is that the line being stripped in should always be controlled by the line hand from behind the rod hand. What often occurs is that the cast is made and the angler grasps the line behind the rod hand and pulls backward, activating the fly. But, if the line hand reaches up and grabs the line in front of the rod hand, this requires letting go of the line in the rod hand, then repositioning the line in the rod hand so it can be trapped under a finger for another stripping motion. But if the line hand strips some line in, then reaches *behind the rod hand* and grabs it for another stripping motion, the rod hand always has the line under control. This same technique applies when you are fighting a fish. Always retrieve line from behind the hand holding the rod—so that you always have control of the line.

Another basic of good presentation comes when you pull off a good amount of line and stand ready to make a cast. This occurs when angling for bonefish, tarpon, or permit. The angler holds a small amount of line and leader outside the rod tip, and the boat moves along, searching for the prey. The fish is sighted and a quick cast is made. But unless one basic technique is followed, the cast will often end in disaster. As the angler first stripped line from the reel and dropped it on the deck, the forward end of the line fell to the deck first. All subsequent line stripped from the

Many boats are a horror for the fly rodder, filled with "line grabbers" such as cleats and equipment that make casting and line control difficult or impossible. Whenever you are faced with this problem, spread a minnow seine over the troublesome items. If you remove the wooden floats on the seine, you can store it in a small plastic bag and carry it with you on distant trips. I always take the seine when I know I am going to be fishing from unfamiliar boats where this might be a problem.

reel fell on top of it. If a cast is made with the line in this condition, the forward portion (underneath the pile) often tangles on the shoot. To make sure that you're going to get a good cast, always cast all line pulled from the reel and then bring it back. This way the back of the line is on the bottom of the pile—where it belongs.

One of the most helpful devices to have in a boat is a line tamer. The line is retrieved into the tamer and the cast shoots freely from it. This eliminates accidentally standing on the line and other problems. Here Norm Bartlett demonstrates its use. Note also that he allows the line to flow through his hand for good control.

Among the rules you want to follow when presenting a fly to any fish is never to be rushed. Many saltwater guides will rant and rave if you don't instantly throw the fly. But taking an extra two or three seconds often means the difference between a controlled cast and one that is presented so sloppily that it spooks the fish. If you see a trout rise, or a bass pursuing a minnow, and you rush your cast, you'll probably throw a poor one. Just slowing down means only a second or two more to make the cast, but it can also make considerable difference in how well the fly comes to the fish.

Another basic premise of good presentation is never to fish farther than you can cast well. Many impatient anglers will throw the fly before they are within a comfortable casting distance. But cast only as far as you can do so comfortably and accurately. To try to throw even a few feet farther means relinquishing control. Some anglers place a one-foot mark with a permanent marking pen at the point where they can make their longest cast. They strip only that much line from the reel.

I am a firm believer that you should fish a long way off for many species. Most anglers and many guides feel, for example, that you should not cast to a bonefish until it is within thirty or forty feet. That gives you one opportunity. But if you can cast accurately at seventy to ninety feet, I urge you to try that. If the bonefish refuses or misses the fly, strip and make another cast, and repeat this several times. Instead of one presentation, you often get two or more. I have hooked many trout on my dry flies at forty to sixty-five feet. If I can see the fly (often against glare on the water), I have no hesitation about fishing at these distances. The advantage of fishing that far away is that you have less chance of alerting a wary fish. There are exceptions. Tarpon and billfish are two. Their mouths are so hard inside that you need to have the fish close so you can really set the hook.

If you fish smallmouth bass in a river, seatrout in a grassy basin, steelhead in deeper pools, bluefish, or many other species in open water, make as long a cast as you can and search as much water as possible. So long as the hook is sharp and the rod held low with a taut line, you'll have no trouble properly hooking the fish. Over the years I have caught many fine fish beyond sixty feet. My longest hookup was in Los Roques with my guide, Alex Gonzales. Returning to the boat at the end of our last day, Alex insisted that I cast to a cruising bonefish. I pulled off the entire fly line and some backing, and with a mild breeze behind me, made a cast and hooked the fish at what we estimated to be 125 feet. There was no trouble hooking the fish with a taut line and a sharp hook.

When you are presenting a fly, another good rule is never to allow the fly line to fall over the fish. A heavy butt section crashing to the water will

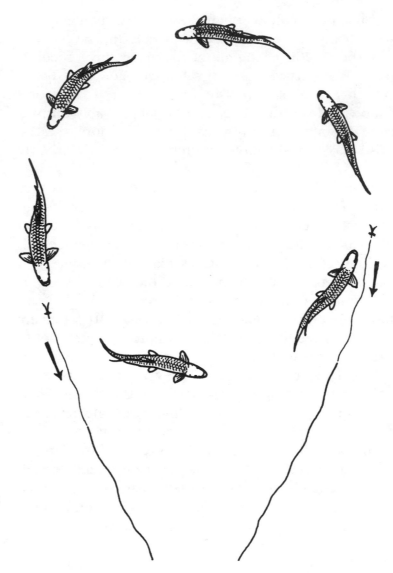

Tarpon frequently swim together in a circle, which anglers call a daisy chain. It is vital to offer your fly properly to these fish. Never cast across the chain or you will spook the fish. Also, the cast on the right side of the drawing is a bad idea, because on the retrieve the fly will appear to be attacking the fish as they come around the circle. Instead, cast to the left, so that the fly appears to be trying to escape.

frequently spook fish. The angle at which you deliver the fly is also important. Many people cast at the surface target. But that often causes the fly to drive heavily into the water—ruining the cast. Most of the time the fly should be cast at about eye level. Thus the energy is expended above the target and the fly falls softly to the surface.

If a dry fly floats over a fish and the fish shows no interest, you need to pick the fly up and make another presentation. The fly is often air-dried by false-casting before it is dropped again to the surface. In rough water there is little concern about where you air-dry the fly. But if you lift a dry fly from a calm surface and the false cast is over the fish, there are two

Trout that live in limestone streams are exceptionally wary. Here Irv Swope uses a very light 3-weight fly line to make a quiet, gentle presentation while he remains hidden.

things that may happen to alert or spook the fish. First, it may see the line in the air. Second, at the end of the back and forward casts, as the line's direction is reversed, water is snapped out of the fly. False-casting over a fish holding in calm water causes miniature raindrops that are flushed from the fly to fall to the surface. It's pretty much the same as throwing pebbles on a tin roof.

There are many situations where a side cast is far better than an overhead cast. In very clear water, if the angler has to false-cast several times, keeping the line very low to the water often is an asset. By false-casting at a low side angle, you keep the line, leader, and fly out of sight of the fish. This is especially true when you are very close to a fish.

Five

FLIES

Regardless of the other tackle we use, we must offer a fly that will be acceptable to the fish. That fly must be tailored to the species, and frequently it must be matched to the habitat. For example, coaxing a fish out of dense vegetation, such as a bass among lily pads, or a redfish down in the turtle grass, demands the use of a fly with some sort of weedless device that allows us to fish there without snagging. In swift current, when fish are lying deep, a fly designed to dive quickly is a necessity. Generally flies are designed to imitate food that predatory fish feed upon—although not always. Those not designed to imitate a food source exactly are called attractor flies. Attractors are patterns that resemble nothing that lives in the water, but experience shows that fish really will strike such flies. Just about any predatory fish is at some time susceptible to them. Attractor flies may be tied with vivid fluorescent colors and may be of radical shapes. Another very different fly type has no special name or designation, so I call it a creature imitation. Such flies don't fall into any of the categories mentioned later on, but they may imitate such food sources as squid in the open ocean and crayfish in fresh water.

For most species we use either a surface fly or one that swims underwater. But for trout we have developed a number of specialty flies that range from those used on top to those that creep and crawl along the bottom. These special flies have names that designate their unique design and purpose. If we disregard trout flies, most other flies used to take fish in salt and fresh water fall into two categories.

Poppers or popping bugs sit on the surface and can be designed to make little noise or a great deal. Most underwater flies are designed to imitate baitfish and are called streamers—although some underwater flies also mimic creatures, such as crabs and crayfish.

Three different types of flies. The top row shows a variety of surface popping bugs. The second row shows a Bend Back (on which the hook rides up and is fairly weedless) and a Dahlberg Diver, which can be worked on the surface or just below. The bottom row shows three types of flies that run deep.

Some Observations About Flies

If we discount dry flies, there are some general comments that can be made concerning most fly patterns. There are certain criteria that govern whether a fly will be productive or not—and if it is properly constructed for the job at hand. Certain characteristics prevail among almost all flies that are fished underwater.

Silhouette. Whether you are fishing a nymph, streamer, or squid pattern, the overall shape of the fly, when viewed by the fish, is important. Bonito and tuna, for example, roam the open seas. Among their favorite prey are small baitfish. Even though these predators may be hefty specimens, they will be more likely lured to the fly if the pattern is a sleek, small one. Large steelhead often prefer small flies, as do Atlantic salmon when the rivers run low and clear. The reverse is true of trophy-size largemouth bass, or cobia. Bigger fish usually want something that appears to be large and worth chasing. The silhouette should also duplicate the general shape of what the pattern is attempting to simulate. Overall shape is often critical to success. A sculpin has a large head, with a tapering body. Flies tied to resemble this favorite food of bass and trout should have a large head and tapering body.

Balance. A skilled fly tier will construct a fly with proper balance. Balance means first that the fly is tied on a hook size that is proper for the pattern. You wouldn't tie a small fly on a large hook, or vice versa. Flies constructed with hooks too large or too small don't swim properly. Hooks too heavy kill the action, and hooks too small often cause the fly to swim unnaturally or roll over on the retrieve. Proper balance or proportions also assure that water flows properly over the pattern, creating the desirable action designed into the pattern. With correct balance the fly is also easily transported through the air on the cast.

Bulk. The amount of bulkiness, or slenderness, constructed into the fly will also determine how effective it is. Sand eels are sleek creatures that stripers, bluefish, and many other species feed upon voraciously. To be effective, a sand eel pattern should be tied so sleekly that in the water it looks as though the tier didn't finish the job. The same can be said for needlefish imitations—they should be long, sleek, and tied very sparsely.

Bulk is often desirable in other situations. If you fish at night, whether for brown trout, snook, or tarpon, a fly that has considerable bulk and will push through the water, creating vibrations that the fish can pick up, is much more effective than the same pattern dressed sparsely. Roiled or dirty waters almost always demand that the fly be tied with a lot of bulk.

Color. The color of the fly is often critical, for several reasons. Most important is that generally the color should be close to what the fish are feeding upon. On the open ocean and in many inshore waters, almost all baitfish have either a blue or green back and a white belly. If you seek bonefish anywhere in the world, you'll find that most of the time a fly that is similar to the bottom coloration where the bones are feeding is the right choice. If the bottom is of light sand, then a light-colored fly will generally be best. If the bottom is carpeted with dark green turtle grass, then flies of that hue will often do better. Attractor patterns, those that contrast radically with the environment you are fishing, are often so different that fish find them enticing. And when a fisherman can see a bright fly well, it will sometimes outproduce one that cannot be easily detected. Fluorescent chartreuse flies can be seen from a great distance and I believe it is one reason why this color is so effective.

Flash. Many flies, especially those that imitate baitfish, are generally more effective if a small amount of flash is added during the tying procedure. Krystal Flash, Flashabou, and similar reflective materials often induce strikes that will not come if the fly is devoid of flash. But swimming baitfish do not resemble blinking mirrors as they move through the water. You see only an occasional flash. Bear that in mind when tying or selecting flies with reflective material in them. The best flies have just a moderate amount of flash. It is not a good idea, either, to attach material such as Krystal Flash or Flashabou, then trim all strand ends at one spot. This leaves most of the reflection at one location—where the strands were severed. Instead, clip off the strands at different lengths along the entire body—that way you'll see little sparkles of light throughout the pattern. Since few things in nature are one color, it pays

A small, slow-sinking fly allowed me to take this big tarpon.

to mix several colors of flash material in a pattern. While other fly fishermen have been using the technique, famed outdoor writer Dan Blanton has popularized the trick of letting a number of strands of Mylar extend beyond the wing or tail of a streamer. He coined the term flashtail, and there is no doubt that at times this extra flash at the end of the pattern will draw more strikes.

Sink rate. One of the most important factors when selecting flies is the sink rate. A fly that won't sink quickly enough, or one that dives too fast, is often useless. Several examples come immediately to mind. If you are fishing in water less than a foot deep, where the bottom is carpeted with grass or rock rubble, a fly that is heavily weighted will be constantly snagging on the bottom. An unweighted nymph cast into calm water may sink properly so that it travels through the water column at the same level as the trout. But this same nymph, when fished in swifter currents, will be carried along high above the fish and never descend to the proper depth. A tarpon fly, such as a Whistler, is usually designed with heavy bead chain or lead eyes. It sinks quickly. Since it is heavy and bulky and lands with a bit of a splash, a weighted Whistler is rarely used when seeking tarpon in the Florida Keys. In such clear waters the wary fish would spook from the heavy impact. If the fly is thrown far enough in front to prevent the cautious fish from becoming alarmed, it then sinks too fast and will have descended too far by the time the fish arrives near the fly. However, the same pattern tied unweighted can be effective. In another situation you might want to fish a fly very deep, crawling it along just above the bottom. You can tie a fly with very buoyant wing, such as bucktail, and then fish it on a fast-sinking line. The sinking line will snake along the bottom, while the buoyant fly will ride a few inches above the bottom—and in front of the nose of a fish. There are cases where sink rate is vital to success.

Trout Flies

Before examining in detail the other types of patterns just mentioned, let's look at trout flies. There are more than a dozen special designs for dry flies for trout. Among the most popular are the conventional dry, terrestrial, thorax, Paradun, parachute, Griffith's Gnat style, No-Hackle, spinner, Renegade or Fore-and-Aft style, skater, Variant, caddis, and stonefly.

Some General Observations

Like many flies used in other areas of fishing, dry flies fall in two categories: imitators and attractor or exciter types. It is worth noting that truly exact imitations are often not effective. In fact, the more closely the pattern resembles the insect, generally the less effective it is. The best patterns seem to be those that more or less imitate the insect fairly well. But they do not look exactly like the insect. There are some accomplished tiers who can now create flies in their vises that look as if they could crawl, fly, mate, and eat. Such flies are certainly to be admired as works of art, but they generally do not fish well.

Conventional dry flies are those most of us use, such as the standard Adams and Light Cahill. The tail is usually of hackle tips, although I really

The drawing shows the three major types of fly patterns that imitate mayflies and cad-disflies. Top row, left to right: Paradun, Renegade or Fore-And-Aft, Variant, conventional Catskill-style dry fly, parachute tie, and thorax.
Bottom row, left to right: Elkhair Caddis, Goddard Caddis, spider, Griffith's Gnat, and spinner imitation.

like Microfibetts, which are more durable and stronger than hackle tips. They come in different colors to match the patterns being tied. One important factor when tying such flies is that tiers often will clump the hackle tips together for the tail. This will cause the rear of the fly to drown. Capillary action sucks water up along the bunched strands, much as a teenager would draw a milkshake through a straw. By spreading the fiber tips, you eliminate this problem, and also the spread fibers give the fly better stability as it floats on the surface.

On conventional dry flies the body is constructed of either synthetic or natural furs. The wings are spread at about a 30-degree angle on top of the fly. The wings are usually made from either feathers or hair. What many anglers are also discovering is that fluorescent polypropylene yarns make fine wings—and are much easier to see. On overcast days or when I'm fishing where there is a lot of glare on the water, I have great success with pure black poly wings. An even more visible wing can be made from pearl Krystal Flash, and even in my late seventies I can see a parachute dry fly with such a wing at least thirty feet away.

On the conventional dry fly, two or three quality hackles are wound around the shank to support the fly above the surface. The fly is tied in two styles. One is very sparse and with a minimum of body materials. This is called a Catskill tie, since it originated in that area. The other is generally referred to as a western tie of the conventional dry fly. Such flies are usually tied with nearly twice the dressings. They float much better and are more durable. But on calm waters, where wary fish can take a long look at the fly, the sparsely dressed Catskill pattern may have advantages. The western tie is better on heavy or turbulent waters, where the more lightly dressed pattern would probably soon sink. The conventional dry is used more than any other type of dry fly. It has served generations of anglers and belongs in everyone's box.

The parachute dry fly is rapidly becoming more popular. In waters that are hard fished, where the trout are more wary, a parachute tie, which sits on the water in a more realistic manner than a conventional dry fly, will catch more fish. If you are having refusals on a conventional dry fly, switch to a parachute style. One of the most important tips for tiers is that when you wind the parachute hackle, each turn should be made beneath the previous one. Spiraling each turn on top of the last makes for a poorly dressed fly.

The parachute fly is exactly like a conventional dry fly, except that the hackle is wound horizontally around the base of the wing, rather than being wound vertically around the hook shank in the wing area. It has several advantages. First, you don't need the highest-grade hackle to construct the fly. A #3 dry fly neck will do about as well as a #1, which will cost much more. The fact that the hackles radiate outward from the hook means they will better support the fly on the surface. I personally feel that parachute flies give a more realistic impression of an insect to the fish that views the fly, since the hackles are in the same position as the insect's legs. And when tied with brightly colored hackles, these flies are easier to see on the float. A final advantage is that in rough water, a parachute-hackled dry fly will float longer and better than a conventional one.

The upside-down dry fly is a variation of the parachute fly. John Goddard, the English writer, whom I regard as the best trout fisherman I ever fished with, gave me some of these to try. Under very difficult conditions,

On the left is a conventional Catskill-style dry fly, which rides up well off the water on its hackle tips. In rough water this is okay, but a natural mayfly is normally flat, with its body in contact with the surface. In calm water, trout take a longer, better look at your offering and will often refuse a conventional dry that sits up unnaturally high. But the parachute-style fly (middle) and the Paradun (right) present a more realistic appearance. Under tough conditions these latter two styles usually outfish conventional drys.

I firmly believe, an upside-down dry fly will outfish either a conventional or parachute dry fly. The upside-down dry fly is tied with the hook point reversed, so that it rides upright and out of the water. Standard dries often have the hook protruding below the surface and easily visible to the trout. Upside-down flies have the hook well above the surface and pretty much hidden by the fly body. Upside-down flies are also tied in the parachute style. If you encounter some difficult fish, especially on calm water, you may do a better job with an upside-down fly. It is a little difficult for me to tie, and I find that I need a gallows tool for my vise to tie this one.

Thorax-tied dry flies are now becoming popular. They were first described in the 1930s by Dr. Edgar Burke, and more recently by Vince Marinaro. Thorax dry flies are also more effective in most cases when fishing becomes difficult. In all my years as a trout fisherman, I have seen only a very few mayflies floating along with their wings spread apart, as is so common on most imitation dry flies we tie. Instead, the wings on a natural mayfly as it floats along are clumped together as a single unit. Thorax ties are the same—a single wing protrudes above the surface. The hackle supporting the body can be attached in several ways. I prefer the parachute style. A parachute tie on a thorax dry fly is one of my favorites when fishing difficult waters.

The Paradun is a variation of the Haystack, a favorite dry fly variation of the northeastern United States. The Haystack has a tail spread wide to help support the fly. The wing consists of a bunch of deer hair that is raised in a fan shape at the front of the body. The Comparadun is an offshoot of this, developed by Al Caucci. The Comparadun has two tails of two strands that are spread in a wide V to give the fly support. The body is made of material (usually natural, but sometimes synthetic) that floats well. The wing is usually of deer hair and is positioned just forward of the center of the body, much in the same style as a thorax tie.

The Griffith's Gnat is a different fly—and it belongs in every serious fisherman's box. There are times when trout will be sipping on minuscule flies, often difficult for the angler to even see. While minute imitations that exactly match these emerging insects will certainly do well, the Griffith's Gnat is usually just as effective. Best of all, just about anyone can tie this pattern.

I use a No. 16 through 24 light-wire dry-fly hook. Attach one of the smallest hackles to the rear of the hook shank (the favorite color is a grizzly hackle, from a good dry-fly neck), then simply spiral the feather forward, palmer fashion. Tie off and that's it! To the tier it resembles a minute caterpillar. But to the trout it must appear as one of many small emerging insects. It just looks buggy! I can't tell you how many times this fly has saved the day for me when trout were sipping on extremely small stuff. Another method of tying the Griffith's Gnat is to first wrap an ultra-small tip from a peacock herl on the hook shank, wrap it forward to the eye, then palmer a grizzly hackle down the shank. I urge you to carry at least a dozen of these in various sizes, ranging from No. 16 to No. 24. If you clip the hackles from the bottom of this fly, it makes a great imitation of a midge or an emerger.

Another dry fly, similar to the Griffith's Gnat, which used to be fished a great deal and modern fly fishermen have disregarded, is the palmered fly—which may have been the design of the very first of all dry flies. Nothing in dry-fly construction could be simpler. A good dry-fly hackle is attached at the rear of the hook and spiraled forward to resemble a caterpillar without a body. With only a hook to support, this fly floats extremely well. Some people use two feathers. The first is spiraled forward to within about ⅛ inch of the hook eye. Then a much brighter feather, usually white, is wrapped around the pattern at the front. This is sometimes called a Bivisible, and the white front collar certainly aids the angler in seeing his fly during the drift. The palmered concept can be added to a number of dry flies to aid in the float, and the many radiating hackle points also give the impression of an insect moving its legs.

The Fore-And-Aft is an old pattern, quite similar to the palmered fly. Instead of the feather being palmered the full length of the hook shank, the Fore And Aft is made with two feathers. One is wound around the hook at the back, then a body material is wrapped around the center portion, followed by another feather spiraled forward to the hook eye. The Renegade, which Dennis Bitten, an avid Idaho Falls angler, has proven many times to me to be a deadly trout fly, is a good example of the Fore-And-Aft. It looks like a beginner's tying effort, but for some uncanny reason this fly really works.

Doug Swisher and Carl Richards have made famous a rather old pattern, the **No-Hackle**. This is a fly with a body and splayed wings and stiff tail feathers to support the fly, but no spiraling hackle, as is standard on most other flies. If you carefully observe a floating mayfly, you will note that the natural insect sits with its body on or in the surface film. It does not sit high above the surface, as is characteristic of so many dry-fly imitations.

When you are fishing supersmart trout, especially in slow water, the No-Hackle offers a much better imitation of a drifting insect, and at times it will score when few other patterns will. One caution: I've found that these flies are especially difficult to tie (at least for me), if you want them to float properly. It is one of the few flies that I buy.

Spiders or skaters are another fly that many anglers don't use, but I find these at times to be the most exciting of all dry flies to fish. I always carry a few of these. Spiders and skaters are simple flies, usually on a short-shank hook, with large, stiff dry-fly hackles wrapped around the hook for a short distance. The way to fish them to draw the most excitement is to skate them over the surface. I suppose that they imitate an insect trying to lift off the water. Dress the leader and the fly with a good paste floatant. Cast slightly across and downstream. Hold the rod high and allow the water to push the fly line, leader, and fly sideways and downcurrent. This causes the fly to skitter on its hackle tips across the surface. By waving the rod tip back and forth while the fly is skating across the surface, you can add additional action to the fly and also manipulate it in front of a hungry trout.

The Variant dry fly is different from a conventional dry fly in that it has hackle supporting the fly that is two or three times larger than the hackle on a conventional dry fly, and rarely are wings attached to a Variant dry fly. There seems to be no logical reason why this fly is so effective at times. The fact that it is a very old pattern may explain why it is rarely used anymore. Even so, it is a fly deserving to be in anyone's box for those situations when other dry flies are not doing the job. Years ago a problem in tying this fly was finding large enough hackle that was properly stiff. Today, superior dry-fly necks are commonplace, and this problem no longer exists.

There are many other specialty dry flies. One is the spinner. After mayflies have mated and the eggs have been deposited on or below the surface, the insects die and fall to the water with their wings outstretched. In fact, some people refer to the insects at this stage of the hatch as spentwings. The surface at times can be covered with their bodies, and trout (often big ones) will go on a feeding binge that anglers should take advantage of.

Many people tie the outstretched wings with hackle tips. But careful observation will show that such wings simply mat the fibers against the quill and usually don't give any representation of a spentwing. Hair wings do a better job, but they are also very bulky, and individual "spines" of hair also don't do as good a job of representing the outstretched wings of the spinner.

George Harvey, whom I believe to be the best American trout fisherman I've ever known, is also a superb and innovative fly tier. George has developed a spinner that has the most realistic wings. Best of all, when dressed this way the fly can be seen for a long distance. Visibility can be a problem when fishing smaller flies that sit flush on the surface. George uses Krystal Flash, which is ultrathin strands of twisted, flashy Mylar. He uses the pearlescent Krystal Flash, which exactly imitates the coloration of most spinner wings. About six strands are used during the tying procedure. Because the strands are spiraled, no matter the viewing angle you will see light reflected from the wing. I have been able to make a cast of fifty feet and clearly see a No. 20 spinner floating along. This is a terrific asset when fish are barely sipping such small insects from the surface and it's hard to detect a take.

Using George's idea, I have for several years been tying all my parachute-type flies with the Mylar wing instead of conventional materials. It's amazing how much farther and easier you can see even a small parachute on the surface.

Terrestrials offer another form of dry-fly fishing. Terrestrials are land-based insects that fall into the stream, and include leafhoppers, grasshoppers, ants, beetles, and many other kinds of insects that either fall to the surface or crawl accidentally to a place where they are deposited on the water.

The major difference between conventional dry flies and terrestrials is that dry flies sit above the surface, while terrestrials float awash in the surface film. When especially large hatches of a particular insect are falling on the surface, the fishing can be frantic. A prime example of this is in late August, especially out west, when grasshoppers are tossed by strong winds into the streams. Grasshoppers represent a real chunk of protein food, and all of the trout in the stream eagerly take them.

If there is one terrestrial that every angler should carry, it's the ant. Just about anyplace you find trout, you'll find ants. And trout seem to go out of their way to take them. In September in many parts of eastern North America, ants will fly in great migrations. If the water's surface is wide, or the wind gets up, millions of these ants will fall to the surface. It creates one of the best trout feeding binges you'll ever see. Usually during September in the mid-Atlantic area, the big limestone rivers, such as the

A head-on view of a standard dry fly (left) and a terrestrial. The standard dry sits high up off the surface, while the terrestrial sits right in the surface film.

Susquehanna, Potomac, James, and similar rivers, often are subject to millions of migrating ants falling to the surface. Some of the finest smallmouth bass surface action of the year occurs at this time.

If I had to choose only seven dry flies for all my fishing, two of them would be terrestrials: ants and grasshopper imitations.

Another dry fly, the caddis, doesn't imitate mayflies. Rather, it imitates the large body of caddisflies that inhabit most trout rivers. As water equality declines in many rivers, mayflies (which need very clean waters) are declining. **Caddisflies,** which can tolerate less pure waters, are on the increase. This means that anglers should become more alert to the possibility of using the caddis dry fly.

The basic difference between a mayfly and caddisfly is that mayflies hold their wings vertically above the water as they float along. Caddisflies fold their wings along the body in the shape of a pup tent, with the wing protruding well behind the body as the fly sits on the surface.

Caddisflies can be found in many sizes, from those dressed on No. 8 hooks to some so small that a No. 18 or 20 hook is appropriate. Most effective caddisflies are dressed on No. 12 and 18 hooks. However, a mistake that many fairly skilled fly fishermen make is they often use imitations that are not small enough. There is often a hatch of very small caddisflies, which some call microcaddis. Always carry a few patterns to match these. I like Gary Borger's polypropylene imitation. It is simply a little polypropylene wound on a hook for a body, one hackle spiraled forward to help support the fly, and a wing of the same polypropylene laid back along the body.

While caddisflies hatch in many colors, I feel that all you need are dark and light brown, and a few in light gray. With these colors in various sizes you'll find that you can handle most caddisfly action.

Of all the caddis dry-fly patterns, the most popular, and deservedly so, is one developed by Al Troth, called the Elkhair Caddis. It is not suitable for imitating the very tiny microcaddis, but for all other caddisfly hatches I find this fly does the job very well.

Stoneflies usually crawl out on rocks changing from nymphs to winged adults, and then fly away to mate. For that reason few stonefly patterns have ever been developed. But there are local conditions that can make stoneflies a very desirable pattern to have with you. Two examples come to mind. When the tremendous willow fly hatches occur on western rivers in late spring, the fish feed on these huge stoneflies and ignore virtually all other foods until the hatch is over. This is the time to match the hatch with a stonefly imitation. Another time when stoneflies can be effective, though many trout fishermen are unaware of this bonanza, is in the dead of winter. At this time a small (No. 18) black stonefly hatches in prodigious numbers. The trout are tuned into these emerging insects. I've had some great dry-fly fishing in Maryland, where I live, in mid-February, when these small black stoneflies emerge.

Underwater Trout Flies

Aside from streamers, which will be discussed separately, there are three major groups of underwater flies that take trout: wet flies, nymphs, and soft-hackle flies.

Wet flies are imitations of drowned insects and were probably the first artificial flies used for catching trout. They have fallen from popularity. Some of the wet flies of old are still every bit as effective as they once were. One of the most effective methods of fishing wet flies is to fish what is called a "cast," or a series of two or three flies on the same leader. The fly on the bottom (usually the heaviest or largest) ensures a good turnover of the leader. The other patterns are attached with short sections of leader, called droppers.

One of the real tricks to fishing a cast of wet flies is to make sure that the droppers are no longer than four inches—or about the width of the average man's palm. If they are longer, they will frequently entangle in the leader. A great advantage to using a cast of flies is that you can offer the trout several different colors, styles, or sizes of wet flies at the same time. Often it will become evident that the trout definitely prefer a particular one.

Nymphs are perhaps the single most effective flies for catching trout. Nymphs are imitations of the underwater stages of many aquatic insects. When you consider that nymphs make up perhaps 90 percent of the total diet of most trout, then it makes sense to fish these imitations.

Nymphs are imitations mainly of mayflies, but also stoneflies, caddisflies, and other aquatic insects. They range in size from those dressed on tiny No. 24 hooks to monster nymphs dressed on No. 2 hooks. Most nymphs are tied on hooks that are slightly longer than standard length, since the bodies of the naturals are usually long and thin.

It is good to remember that trout will often refuse a dry fly that doesn't float naturally. But trout understand the currents beneath the surface maybe even better than they do those above, since that is where they do most of their feeding. *For that reason, the better you can drift a nymph drag free to the trout, the more strikes will be forthcoming.* Another important factor in nymph fishing is to realize the various techniques used to offer a nymph to a trout. These will be discussed in much detail in chapter 8, special fishing techniques.

Best of all, you don't need a huge array of nymphs to fish them success-fully. If you have several nymphs in light, medium, and dark tan, but in assorted sizes, you can usually score well. Again, the selection of nymphs will be discussed in chapter 8. As fish become smarter, we need to fish with smaller nymphs. The standard a decade ago was to fish nymphs in sizes from No. 10 through 16. But today, you will find that sizes No. 16 through 22 are often more effective, even on very large trout.

Soft-hackle flies are unique in that they don't imitate a specific insect. Instead they offer something to the trout that has appeal in shape, color, and action. Some anglers insist they are better imitations of a drowned insect; others feel they are counterfeit nymphs. This is an academic argument, and irrelevant so far as I am concerned. What is important is that soft-hackle flies are deadly. They certainly are more effective in most cases than wet flies, and in many situations I can outfish my nymphs with them. As with nymphs you only need a few soft-hackle flies to be effective. You will need them in assorted sizes from No. 10 through 16.

Another fly that trout fishermen are beginning to use more, and that has resulted in catching trout at times when anglers used to fail, is the emerger. Emergers are patterns that represent that stage of an aquatic insect as it emerges from the nymphal stage to become an airborne adult.

Emergers can be tied so that they can be fished in the water column, or as floating nymphs still held captive in their nymphal shucks as they struggle on the surface trying to free themselves. When you are tying this fly, selection of the proper hook and correctly dressing it are vital to success. The fly should not be tied so that it sinks like a nymph, nor should it float like a dry fly—it really represents a fly that either is swimming up through the water to emerge, or has already reached the surface and is trying to rid itself of the nymphal case and fly away.

Streamers

The dry fly has captured the soul of most writers who address the sport of fly fishing. Nymphs and wet flies perhaps have received the next most attention. But strangely, streamers, which are the most versatile flies any fisherman can use, have received very little notice over the years. Yet streamers are used to catch everything from bluegills to blue marlin. I know for certain that if I had to choose a style of fly for all my fishing, the streamer would be my first choice. Somehow streamers have gotten a bad rap.

The dry fly is regarded as the ultimate way to take fish on a fly, especially trout. Wet flies and nymphs are regarded by many purists as not quite ethical methods of catching trout. Streamers are ignored. Streamers can be trolled (as they are traditionally in New England and other parts of the world), but they are more often cast. They range in size from less than an inch for trout, bluegills, and crappie, to those dressed on No. 5/0 to 7/0 hooks, used to take ocean species such as sharks and amberjack.

There are two basic types of streamers: exact imitations and attractor patterns. Both are effective, often in the same place, at the same time, and on the same species.

Imitations. The original streamers were imitations of baitfish that various predatory fish fed upon. Fly fishermen soon realized that fish often fed on minnows and small swimming creatures. Tying undulating feathers or hair on a long-shanked hook to represent a swimming baitfish was so successful that hundreds of patterns were developed to more closely imi-

Barracuda are spectacular gamefish and offer a great fly rod target on tropical flats.

tate the local species of baitfish. The first streamers were probably tied with a chenille body and a wing of either feathers or hair. Two examples that over the decades have taken many fish are the Black Ghost (feather wing) and Black-Nose Dace (bucktail wing). In recent years some incredibly good imitations have been developed, using older standard materials along with modern materials, such as Mylar and epoxy.

Attractors. This kind of streamer is often outlandish in color and shape, and even experienced anglers don't know why there are times when such a fly produces so well. Such flies range in color from all black through some brilliant fluorescent combinations. Often, very flashy materials are used, too.

The shapes of streamers vary widely—and there are good reasons for this. If the angler is forced to fish at night, when waters are roiled and dirty, or any time that the fish's vision may be impaired by local conditions, the shape of the fly becomes very important. The most effective flies for such fishing have large heads, which "push" water. The head and forward portion are wide, and the wings are usually very bulky. All of this is an effort to create something that when retrieved through the water will create vibrations that the fish can sense and locate. Most streamers that are supposed to represent baitfish should have the general shape of a baitfish.

Streamers that have stood the test of time have a unique design that is critical to their success. One example is the hackle fly, which was developed in the 1800s by bass fishermen. Joe Bates, in his 1950 edition of *Streamer Fly Tying and Fishing,* called it the Homer Rhode, Jr. Tarpon Streamer. Today it is known as the Seaducer. It is one of the most effective flies you can use in the shallows in fresh or salt water. Such a fly has been in use for perhaps a hundred years—or more. You can sell a fisherman one bad fly pattern, but you'll never convince him to buy a second one. The long-term use and success of the hackle fly proves it has some very good design factors.

Let's discuss those factors: The tail of this fly has six to eight saddle or neck hackles. They are tied splayed (like a pair of frog's legs) so that when the fly is moved through the water, these legs close, and they spring apart when the fly is stopped. They also continue to undulate for a brief time. That alone is attractive to many species. But this fly has the full length of the hook shank palmered densely with wound hackle. This hackle accomplishes three things: It presents a bulky shape, which to a fish must make it look as if it's a relatively large morsel. Second, the many hackles extending out and around the hook shank act much like outriggers. They support the fly in the water and resist letting the fly sink. These hackles also allow the angler to fish in very shallow water without fear of snagging the bottom. On the retrieve the fly can be brought to a stop, and will sink so slowly that it can be allowed to pause in front of a fish. Then a short twitch to get tail and collar moving will often trigger a strike. The third attribute of the hackle fly is that the wound collar creates mini eddies as the pattern is retrieved. Water tumbling through and over the many spines of wound hackle sweeps back, eddy fashion, over the tail feathers,

Size is often important in streamers. The author caught this 19-pound peacock bass after switching to a 10-inch, bulky streamer pattern.

The hackle fly, also called a Seaducer, is one of the most versatile shallow-water flies for both fresh and salt water. It is a very old American pattern, first developed for bass fishing in the late 1800s.

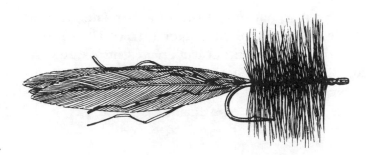

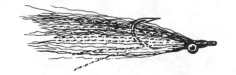

The Clouser Minnow is the single best underwater fly I have ever fished. It can be tied in lengths from ½ inch to 12 inches, and will take any predator that eats minnows.

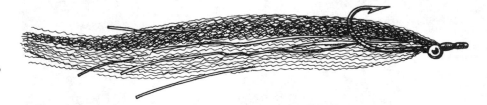

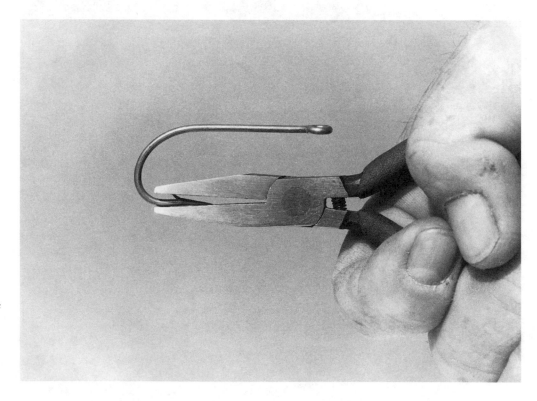

To prevent a hook from breaking when you crush the barb, grasp it with the pliers as shown. This way the jaws support the hook on either side of the barb, making breakage much less likely.

giving additional motion to them. This is a good example of how fly design is important.

The best streamer that I have ever used around the world in fresh and salt water is the Clouser Minnow, developed by Bob Clouser. Several years ago in his shop on the Susquehanna River in Pennsylvania, Bob handed me a crude sample and urged me to try it on smallmouths. I quickly saw that the design of this fly was superb. I encouraged Bob to work on this fly, and I added input. I don't keep records on fish I catch, but the Clouser Minnow is so effective that to date, I have caught eighty-six species of fish, swimming the fly through waters in many parts of the world. They range from wary brown trout in small streams to many ocean species, such as a Spanish mackerel of twenty-five pounds off Australia. Even permit have fallen for it.

Best of all, a complete novice fly tier can construct this pattern in a few minutes. A pair of lead eyes are tied in just back of the hook eye. Then the fly is turned over and repositioned in the vise. A wing of bucktail or artificial material is added. On top of this are placed a number of strands of Krystal Flash or Flashabou (I favor Flashabou since it is more supple). Then a top wing of bucktail or synthetic materials finishes the fly.

Because the fly is designed with lead eyes and a minimum amount of wing material, it sinks like an anvil in a swamp. This is a major drawback to most streamer flies—they don't sink well. With a floating line and a long, ten- to twelve-foot leader, a Clouser Minnow can easily be fished six feet or deeper in a river. That's several feet below what most streamer flies will do. Because the wing is sleek and the hook carries lead eyes, it is surprising how well the fly casts. When cast into the wind, the bulk and buoyancy of most streamers often cause them to fall back on the leader. The lead eyes on the Clouser Minnow, if a good cast is made, will maintain enough inertia to pierce the breeze and turn the fly over.

The sleek dressing gets the fly deep, where the large eyes attract the attention of predatory fish. I believe that eyes often act as bull's eyes for predators seeking baitfish. Experiments over the years have proven to me that in clear water, the same pattern with much larger eyes will draw more strikes than a conventional tie. The Clouser Minnow has eyes that stand out.

As a guideline for tying this fly, use $\frac{1}{100}$- or $\frac{1}{50}$-ounce (twice as heavy) lead eyes for small flies used for crappie, trout, bonefish, and other species that would be attracted to such a fly in the shallows. For most smallmouth and largemouth bass, for bonefish in deeper water, for permit, and for where I want to get down deeper or faster with a Clouser Minnow carrying a wing 2½ to 4½ inches in length, I use $\frac{1}{36}$- or $\frac{1}{24}$-ounce lead eyes. For fast-sinking patterns and larger flies, I use either the $\frac{1}{18}$ or $\frac{1}{10}$-ounce eyes. A caution when using these heavier eyes is to keep your cast tilted to the side. They smart when they hit you in the back. But when you want to get down deep and fast, these two sizes will do the job. On a fast-sinking line you can fish in lakes or saltwater reefs with such flies, in twenty to thirty feet of water. For anyone who doesn't want to use lead eyes, there are metallic eyes that many find acceptable. I suggest using one size larger to get the same sink rate as a lead eye.

The three most effective color combinations for the Clouser Minnow, I think, are an underwing of white or yellow with an overwing of fluorescent chartreuse; a white underwing with dove gray overwing; and a white underwing with tan or brown overwing.

The sink rate of a streamer is vital to success. The hackle fly and Clouser Minnow are exaggerated examples. One barely sinks; the other bombs to the depths. Streamer imitations, to be effective, must sink at the proper rate. Two examples come to mind. There are two basic types of tarpon flies: the Keys style and the Whistler. The Keys style tarpon fly is a short (rarely longer than 2 ½ inches), sleek, sparsely tied fly with only a few hackles at the rear and a thin collar. The Whistler is the exact opposite design. It can have a weighted or unweighted body. The shank usually has a heavy chenille body with an extra amount of bucktail tied in around the hook shank, with several hackles flared on each side. It is completed by adding a pair of large bead chain eyes, and the finished head is tied deliberately bulky. Though completely different, both types are designed for tarpon.

Fishing conditions determine which pattern to use. In the Keys, tarpon are first seen in clear water, and an exact cast close to the fish is made so that on the retrieve the fly arrives exactly on a level with the fish. It's a good rule of fly fishing that excepting bottom-feeding species, predatory fish will almost never descend to take a fly—but will often rise slightly to do so. The conventional Whistler pattern is generally not used when sight-fishing tarpon in clear water. It sinks too fast, and the heavy fly crashing to the water doesn't allow a quiet entry—something demanded when sight-fishing in clear waters. But the Whistler is vastly more effective when fishing in such places as Casa Mar, the famed tarpon camp in northeast Costa Rica, where Dan Blanton designed this fly.

Here conditions are exactly the opposite from the Keys. The waters are usually roiled from jungle rains, and visibility is severely limited. The bulk of the Whistler creates sound vibrations so that tarpon can locate it in these poor conditions. A sleek Keys style tarpon fly would be nearly useless in such waters. It wouldn't sink fast enough and couldn't be located. Another example of the importance of sink rate is when tying a sculpin pattern. Sculpins are a favorite food of bass and trout. They have no air bladder, so they sink to the bottom when not actively swimming. That means that most of the time fish find them on the bottom. Sculpin flies should have a rapid sink rate, so that when the caster offers his fly to a fish, it goes very close to the bottom.

The sink rate can be controlled in several ways—and it's important to realize that the same pattern can be tied to obtain a slow, fairly fast, or rapid sink rate. Let's take a plain bucktail streamer, for example, with a white underwing and an overwing of blue. If the hook shank is left undressed, or wound full length with very light tinsel or Mylar, and a relatively heavy wing of bucktail is dressed, this fly will fish almost in the surface film. A second method, which will cause it to sink faster, is to dress the hook shank with a few wraps of .010 lead wire and chenille. Then a wing more sparse than the first tie is made. If you want the same pattern to dive deep, wrap the entire hook shank with .030 lead wire, add chenille over the lead, tie in a rather sparse wing, and add a pair of lead eyes at the head. All three of these flies are the same basic pattern—but each sinks quite differently.

Styles of Streamers

There are a number of different styles of streamers, all designed for special fishing situations. The most conventional, of course, is a relatively long hook shank, usually dressed with chenille or similar material, and a wing that lies along the top of the shank. A variation of this is the well-known Matuka style, where the wing is secured to the shank, eliminating the possibility of the rear of the wing fouling around the hook. The Zonker represents another variation of the conventional streamer, in which a rabbit fur wing is placed on top of the body.

The hackle streamer or Seaducer is another style. The Clouser Minnow is another type. The Lefty's Deceiver is another style, where the wing is secured at the rear to prevent under-wrapping the hook. A collar that flows beyond the rear of the hook helps to form a minnow shape in the water. This collar also forms mini currents that increase the action of the wing. The fly is very sleek out of the water and easy to cast.

The Bend Back, a very old bass fly that was developed to fish in the thick vegetation of the South, has become a very popular semiweedless fly. The use of either monofilament or wire weed guards is still another method used to prevent a fly from snagging during the retrieve. The woolheads and the famous Muddler Minnow are streamer variations. Carrie Stevens, a famed New England fly tier, designed a fly that I have found extremely useful over the years. It has been renamed the Thunder Creek Fly. Bucktail is tied in so that it faces forward, and then it is brought back and secured again on the hook shank. This fly is exceptionally easy to cast and never tangles in flight. It has been one of my favorite smallmouth flies since the late 1940s, when I first found a sample in Maine. The leech patterns are imitations of a food many fish desire, and they really are a form of streamer fly. Even the Woolly Bugger would be considered a streamer, since it is often fished like one. Bob Popovics developed the Surf Candy, a streamer made from standard materials with a head coated in either epoxy or silicone that is extremely effective on many saltwater species. There may be more styles of streamers that I have forgotten, and certainly more are yet to come.

Fishing the Streamer

Streamers can and should be fished in a number of ways—depending upon the situation. But there are some simple guidelines that apply to almost all fishing situations. First, streamers are often retrieved so that undesirable slack accumulates in either the line or leader. If a fish strikes, a hookup becomes more difficult. Perhaps the greatest fault in fishing streamers is that most anglers hold the rod tip too high. The fly will never completely stop if the rod is held high on a windy day. In good streamer fishing technique, the rod tip should be held lower than the belt. Many fish have eluded anglers who used the rod to help impart action to the streamer. Flipping the rod tip up and then dropping it causes the fly to dart forward (often several feet, which is unrealistic). Several feet of slack is formed each time the rod is dropped. Should a fish strike then—and they often do—it's difficult to remove the slack and set the hook. When retrieving a streamer, I try to keep the rod tip either in the water or no more than a few inches above the surface.

When you are casting across a current (river or tidal flow), a good technique is to throw the fly approximately at right angles to the flow. And on the retrieve, drop the tip below the belt and rock the rod hand slightly. This will cause the rod tip to undulate only a few inches, and it imparts a short, darting motion to the fly. After each rise and fall of the tip, strip in the accumulated slack, making sure that the line remains taut.

A major fault of streamer fishermen is to make a cast and leave the rod pointing in the direction where the fly fell to the water. If a current flows south and you cast directly east across the current, don't allow the rod to remain pointing east. Instead, as the line drifts downstream, move the rod in that direction. Attempt to keep as much slack out of the line as possible. On extended drifts I often switch the hand holding the rod and continue to sweep the rod slowly until it points almost downstream—all in an effort to keep out slack during the drift.

Here's a tip for fishing a shoreline from a boat, be it a river, lake, bay, or canal. Most fishermen will cast at approximately right angles to the shore.

If the cast is made to the bank, the fly lands; once the retrieve starts, the fly swims almost directly away from the fish. The fish views such a fly from the rear, or almost as if looking down the length of a knife blade. And much of the bank is not covered by the fly, since the fly is cast, retrieved, and then cast back a few feet farther along the shore.

A much better method would be one where the fly travels along the bank. This would allow it to swim along the entire bank and show a profile (instead of an end view) to the fish. This is relatively easy to accomplish. Make a much harder than normal side cast toward the shoreline, stopping the rod very abruptly at about halfway between a right angle from the angler and the bank. The rod will make the stop, but the tip will curve deeply inward toward the angler. This will cause the line, leader, and fly to follow a similar curve. With a little practice the fly drops on the water with a considerable amount of line and leader lying parallel to the bank. On the retrieve the fly will travel along the bank before it makes the turn and starts toward the angler. This cast is easy to do if you make sure to make an extra hard side cast, and stop abruptly. Make sure that the forward stroke of the rod is absolutely parallel to the water. If the final speed-up-and-stop of the rod tip starts three feet, two inches from the surface on the forward stroke, the stroke must end three feet, two inches from the surface.

Streamers can be fished on floating, slow-sinking, and fast-sinking lines. Two lines are especially helpful in streamer fishing when you need to cover a lot of water. A shooting taper allows the caster to obtain more distance and thereby search more water. And many sinking lines are specially designed so that the tip sinks at the same rate as the rest of the line; this will result in more positive hookups when fishing deep. One line that is not a good choice for underwater fishing with a streamer, where longer casts are being made, is the sinking-tip type. The first ten feet or so sinks, while the rest of the line floats. With every strip on the retrieve, the floating portion tends to loft or draw the sinking portion toward the surface. If you want a streamer to run at about the same depth underwater, a full-sinking line or a shooting taper is best. Streamer flies, because you can alter size, shape, and sink rate, appeal to all predator species and can help you catch more and bigger fish.

Creature Imitations

There are a few underwater flies that really resemble nothing specific, nor are they attractor patterns. But they are deadly. I suppose if most trout fishermen were limited to just a single fly pattern to be fished underwater for trout, and maybe bass, they would select the Woolly Bugger. This is not a streamer. It's not a nymph. In fact, it is sort of a combination of both—and also resembles a leech, a favorite underwater food of several predatory fish species.

The Woolly Bugger is nothing more than the old Woolly Worm pattern, with a flexible, soft tail, usually of marabou fibers. It can be dressed on hooks as small as No. 14, and as big as No. 2. Usually Woolly Buggers are dressed on hooks that are 2X or 3X long, rather than on standard-length hooks. The body is typically chenille, but I've determined that one of the best body materials is several strands of peacock herl twisted into a rope and wound on, with a dark, soft, webby hackle spiraled over this body. To prevent the herl from breaking, I usually wrap fine copper or gold wire with the twisted herl. For larger flies, marabou is used for the tail. But for smaller flies I find that using the fluff at the base of a neck or saddle hackle lets me tie a better, fuller tail that is exactly the same as marabou. Woolly Buggers can be dressed so that they are unweighted, or weighted with beadheads, coneheads, or lead wire, depending upon fishing conditions.

While Woolly Buggers are tied in colors that range from bright salmon-pink fluorescent (great for Alaskan salmon) to subtle, dark hues, two colors are by far the most popular with trout fishermen. All-black Woolly Buggers are fished more than all other color combinations. Next choice is olive.

The fly can be fished in several ways. In lakes and deeper water it is often tied with various weights, then cast out and allowed to sink slowly. The angler watches the line as the fly descends, since fish will often take the Woolly Bugger as it falls. If not, at the desired depth the fly is slowly retrieved. In shallow streams it is sometimes allowed to fall to the bottom, and then brought back so that it crawls along the bottom. It can also be cast across current and allowed to sweep along with the flow, and the angler can allow it to dead-drift or give it slight movement with the rod tip. The Woolly Bugger can also be fished as a streamer: cast out and brought back slowly or rapidly.

It is one of the most versatile flies I have ever used, especially in fresh water. It has helped me catch a host of species, including northern pike, bonefish, mangrove snapper, bluegill, trout, bass, and striped bass.

The sculpin is another pattern that I'd class as a creature imitation. It's not really a streamer, but it does represent a small minnow that lives on the bottom. The sculpin has no air bladder and will rest on the bottom when not swimming. It also feeds mostly during the very early and very late hours of the day. *Thus, sculpin imitations are not as effective at midday as they are early and late.* Almost all sculpins are tan, brown, or olive. I prefer to tie my sculpins weighted, and I much favor patterns dressed with materials that tend to sink. While many sculpin flies have been dressed with deer hair, I personally favor flies tied with a material that tends to sink better, such as wool. Since sculpin flies are most effective when fished close to the bottom, it is desirable to have the fly tied in reverse, so that the hook rides up. If not dressed reversed, then they should carry a weed guard to prevent snagging the bottom on the retrieve.

Surface Flies and Popping Bugs

Nothing appeals to some predator fish more than a creature struggling on or near the surface. Insects that are somehow trapped in the surface film and trying to free themselves, and crippled baitfish straining to swim away, just can't be ignored by many fish.

Perhaps the best thing about popping bugs is that you see the strike. The fish has to break the surface to take the offering—and that's exciting. One other reason for using popping bugs is that many times they will catch you bigger fish. Many trophy-size species will ignore an underwater streamer, no matter how large it is. But a good-size popping bug worked noisily over the surface creates such a disturbance that a big fish is convinced that what you are offering it is really larger. Some species of fish are suckers for a surface fly or popping bug. Largemouth bass, jack crevalle, striped bass, and amberjack are all fish that just can't seem to ignore a gurgling bug.

For years the most common materials for building popping bugs were balsa wood and cork. Cork remains the most common material used today. But when casting on salt water, where wind, distance, and a large

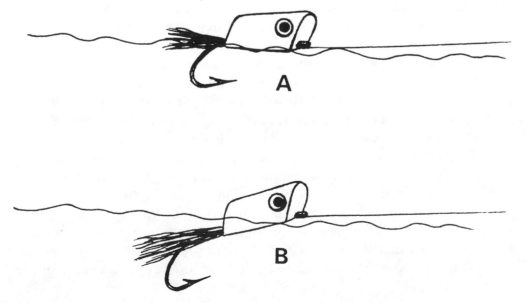

Poor and good popping-bug designs. Drawing A shows a bug with a short-shank hook, on which the point sits underneath the bug's body. This requires that the fish swallow the entire bug before it can be hooked. Drawing B shows the same bug on a long-shank hook that places the point well behind the bug, and tilts the point down, too. This greatly improves the chances of a hookup.

bug all complicate casting, newer space-age materials are used. Ethafoam, a material made by Dow Chemical, is preferred by many of us for larger popping bugs. A mistake made by many people new to tying poppers is to put too many tail materials on them. A bug should be sleek, as this will help it cast better and increase its action on the surface. Unless you want a bug to sit for long periods and be examined by the fish below, make your bugs sleek, and with minimal dressing at the back of the body.

Good popping bug design is critical to successfully hooking fish. Hooks should extend beyond the bug body. Poorly designed bugs have the hook point underneath the body, which means that the fish has to engulf the entire bug before the hook makes contact. Bugs with the hook extended back of the bug body also tend to sit in the water at a slight angle, with the hook point well below the surface. This ensures better contact with the fish as it strikes. It also makes it easier for the angler to lift the bug from the water.

For many years I've been using a largemouth bass popping bug that I feel is superior to any other. Many largemouth bass situations require that you leave the popping bug motionless on the surface. The bass will frequently study the offering for some time before deciding to strike it. If you had a bug that, long after you had twitched it, would still display some movement, you would have a better bug. Norm Bartlett, a well-respected Maryland fly rodder, many years ago designed a bug from an old pattern called the Gerbubble Bug. The original bug was tied so that chicken hackle fibers radiated out from the sides. Norm substituted marabou for the stiffer, skimpy hackle fibers. After the bug is popped, mini currents are created around the bug. The marabou, incredibly supple, continues to undulate long after the bug is stopped. I find that strikes are radically increased by using Norm's special popping bug.

Another specially designed bug is the Pencil Popper, which I think was developed by Jerry Jarosik. The fly is a tube of balsa wood, tapered at the rear. (Jerry used a pencil sharpener to shape it—hence the name.) It is usually tied with a monofilament weed guard. The Pencil Popper has three attributes important to bass fishermen. First, its thin profile allows it to be cast much easier than a standard popping bug. Also, a Pencil Popper's sleekness allows it to slither through lily pads and vegetation, where wide-faced bugs may get tangled. And the third attribute is that the long, thin body closely resembles a crippled baitfish. I might add that it works well in a number of inshore saltwater fishing situations, too.

Popping bug bodies are also made from deer hair. While there are some special fishing situations where deer-hair bodies work well, in most cases I've found that the fishermen who enjoy and promote using them are fly tiers. Balsa wood, cork, and closed-cell foam bodies float much better than deer hair, which tends eventually to soak up water and becomes heavy to cast and loses some of its inherent action.

Another surface fly, which is a combination of a popping bug and a streamer fly, is the Dahlberg Diver. This fly has a head of deer hair and the feathered body of a streamer. The head has a special shape. It tapers to the hook eye like a blunt cone. Behind the cone is a deer-hair collar and behind that, the streamer-fly body.

When the Dahlberg Diver is fished, it lies on the surface. A pull on the line causes it to dive under slightly and make a popping sound, much like a popping bug. Because the head is of deer hair, it immediately floats back to the surface, where the action can be repeated. It has another attribute that makes it a very special and effective fly. If tension is kept on the line, and the retrieve continued, once it dives beneath the surface, it will swim underwater. If the retrieve is stopped, during the pause the Dahlberg Diver again rises to the surface. Thus by varying the retrieve, the angler can cause the Dahlberg Diver to make a series of pops, followed by an underwater swimming motion (duplicating a streamer), and then let the bug come back to the surface, where it can again imitate a popping bug.

Six

HOOKING, FIGHTING, LANDING, AND RELEASING FISH

Once the fish has accepted the angler's offering, he must hook, fight, and land it. There are techniques for accomplishing these things. It is a sad but true story that many anglers who finally hook a trophy fish often lose it. The loss can be from improperly setting the hook, not knowing how to fight the fish, or landing it incorrectly.

Bringing a fish to your boot tops or into the boat begins with selecting and preparing your tackle. The size of the hook is important. And it must be matched to the fish. Sailfish, for example, have a mouth almost filled with solid bone. The rim of the mouth is large and very tough. A hook smaller than No. 3/0 (the absolute minimum size) simply can't find a purchase. Giant tarpon inhale a fly, so a smaller hook can be used, but they have strong jaws and will frequently crush hooks smaller than No. 1/0; the most popular are No. 2/0 and 3/0. When you are fishing for very large trout while offering them small flies, such as Tricos, it's to your advantage not to tie your flies on the conventional No. 20 or 22 hooks. Such thin, fragile hooks will often straighten during the battle. You need the strongest hooks you can use, and still get the fish to accept the fly. Some experienced anglers will tie a No. 22 Trico, midge, or other small pattern on a thin-wire, No. 18 hook. If you fish for hefty saltwater species or any large fish with light, fragile tippets, you will need the softness of a smaller-than-normal rod, such as one that would cast a 5- to 8-weight line. And the hooks should never be larger than No. 1/0. The larger hooks have a

This Argentine guide is directing the angler to the best position from which to cast to a wary trout on the Mello River.

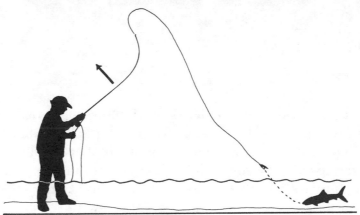

When fishing an underwater fly in shallow water, never strike upward when the fish takes the fly. If the fish misses, the upward movement takes the fly right out of the water. This means you have to throw the fly back at the fish—never a good idea.

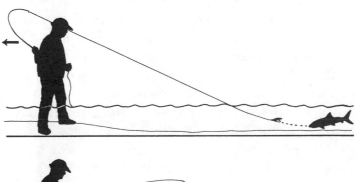

Instead, move the rod to one side (middle drawing) or make a strip strike by pulling sharply back on the fly line with your line hand. Even if the fish misses, the fly remains near the fish, and you have a chance at another strike.

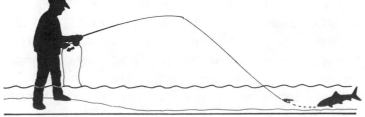

Simply flipping the wrist to set the hook won't do the job for large fish like this barracuda.

thicker wire diameter, and the stiffer rods won't bend easily, so the light leader will break. Nymphs that you need to sink should be dressed on heavy-wire hooks. Consideration of the type of hook you use in seeking your quarry is often a vital point in scoring well.

Once you have selected the hook, it should be sharpened. I firmly believe that the greatest fault of all fishermen is that they don't fish with sharp-enough hooks. There are some new hooks that are chemically sharpened, and they do a good job. But many hooks you buy are not sharp enough to fish with. It's easy to check. Drag the point across your fingernail with very slight downward pressure (it doesn't hurt). If the point doesn't dig into the nail, it needs sharpening. There are many techniques for sharpening hooks, and it's a personal matter which you choose. But sharp hooks are the first step in making contact with fish.

Striking

The angler should carefully consider his casting position, not only for a good presentation, but also for when he hooks the fish. Is there room to follow the fish as it takes off? Are there obstructions or hazards that might not be encountered if a different casting position was taken? Where is the best place to land the fish, and can you get to it easily? The angler should ask all these questions before making the cast. It does no good to hook a fish and then have no way to win the fight. When you are trout fishing, for example, where large fish may be taken, the best place to land them is usually at the tail of the pool. Here the river will be shallow, so the fish has less water to fight in, and you have a better chance of bringing the fish close to shore. If you can get the fish into very shallow water, you restrict its ability to swim, and you better your chances of landing it.

During the retrieve, whenever possible, watch the fly. You should set the hook only after you are convinced that the fish has taken it well. There are a number of ways to strike, or set the hook, and they vary with the fish being sought, the line used, and sometimes the fishing conditions. But certain rules govern good striking technique.

Rules for Striking

Never strike too hard. The instant reaction of any fish is to try to flee the moment the steel is felt. If the angler's rod is traveling one way on the strike, and the fish is going in the other direction, attempting to flee, that sudden jolt on the leader is almost surely going to break it. Some anglers set a hook in a large fish as though they are trying to tear the fly free from the bushes. This can lead to a broken leader or pulled hook. Set the hook with just enough pressure to fully bury it in the fish's mouth. Once the hook has been set, forget the fish if it's a long-running or big one, and concentrate on clearing all loose line off the deck and from around your feet. Once all line either is on the reel or has cleared through the guides, you can start thinking about fighting the fish. A major mistake is to try reeling in the slack line when the fish stops running. Either move away from the fish or wait until it runs again, until all line is outside the guides. Invariably when you try to fight the fish and reel in loose line, the game is lost.

When fishing an underwater fly in shallow water, never strike upward with the rod tip. Fish in shallow water are easily spooked. Any additional

This dry-fly angler will have to strike fish much differently here than he would when fishing in calm, slow water.

cast to such a fish means a good chance of alarming it. This rule applies to both fresh- and saltwater fishing situations. If you sweep the rod upward and the fish is missed, the line and fly will leap out of the water. This will necessitate throwing the fly back to the fish—something you want to avoid.

Instead, when you think the fish has taken the fly in shallow water, make a side strike, or a strip strike. If the rod is moved gently to the side a short distance, and the fish is missed, the fly simply slides a short distance across the bottom and remains near the fish. If a strip strike is used (the hand pulls back on the line to set the hook), and the fish is missed, the fly moves only a few inches. With either method the fly remains near the fish following the strike and is not removed from the water. Many times the fish will take the fly again.

To better understand how the rod helps or hinders you when striking and fighting a large fish, try this simple experiment. Extend about fifteen feet of line through the rod and grasp the line end firmly. While you hold the line end, have someone apply full pressure as the rod is lifted or brought to the side. The results will be the same. As the rod begins to rise or is moved sideways, only the butt section of the rod is bent and considerable pressure can be felt by the person holding the fly line. As the rod rises or is moved backward the bend in the rod moves toward the tip. Immediately pressure begins to drop off. When the rod is held vertically, only that part of it near the tip is bending, as only a few ounces of pressure are being applied.

What this means is that when using fairly strong tippets, from say, twelve to twenty pound test, you should strike and fight a fish with the butt of the rod. If you are using fragile tippets, such as when freshwater trout fishing, you should use the tip of the rod to set the hook—and fight the fish.

With large fish such as giant tarpon, sailfish, cobia, or similar species, don't strike by flipping the wrist or forearm. Generally for such fishing a heavy rod is used, almost never lighter than 10-weight, and often a 12 or 13. These rods are heavy and difficult to move rapidly with just the wrist or forearm, and such heavy fish often possess bony, hard mouths that resist the hook's penetration. You need to drive the hook home with much greater force by utilizing the butt section of the rod.

For large or powerful fish, use the body and arms to make the strike. It takes a lot of power to drive a large hook into the bony mouth of such species as billfish and tarpon. During the retrieve, when the fish strikes, bring the arms in close to the body. Grip the rod firmly, and with the arms held against the body, rotate the hips away from the fish. This allows you to use the arm, back, and full body to assist the butt section in setting the hook. Another technique favored by many top fly rodders is to grasp the line firmly in the hand, point the rod directly at the fish, and give a sharp pull backward away from the fish. But be ready to release the line instantly after you have jabbed the hook home. Strike with the butt—not the rod tip.

When you are retrieving underwater flies, most of the time a more efficient strike occurs if the rod tip is held low and pointing toward the fish. The lower the rod on the retrieve—especially if the rod can be pointed at the fish—the less slack develops in the line between angler and quarry. On the strike all slack must be removed before the hook can be driven home. A good basic rule for getting an effective strike is to eliminate all slack before you strike.

That means a low rod that is pointed at the fish. There are some exceptions to this, of course. When you are fishing with nymphs in pocket water and riffles in a trout stream, the best technique is generally to elevate the rod and keep as much line off the water as possible. When you are drifting a fly for steelhead or Atlantic salmon, a large, slack mend is thrown upstream in the line to get a controlled drift, often necessitating a high rod angle. But most of the time when you are fishing underwater flies, it's best to keep the rod low and pointing at the fish during the retrieve.

When dry fly fishing, you strike differently under various fishing conditions. Trout live in different environments, which require them to feed differently. The angler has to adapt his striking technique to score consistently. Look at two examples: A rainbow is holding in a swift riffle in a large river. An insect is swept by quickly. The trout sees it and has to make an instant decision. Hungry, it sweeps up, inhales the fly quickly, and dives below, out of the current. It doesn't take the fly gingerly. It is forced to grab it in its mouth before the fly can sweep away on the current. The other extreme is another trout that lives in a slow-moving stream—such as a limestone or spring creek—or a lake. The feeding situation is entirely different. A fly settles to the slow-moving surface, and the trout rises carefully and leisurely to inspect it. There is plenty of time to look it over and decide if it should be eaten. And if that decision is made, the trout slowly sucks the fly from the surface, instead of gulping it down.

In the two situations, the trout are forced to feed differently. The rainbow, because the fly was in its vision and soon would be gone on the fast currents, had to make an instant decision. It could get only a brief look at the quarry and then had to open its mouth and gulp the fly in, inhaling it deeply to be sure it didn't escape. But the trout in slow water has no need for haste. This fish is more leisurely and has no need to grab the fly. The fish moves under the fly and slowly sucks it down.

The fish in swift water takes the fly so deeply that an instant strike will usually result in a hookup. If there is not a quick strike, the fish will often spit out the imitation. But when fish are feeding on surface flies in slow-moving or still water, the strike must be delayed briefly. As the fish accepts your offering, count mentally "One, two, three," then lift the rod gently. The English used to say before striking "God save the queen." This gives the fish time to suck the fly deeply into its mouth. *Of course, you can delay too long, but you'll hook more trout in this case by striking too late rather than too early.* I have watched hair-trigger fly fishermen set hooks on fish sipping flies off a slow current who missed perhaps 75 percent of what should have been solid hookups. The major reason for the delay is that the trout is slowly inhaling the fly and the water around it. The mouth is open as the water and fly go inside. If you make a quick strike with the trout's mouth open, you stand a good chance of pulling the fly free. The fast-water fish grabs the fly and closes its mouth quickly, so that the insect can't escape; thus you can strike much faster.

There are times when a "non-strike" can be very effective. Sometimes, if the line and leader are taut between the angler and the fish, it's desirable not to strike. Instead the angler firmly grips the line and simply holds on. The rod is usually held at a slight side angle to the fish, but it is not swept away from the fish, as in conventional striking.

One example is when fishing dry flies for steelhead in big rivers. As the floating line and surface fly drift downstream from you, the steelhead pokes its head out of the water and sucks in the fly. The fish is usually pointed toward you, and the mouth is open so that the fly can be inhaled. If the angler strikes as the fish is inhaling the fly, it is simply pulled from its open mouth. The angler has to wait until the mouth has closed to ensure a hookup. The line and fly are being swept downstream and usually to the side as the fish takes the fly. If the angler doesn't strike but simply grips the line, with the rod pointed at the fish, the current will help sweep the fly deeper into the steelhead's mouth. Some steelheaders are so adept that they actually feed a slight bit of line to a steelhead taking a dry, in order to get the fly deeper into the mouth. That takes experience!

There are two schools of thought about how to set the hook on tarpon and sailfish. One group believes that you should either use the body, as explained earlier, or a strip strike. Another group feels that when a tarpon or sailfish takes your fly, a no-strike method is better. I have used both methods, and experience tells me that with sailfish I have better hookups with the no-strike technique. But both systems work. What is important is that you realize that both techniques exist. If one method isn't working for you, perhaps the other would.

The body and the strip strike have been explained earlier. The no-strike is a simple procedure. Of course, it is assumed that your hooks are always very sharp. As the tarpon or sailfish accepts the fly, the angler moves the rod parallel to the water and off to the side of the fish, at nearly a 90-degree angle. The line is firmly gripped, and the rod simply held stationary. With the fly in its mouth, the fish begins to rock its head back and forth or swim away. The angler, holding tension on the line, actually allows the fish to bury the hook by its own thrusting motions. This method is very effective, but one vital trick must be mastered. When the fish realizes something is wrong, it is going to get out of there—and fast. Should you continue to hold onto the line, the leader is going to break. The moment the fish tries to escape, you must give line. But line should be released so that the angler has control of both it and the fish. To do that, simply form an O ring with the first finger and thumb of the line hand. It is, in effect, a substitute for a large butt guide. As the line streaks away, you feed it through the O until all loose line is gone, and the fish can be fought from the reel.

If a knot forms in the fly line between the reel and the first rod guide after a fish is hooked and the battle begins, turn the rod upside down as the knot approaches the guides. Here is a situation every experienced fly fisherman has faced: A large fish is hooked. As the line peels through the guides, the angler is horrified to see a knot in the fly line coming toward the guides. For most people this ends in disaster. The knot catches on one of the guides and the leader breaks.

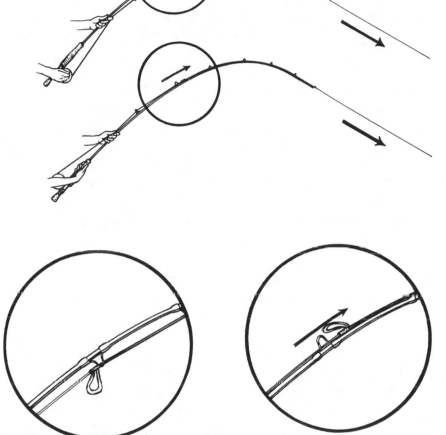

If a fleeing fish is pulling line through the guides and a knot or tangle suddenly jams against a guide, it will pop the leader. A knot will usually pass through the butt or stripping guides, but jam in the thin snake guides. If this happens, you can often prevent losing the fish by turning the rod upside down. This allows the line to run on the smooth rod blank and prevents the knot from catching in the thin wire of the snake guides.

While it doesn't work every time, there is a neat trick that many times allows the knot to pass through. Unless the knot is large, it will usually pass through the round ring guides. It's the snake guides that cause the real problem. Of course, larger guides on fly rods are recommended, and most manufacturers now place them on their rods. The knot will slip through the rounded, smooth edge of the butt or stripping guide. But as the bow forms in the rod from fighting the fish, the line is forced to bind against the wire snake guides. There is a simple solution that works most of the time. When you see the knot approaching the guides, roll the rod over, so that it is in an upside-down position. Now the line, instead of binding against the snake guides, actually is running along the smooth surface of the rod blank, and it will very often slip through all the guides. Since the battle will almost surely be lost if you don't do this, it's a trick worth trying.

Fighting and Landing

The most important thing to do after a strike is to clear the line that remains around your feet. Experienced anglers never pull any more fly line off the reel than is needed to make the anticipated casts. If extra line lies at your feet, it is only a source of trouble when the fish tries to flee. Of course, there will usually be some excess line, and that must be manipulated so that during the fish's first escape attempt, that line is cleared. You can usually accomplish this by using the O-ring finger trick. The maneuver is as follows: Once the hook is set, forget the fleeing fish and concentrate on using the O-ring to manipulate the line off the many things that tend to grab it, and also from under your feet. Also, as the final bit of line is being cleared, make sure that you feed that line toward the first or butt first guide. Some anglers will keep the fingers forming the O ring near the reel. This can cause the line to catch on the reel or around the butt of the rod.

Almost always, the longest, hardest run made by a hooked fish is the first one. Fear and a desire to get away cause it to flee, burning up vital energy. On the first panic run, let the fish go under light pressure. Most fish are lost either at this time or at the very end of the fight. As the fish slows down, the angler can begin retrieving line.

In most situations, unless the fish is very small, it is best to pump the fish in, rather than try reeling it to you. **Pumping** means raising the rod, which will draw the fish toward you, then lowering it to recover line by reeling in accumulated slack. But there is a little more to the pumping procedure than that. It's important to understand that moving the rod farther back doesn't mean you are applying more pressure on the fish. In fact, the reverse is true. If you raise the lower portion of the rod much beyond the horizontal, you begin actually to apply less pressure. And the more you sweep the rod up or back, so that it forms a deep bow or horseshoe shape, the less pressure is being placed on the fish.

What you want to do is a series of short, fast pumps, keeping the rod only slightly elevated. This technique is easy to learn, if you have a spring scale. Attach the leader end to the scale. Then have someone hold the scale and look at the readings. Begin bringing the rod slowly back. As the rod is raised, pressure will increase the reading on the scale, depending upon how hard you have set the drag. As the rod butt passes beyond about a 45-degree angle to the water's surface, the readings will begin to decline. Many people bring the rod back so far that the tip is actually behind the angler. In this case, you may be surprised to find that the scale will be registering almost no pressure. Another very important factor when pumping fish is to reel in slack only as the rod is lowered. Don't pump up and then quickly drop the rod tip. This creates a lot of slack, which might cause the

This drawing shows the proper procedure for pumping in a large fish. Lift the rod in short strokes as shown. Then as you lower the rod, reel in all slack, keeping a slight bend in the rod tip. Don't drop the rod too quickly or you may create slack and lose the fish. Never make long, sweeping pumps of the rod, because when the rod gets above 45 degrees, pressure on the fish actually decreases.

hook to fall out. The key to good pumping technique is to raise the rod, putting a bend only in the butt section. As the rod is lowered and reeling begins, make sure that the tip of the rod always has a slight bend. This will keep the line taut and prevent the hook from falling out.

There are three techniques that should be observed during a fish fight. One is to remember that a steady pull rarely breaks a line; it is a sharp jerk. In fact, I tell people it's the jerk on the wrong end that breaks the line! To demonstrate this, run the fly line and leader through the rod, and attach the leader, preferably about three- or four-pound test, to a doorknob. With a rod that throws a line size 2 through 6, raise the rod. You'll find it difficult to break the three-pound leader with a steady pull. If you give it a sharp jerk, it snaps instantly. The key, then, is to never allow a jerk to occur on the leader. Watch the fish during the fight. If it surges away, even in the middle of a pumping situation, immediately drop the rod toward the fish. By pointing the rod at the fish and forcing the fish to pull straight off the reel, you reduce the possibility of a jerk occurring, and the fish will be running against the lightest possible drag. Once the fish slows, you can return to recovering line.

The second technique is as follows: When a fish jumps, you need to throw controlled slack. A fish underwater trying to escape is somewhat like a person trying to run in a swimming pool. As the fish lunges sideways against the line, it also has to fight the water, which cushions the jerking on the line. But let that same fish rise above the surface and you have a totally different situation. Suppose the fish is lightly hooked in the side of the mouth. Underwater it can't pull hard. But when the fish is in the air, it can throw its full body weight against the hook, and probably break the tippet or tear it free.

We need to throw slack as soon as any fish (rainbow, brown trout, bass, sailfish, tarpon, etc.) jumps above the surface. For years we've taught anglers to bow to a fish; that is, stab the rod in the direction of a **jumping fish**. This creates a lot of slack, preventing the fish from breaking off. But bowing can create other problems. As the fish rocks back and forth in the air, it affects the line. This wavering line can wrap around the fish's head or tangle on the rod tip—causing you to lose the fish. Instead, dipping the rod is recommended. As the fish rises above the surface, *stick the rod tip just underwater in the direction of the leaping fish.* If the tip is underwater, there is the desirable slack, but the line is under much better control when the fish rocks wildly back and forth. With the dipping method few fish are lost. Once the fish is back in the water, go back to fighting the fish in a normal manner.

The third thing to remember, especially when large fish are fought on light leaders, is that you simply must tire the fish before you can bring it to you. Many people think that the best way to fight a fish (this is especially true of trout fishermen) is to hold the rod almost vertically. In most cases that is a rather useless way to fight a fish. Let me give you an example: An angler is fishing downstream and he unknowingly hooks a drifting stick. Anyone who has done this knows that the water pressure against the stick will form a deep bend in the rod. Hold the rod vertically and what is the stick doing? Nothing! Same with any fish lying directly downcurrent of an angler with a high rod. Actually, the fish is resting.

What is needed is some method of making the fish burn up its energy. Side pressure is the answer. But side pressure only works when the fish is closer than forty feet. Beyond that the angle is so small that it really doesn't do much good. Here's how it works: If the fish swims in one direction, move the rod at such an angle that it pulls the fish's head sideways. For example, if the fish is moving north, drop the rod to the west. Keep the rod low to the water for maximum side pressure. This will cause the fish's head to be pulled westward. The fish will resist, but it will finally be towed in that direction. If the fish now starts moving west, manipulate the rod so that you are pulling at a right angle (to the north or south as

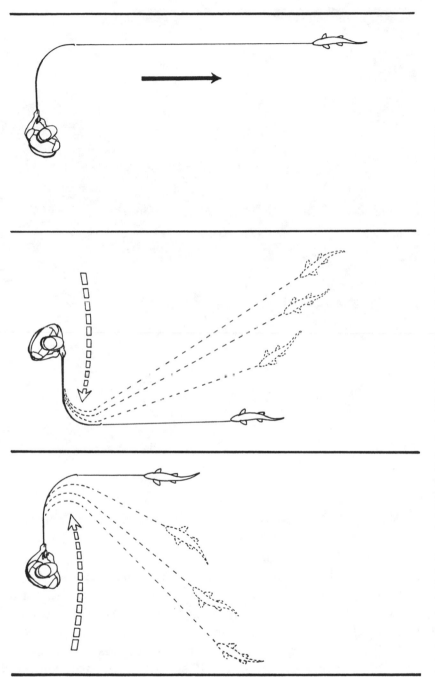

This drawing shows how to fight a large fish on a fragile leader. Anytime the fish is at right angles to the rod butt, the fish is resting. The top drawing shows the fish lying in the current, letting the flow put pressure on the rod while it rests. The same thing occurs with the rod held vertically with the fish directly downstream. This is a common mistake.

If the fish is on the left, flip the rod over to the right side, and low to the water. This turns the fish so that the current washes against its side, forcing it to swim and preventing it from resting. As the fish tries to get at right angles to the rod so it can rest, you can reel in some line.

As soon as the fish is at right angles to the rod on the right side, move the rod to the left and you can recover more line. By applying side pressure in this way, you force the fish to swim constantly and burn up energy. You are also always drawing it closer. It is important to remember that this side-pressure tactic will help you only when the fish is less than forty feet away. At greater distances you can obtain little leverage on the fish.

conditions warrant).This will also allow you to bring the fish closer by recovering some line.

Proper pumping technique, not allowing a jerk to occur to a fragile leader, and side pressure will help you quickly land many trophy fish.

Fish will often dive under the boat while you are fighting them. To prevent a broken line, you must shove the rod underwater and move it around to clear the line. Be careful—don't let the rod touch the boat or the rod may break.

When the fish is finally ready to be landed, be careful: This is one of the two most dangerous periods of a fight. If someone else is netting the fish, make sure that you move behind him, so that he can more easily approach the fish. Lighten up on the drag and use your fingers to control the reel. But be in a position so that you can see the helper and the fish. If the fish suddenly bolts away, be prepared to drop the rod and let the fish flee on a lightly established drag.

As the fight nears an end and the fish begins to tire, one trick that will help you capture it is to lift the head out of the water immediately before the fish is captured. Don't do this unless the fish is tired. But once the head is out of the water, the fish can only push its body farther out with its struggles. It is one of the most important tips for bringing in a good fish.

If the fish is being fought partially on the reel's drag, as is done with many saltwater species, release the drag tension slightly as your companion moves in to land or gaff the fish. If a heavy drag is set and the fish bolts away, the amount of power required to get a drag to release will

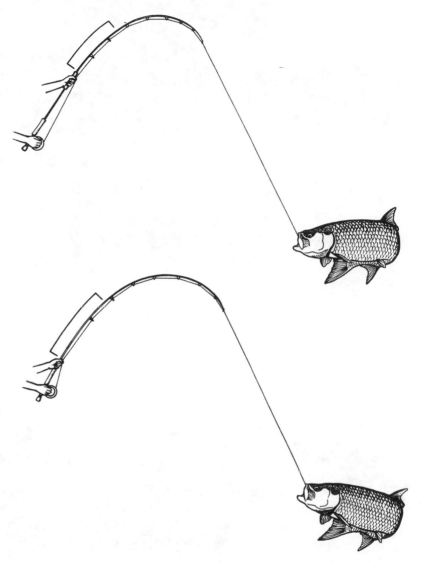

Rods for large fish are often designed with a fighting grip forward of the handle. Many anglers like this idea, but some feel it deprives them of using the most powerful part of the rod—the part below the fighting grip. To exert maximum pressure you can hold the rod as shown in the lower drawing.

often be too much for the leader. By dropping the adjustment to a lighter setting you increase your chances of landing the fish.

Plan ahead what you are going to do when you release the fish—or keep it. If the fish is small, there is no need to handle it. By handling the fish you can remove the protective slime coating from its body, so the less any fish is handled, the better. Small fish can be brought to the boot tops or to boatside, and with either a pair of needlenose pliers or hemostats, the angler can slide his fingers down the leader to within an inch or two of the fish. This will allow him to control its movements. Then he can grip the hook with the pliers or hemostats, and by turning the hook point down, the fish will fall free.

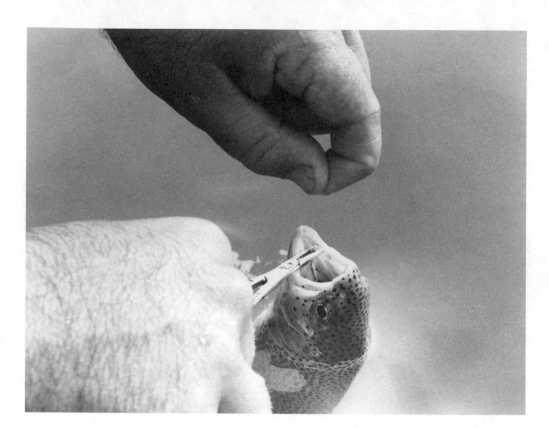

If the fish is landed and is in good condition, try to avoid handling it at all. Grasp the tippet just above the mouth and use pliers or hemostats to free the hook.

You sometimes have to lift larger fish from the water to remove the hook. In these situations the comfort lift, which the author demonstrates here, is ideal. Slide your hand under the fish so it is beneath the center of the fish's body weight. Usually this is a few inches behind the head. Then lift the fish slowly. If it starts to slide, you may have to adjust your hand position. Biologists have told me that this does not hurt the fish. This is better than using a net, which can harm the fish's eyes and remove its body slime. You need not gaff barracuda, bluefish, and other toothy critters. Use the comfort lift instead.

The proper way to use a net is to hold the net motionless in the water and lead the fish into it. Never chase the fish with the net, and never try to net the fish from the rear. When removing the fly from a fish, hold the fish upside down and it will remain motionless.

For many years I have used **barbless hooks** on almost all fish. Two exceptions are tarpon and sailfish, which jump frantically. Here I leave only a small amount of barb. With just about every other species, I either file the barb off or bend it down. I think it helps me land more fish. The hook can more easily penetrate the fish, and when you want to release it, the job is so much quicker and simpler. It is also kinder to the fish.

If you net a fish, there are several things that help make the job easier. First, brightly colored nets will often frighten fish. Either purchase a net of subdued color or dye it with common household dyes. Second, if you place several small sinkers with the little ears on the ends on the bottom of the mesh, the net will fall open better when you bring it to the fish.

There are nets on the market with a rubbery mesh that always fall open and seem to be kind to the fish. Third, and most important, never try to net a fish tail first. If you touch the fish's tail with the net, it increases its frantic efforts to escape. Also, don't chase the fish with the net. Put the net in the water, and permit the angler to draw the fish, headfirst, toward the net. Nets can damage the fragile eyeballs of a fish, and they scour that protective coating. Once netted, a fish should be removed from it as soon as possible and released.

Gaffing fish is recommended *only* when you intend to keep the fish. If the fish is to be gaffed, there are certain procedures that should be followed. Most important of all is that the gaff be sharp. Some gaffs are so dull that most of the time they only serve to wound the fish and increase its chances to escape. Also, use a gaff with the correct size hook. A very small hook, when used to lift a large fish, will often not have enough purchase, and the fish will fall free. A hook too large makes it difficult to properly impale the fish.

When fishing from a boat with high sides, a longer handle will be needed so that the angler can easily reach the fish. Gaff points should be protected when not being used so that injuries don't result. There are all sorts of protective devices, but one of the worst is the coiled spring that is attached to the handle with the gaff point slipped inside the other end of the spring. What happens is that the point is well protected, but often the spring entangles in the leader when the gaff is brought near the fish.

If the fish is very large and must be brought aboard, plan what you are going to do. Have a cleared space where the fish can be dropped after it is lifted aboard. I once saw a top-flight light-tackle angler bring in a sixty-pound cobia. He intended to lift it from the water into a large fish box. But the fish fell off the gaff hook and hit the deck. Its wild thrashing destroyed several good rods as both of us danced away from the fish.

Releasing

Most fly fishermen release their fish. Some people question me about why I put fish back. My answer is "You don't burn your golf balls at the end of the day, do you?"

Proper releasing technique begins before the fish is hooked. It is in the fish's best interest, once it is hooked, for you to bring it in as quickly as possible and free it. Saltwater fish will get lactic acid buildup in their bodies during long fights, which can actually result in a fish dying after it has been released. Freshwater fish often die after being released simply because we fought them for too long. Trout fishermen especially are guilty

If you hold almost any fish upside down it will remain motionless, as this rainbow trout is doing. This is the best way to hold a fish, especially trout. If you grasp a fish with its belly down it will struggle, forcing you to hold it more firmly, which risks damaging its internal organs.

of this. They use ultrathin 8X or 7X leaders and will play a fish for a long time, fearing they will break the leader if they try to bring it in too quickly. But many trout fishermen, myself included, believe that if you can get the leader through the eye of a dry fly or nymph, then the smallest leader you need for almost all fishing situations is a 5X or 6X. Just remember that between a 5X and a 7X there is only .002 inch—and trout don't have eyeballs to measure that difference. Be kind to your trout and use the largest leader you possibly can for existing conditions.

Once the fish has been landed, it should be put back in as good a condition as possible. Holding the fish out of the water for more than a brief period is like holding a person underwater. Don't hold the fish out of water longer than you can hold your breath. Get the hook out as quickly as possible and handle the fish as little as you can. If the fish seems to be exhausted, try reviving it. The best method is to get a good flow of oxygenated water flowing across its gills. Many anglers will hold the fish underwater with the head pointing into the current. That restricts the flow of water across the gills, since only what little water enters the mouth gets to the gills. Instead, with any fish that has no sharp teeth, grasp the tail of the fish and insert the thumb in the mouth, with the first finger gripping the jaw. This forces the mouth open. Now gently rock the fish back and forth. Each time the fish is drawn backward, the gills flare open, flooding them with oxygenated water. You can often revive a fish several times faster using this technique.

The most efficient way to revive an exhausted fish (if it does not have sharp teeth!) is to hold it by the tail with one hand and grasp the lower jaw with the thumb and forefinger of the other. Move the fish swiftly backward in the water. This forces the gill covers to flare and forces a large quantity of oxygen-laden, life-giving water over the gills. This method will revive a fish much faster than will holding its face into the current.

If the fish is now ready for release, be sure to free it in shallow water, if that is possible. That way the fish can be retrieved if it appears to be in trouble. If the fish is let go in deeper water and it starts sinking or turns belly up, you may have trouble recovering it. If a fish begins to swim off in deeper water and then appears to be having troubles, often touching it with a paddle, boat pole, or fishing rod will stimulate the fish enough to try swimming. This often does the trick and the fish swims free. One of the great satisfactions of fly fishing is that we can have all of the thrills of the hunt and the capture—but we can put the fish back.

Always release fish in shallow water when possible. This way, if the fish needs more help, you can recover it easily. If a fish released in deeper water appears to be in trouble, touching it with a rod or paddle may be enough motivation to get it going.

Seven

KNOTS

Fly fishermen are fascinated with knots—especially when they begin fishing in salt water, where they quickly find that strong knots are vital to success. Unfortunately most freshwater fishermen don't realize the value of good knots until they hook a trophy—and then lose it.

There are hundreds of knots. And while they can fascinate you, only a few are needed to cover just about every fly-fishing situation in salt and fresh water, from taking a wary brown trout sipping No. 22 dry flies from the surface to landing a northern pike, sailfish, or giant tarpon.

The most important factor in good knot building is that no knot breaks until it slips, and that includes a two-inch hawser that holds a steamship to the dock, or an 8X leader attached to a fly. It is vital that knots be drawn securely. If the knot is lubricated (dipped in the water or moistened in the mouth), it will draw down smoothly. Good knots that are drawn correctly tight do not need Krazy Glue, overhand knots, or other additives. Tying overhand knots in the tag end or adding glue to a knot is an indication that the tier isn't using a good knot, or the knot is not being drawn tight enough to keep it from slipping. While silicone and other such lubricants will help you draw the knot tightly, these lubricants are extra smooth, and unless extreme care is taken, they sometimes allow the knot to slip. Laboratory tests have shown that it's impossible to close properly any knot with bare hands when monofilament larger than fifteen pound test is used.

A very important factor in tying knots is to follow the instructions carefully. Especially critical is the number of turns made around the standing line. The Improved Clinch Knot, for example, should have five turns around the main line for lines testing roughly from 8X to six pounds, and four turns for eight to twelve pounds. For lines heavier than fifteen pound test, the Improved Clinch Knot is difficult to close with most monofilaments and is not recommended.

If you use six-pound line or lighter to tie this knot and make only four turns, you may not have enough turns around the standing line to keep the knot from slipping. And if you make seven turns (five is recommended), then you may have too many turns to draw the knot properly tight to keep it from slipping. All of this is said to impress the reader that instructions on how the knot is tied should be followed exactly. Most knots are tested over and over on machines, which have no opinion, before they are published for use. These tests determine the best way to tie them.

Here is another important point for anglers who connect two different sizes of monofilament. The knots will close better if you use monofilaments with similar stiffness or limpness characteristics. If instead you use two different stiffnesses of mono, you will find that it is more difficult to close the knot properly. When tying a tapered leader use all monofilament from the same manufacturer.

One other tip about tying knots: If you want to test a new knot against your old favorite, there is a fail-safe way to make a comparison. Take two hooks exactly alike and tie your favorite knot to one hook and the new knot to the other hook, being careful to tie the new knot exactly as shown. Then grasp each hook in a pair of pliers and make some steady pulls until one knot fails. But also apply some jerk tests. Some knots are very strong on a steady pull, such as the Spider Hitch, but near worthless if a sudden jerk occurs. Make a number of tests before making a decision about the two knots.

To develop good knot technique, learn to use knots that have a very high line strength, then practice tying them at home. If they are tied correctly, and closed tightly, they will serve you well. Never use a new knot while fishing—be sure to practice at home.

Here are some knots that you may want to use. Learn to tie them properly and there are almost no fishing situations that one of these won't handle well.

Speedy Nail Knot

This or the common nail knot is the preferred method for most anglers to attach their leader to the fly line. The Speedy Nail Knot can be made with practice in about ten seconds or less, but it is difficult to use when connecting the backing to the fly line. The more common Conventional

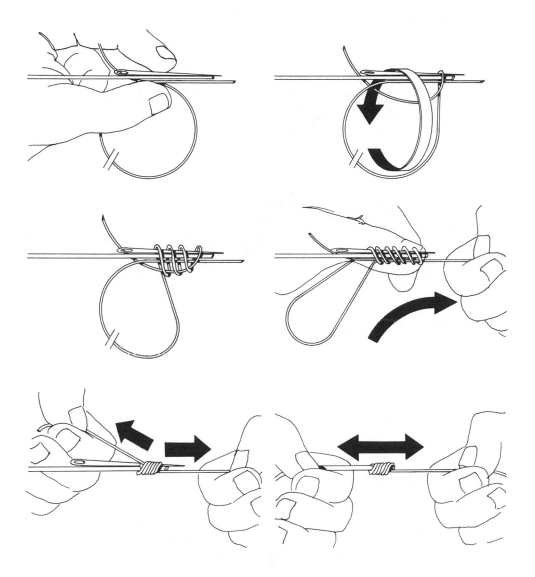

Speedy Nail Knot.

Nail Knot can be used for this, although it does leave a blunt end where the fly line is connected to the backing, and this blunt end can catch on the retrieve.

Conventional Nail Knot

This is slower to construct than the Speedy Nail Knot. But there are some situations where a Speedy Nail Knot will not work. One example is installing a nail knot somewhere along the fly line as an indicator. This is discussed in chapter 2.

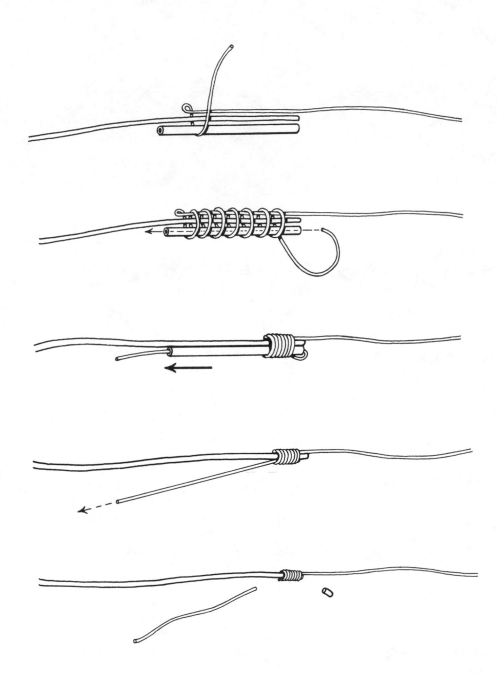

Conventional Nail Knot.

Whipped Loop

This is my preferred way to attach backing to fly line, and leader end to fly. A loop is made in both ends of the fly line by folding the line end back against the main line. And some lines, such as those with a Kevlar core and most clear monofilament lines, do not work well with a nail knot (the knot can slip off). The Whipped Loop works very well. Always test the loop for strength when completed by holding a nail or thin rod inside the loop and pulling on the main line. Properly tied, this loop is stronger than the main line.

These loops never hang up in the guides because of their rounded ends. Properly constructed, they never pull out during the battle. Loops offer the outstanding advantage of allowing you to interchange lines on the reel, or to quickly substitute another leader. The ability to interchange leaders is a vital factor in being able to cope with different fishing conditions. I consider the nail knot a disadvantage in this regard.

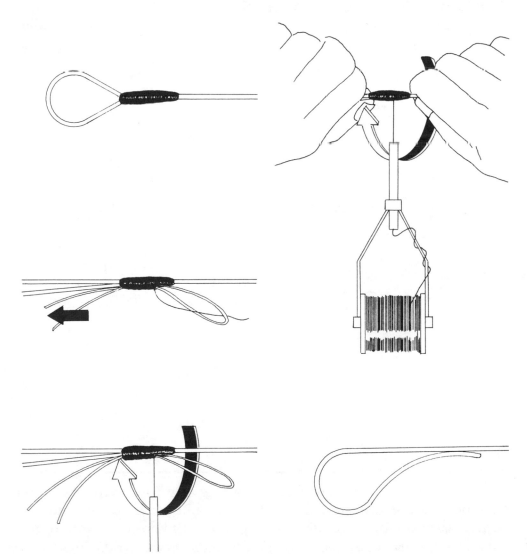

Whipping a loop in a fly line.

Surgeon's Knot

There are many situations where the angler has to connect two different diameters of monofilament together, or in some cases to connect braided wire to monofilament. The Surgeon's Knot will do this quite well in monofilament lines up to sixty pounds in strength—or in connecting monofilament to braided steel wire to forty-pound test. With mono testing more than sixty pounds and braided wire stronger than forty pounds, other knots are recommended. The most important factor in constructing a good Surgeon's Knot is that once the knot has been tied, *all four ends must be pulled very tightly, or a weak knot may result.* You can quickly join six-pound test leader material to 40 pound-test. The drawing shows a Double Surgeon's Knot. But in very thin mono lines, six-pound test or less, I recommend a Triple Surgeon's Knot, which can be drawn properly tight in such small-diameter lines.

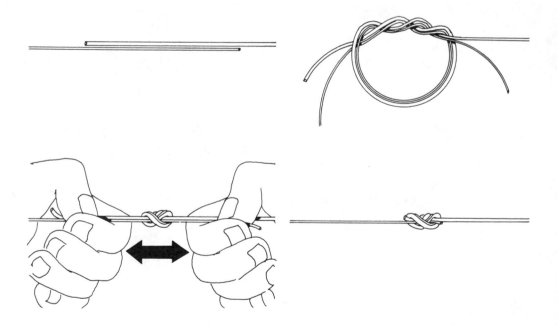

Surgeon's Knot.

Huffnagle Knot

This knot has a number of names, but this seems to be the most common. There are slight variations of this knot, but the drawing shows one of the most popular, which works very well. This knot is superb for joining very large-diameter monofilament (used for shock leaders in saltwater fly fishing) to a thin tippet, or to a tippet constructed with a Bimini Twist.

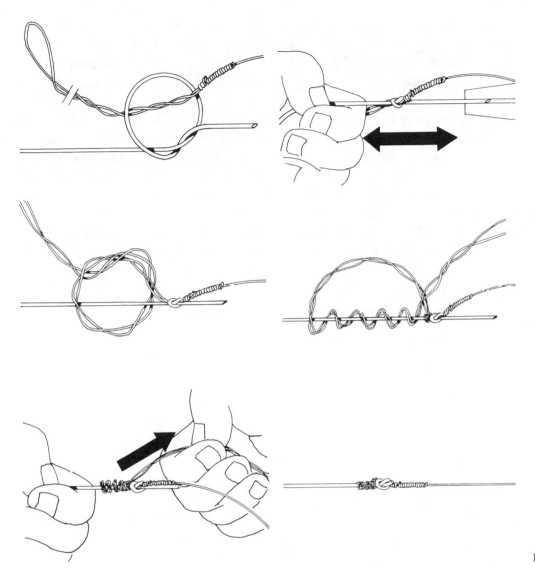

Huffnagle Knot.

One of the advantages of this knot is that it forms one of the smallest connections when joining large (80- to 120-pound) monofilament to a small strand—and it lies straight once the knot is complete, giving the fly improved action on the retrieve.

Bimini Twist

This is the single most important knot a saltwater fly fisherman can learn—and it has great importance to freshwater fishermen who want to tackle large, powerful fish on very light tippets. Most knots result in a connection that is weaker than the line they are tied with. The Bimini Twist will never slip—so it never breaks. When you build a Bimini Twist, you end up with a doubled line or loop extending from the Bimini. That is where the value of this knot lies. For example, if your tippet is twelve-pound test, and you want to join it to a shock leader of one hundred pounds, almost all other connections would result in a knot of less than twelve pounds. But when you make a Bimini (which is stronger than the line), beyond the knot you have two pieces of twelve-pound (or twenty-four pounds) with which to attach the hook or other line. Almost any knot you tie with this doubled strand will be stronger than one made with the single-strand twelve-pound. The Bimini is one knot every serious saltwater fisherman should use (fly, plug, spin, and troll) but more fresh-water fishermen should consider it, too.

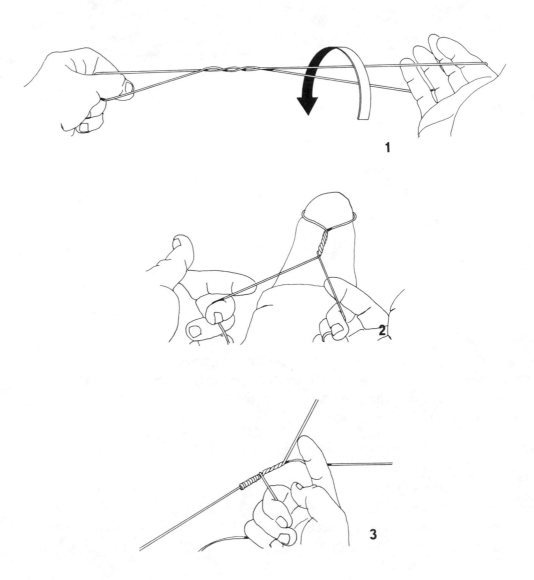

Bimini Twist.

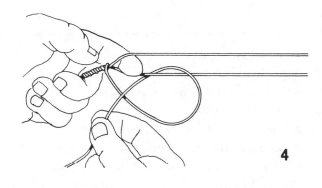

4

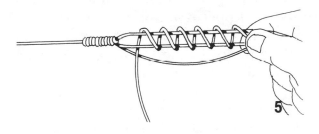

5

6

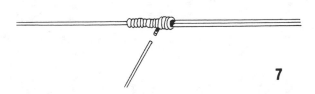

7

Bimini Twist. (continued)

Non-Slip Mono Loop

There are many situations where a loop, rather than a tight connection, is best between the tippet and the fly. This permits the fly to move more freely. This is especially important when tying braided wire or heavy monofilament to the fly, but also many nymph and streamer fishermen prefer a free-swinging loop. The Uni-Knot or Duncan Loop has been used by many fishermen for this purpose. But this knot isn't the strongest loop knot. Actually it is a form of Clinch Knot—one not known for great strength. Another drawback to the Uni-Knot or Duncan Loop is that during a battle with a fish, the knot frequently will tighten on the hook eye, requiring the angler to either move it back to the former loop or retie it.

But the Non-Slip Mono Loop forms a loop that doesn't slip, and most of the time the knot doesn't break—the tippet does. In other words, tied correctly and closed securely, it will usually test as a 100 percent knot. The Non-Slip Mono Loop is vastly superior to the Uni-Knot or Duncan Loop, and every fly fisherman who prefers using loops should consider using it.

For maximum strength this knot has to have the correct number of turns around the standing line. When you are using tippets that test roughly from 8X to six-pound test, make seven turns around the standing line. When you are using line from eight- to twelve-pound test, make five turns; four turns are used in line from fifteen to forty pounds; three turns in fifty- to sixty-pound test; and in eighty- to 120-pound test, only two

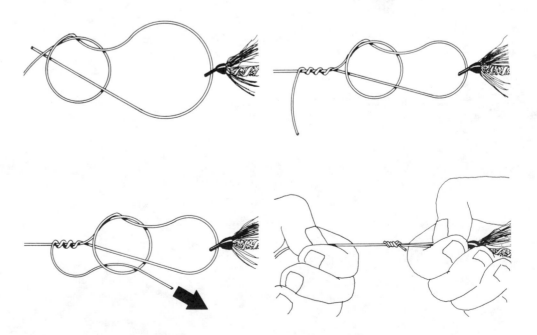

Non-Slip Mono Loop.

turns are needed. Study the knot drawing, for the line should enter and exit the overhand knot the same way for maximum strength.

Trilene Knot

While most people use the Improved Clinch Knot to attach their tippet to the hook eye, a much stronger knot (one that usually breaks at or near 100 percent of line strength) is the Trilene Knot. It is very easy to tie, and with practice is quicker and simpler than the Improved Clinch. What is very important is that you do not "improve" the Trilene, as you do the Clinch. This actually weakens the knot, since it can't be drawn tight enough to keep from slipping when the improvement is added. This knot can be weak if you don't firmly close it.

Maximum strength from a Trilene Knot is obtained when lines testing from 8X to six pounds are made with five turns around the main line. With eight- to twelve-pound test, four turns are recommended, and with fifteen- or twenty-pound lines, three turns are best. The Trilene Knot is not recommended for lines stronger than 20 pounds.

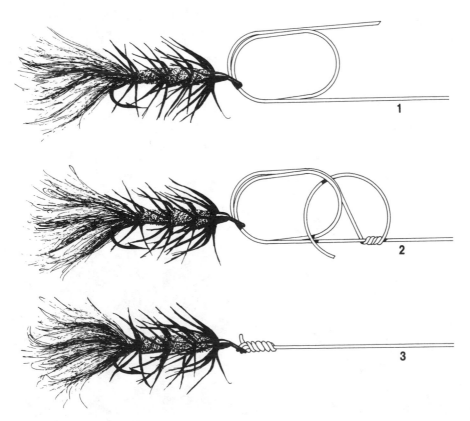

Trilene Knot.

George Harvey Dry-Fly Knot

This knot should never be tied in a ring-eye hook; use only those hooks with down or up eyes. I have also been told that this is a very old knot, but George Harvey showed it to me years ago and I use it exclusively when connecting dry flies to tippets. It has three outstanding advantages: Properly tied, it has near 100 percent line strength. The knot is tied on the thread wrappings of the head of the fly instead of to the thin metal of the hook eye—something I find comforting when fighting a very large trout on a fragile tippet. Maybe the most important advantage is that this knot never allows the fly to tilt to one side, because the tippet enters the hook

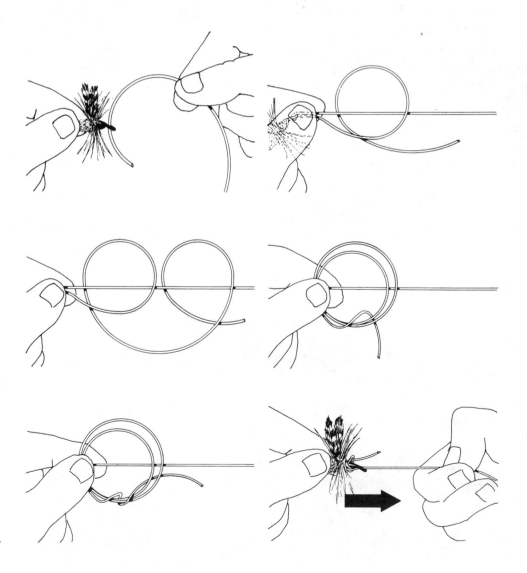

George Harvey Dry-Fly Knot.

eye and grabs the fly around the head. It always floats straight. Many other knots (such as the Improved Clinch) can slip to one side on the hook eye and give the pattern an improper float—the George Harvey Dry-Fly Knot never does this.

Figure 8 Knot

This knot is good only for use with braided wire. It is an excellent connection for braided wire but is a very weak knot when tied with monofilament. It is one of the easiest of all knots to tie, but one important factor must be considered. The final closure of the knot should always be performed correctly. Carefully form the knot. Then, when closing it on the hook eye, *pull all slack wire from the tag end.* This ensures that any kinks formed while building the knot will be pulled outside so that they can be trimmed off. If you pull on both ends, or on the main line end, you will draw some of the kinked wire in front of the hook, and this will cause the fly to twist erratically and spin on the retrieve. When you trim the excess wire away, leave about ³⁄₁₆ inch of wire outside the hook. Then if you decide you want to change the fly, you can carefully "tease" open the knot, remove the fly, and add another, and if you slowly close the knot, the wire will return to its original shape. This knot is very strong in braided wire and never slips. Caution: It is a very poor and weak knot when used with monofilament.

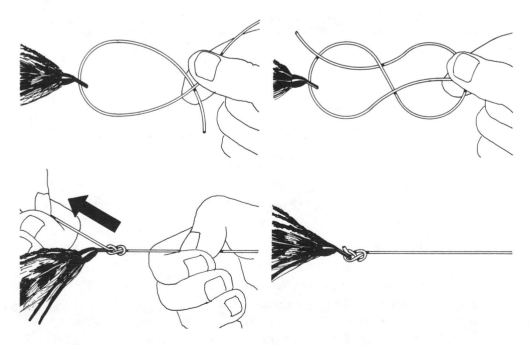

Figure 8 Knot.

Power Gum or Shock Gum Knot

When you are fishing for very large fish with ultra-small hooks (such as No. 22 dry flies for trout bigger than six pounds), any slight jerk against the fragile tippet may mean a broken leader and lost fish. What a number of experienced anglers have been doing is adding a shock absorber in the leader—usually near the butt section.

This material, which looks like monofilament but stretches easily, is called Power Gum or Shock Gum. It can be purchased in some fly shops. A short section is usually tied between the butt section and the next smaller diameter portion of a tapered leader.

However, because the material somewhat resembles a rubber band when worked with, it is difficult to tie when using conventional knots. The drawing shows a method of forming what amounts to two opposing nail knots. If the prescribed turns are used, and the knot lubricated and closed securely, it will not slip. You can also use a Triple Surgeon's Knot, but be sure to close the knot firmly or it will slip.

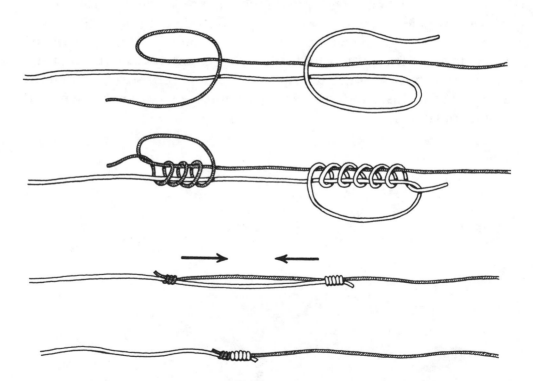

Power Gum or Shock Gum Knot.

Connecting the Leader Butt Section to the Fly Line

There are many ways to connect a fly line to the backing. Shown here are four of them. Each has its proponents.

The top drawing shows the leader butt section glued into the fly line. This glued connection makes the smoothest of all connections and slides

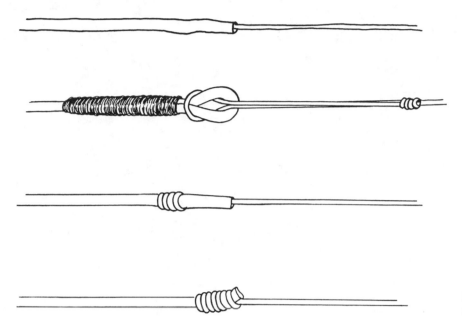

Four ways to attach a leader to a fly line.

freely in and out of the guides. If this is installed by a commercial operation, it can be very strong. Some anglers do this themselves, but unless you have experience the connection may fail for a variety of reasons.

The second drawing from the top shows the loop-to-loop method. I personally favor this way. First, the connection is very strong. Second, loop-to-loops always flow freely through the rod guides. Most importantly, I favor the loop-to-loop because it allows me to quickly disconnect a leader and replace it with one better suited to existing fishing conditions.

The third drawing from the top shows the Needle Knot. The leader is drawn inside the front of the line and then a three- or four-turn nail knot is made encircling the fly line. It is about as smooth a connection as the glued knot and works well.

The bottom drawing shows a Conventional Nail Knot, the one most commonly used by fly fishermen for attaching leaders.

Knot Summary

A final reminder about knots is that no knot breaks until it begins to slip. A poorly designed knot that is closed firmly may be stronger than a well-designed knot that is not securely closed.

Eight

SPECIAL TECHNIQUES

Each kind of fishing requires special techniques for catching various species. That's one of the things I find interesting about fly fishing. The methods used for catching snook are totally different from those for luring a bonefish, tarpon, or northern pike to a fly. It is mastering these subtle differences that makes one angler stand out from others pursuing a particular species. The special techniques can involve certain patterns of flies, modifications of those flies from normal patterns, or using them in a different manner. They also involve special tackle, even altering the gear. Quite often, doing the reverse of what most anglers do to catch certain kinds of fish is more productive. In short, the top fly rodders are anglers willing to not follow the norm or tradition. They are constantly developing innovations.

Trout Tricks

Dry Flies

For most anglers who tempt trout, catching them with a dry fly is considered the ultimate method. Actually, it is one of the easiest methods to master for taking trout on flies. Yet there is no denying that seeing a large trout break the surface and accept your offering is one of the thrills of fly fishing not soon forgotten.

I believe that there is more mystique and more plain misconceptions concerning fishing for trout than any other area of fly fishing. Many people who are not really experienced in the sport have either written or spoken about it, and have attempted to create the concept that this is a very difficult sport to master. That simply isn't true; learning to catch trout on dry flies is really simple. What is needed, I think, is an understanding of how a trout feeds on the surface. Once that is understood, much of the simple technique needed to become a proficient dry-fly angler is easy to conquer.

It is important to understand that a trout does not have a brain the size of a gallon bucket. It doesn't have a computer in its head to identify and catalogue thousands of insects. Trout do not speak Latin. And you don't have to. Keep remembering that trout (and all other fish) need and desire only three things out of life (if we disregard the spawning season). They need a place to hide from predators, a good place to rest near a food source, and something to eat. These three simple factors govern a trout's life—and also how it feeds.

The following is my own concept of how trout feed on the surface in flowing water. If you are driving a station wagon on a dirt road and traveling north, the dust will come in the rear of the car—if the back window is open. If you are traveling north, most of the dust will remain behind the car. But some of the dust that the car kicks up is swirling so that it travels in the same direction as your car. You can equate this with the currents on the bottom of a stream. If a current is flowing north and there are boulders and rocks lying on the bottom, some of the currents downstream of

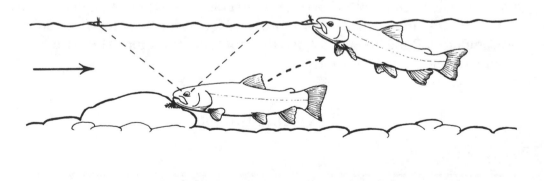

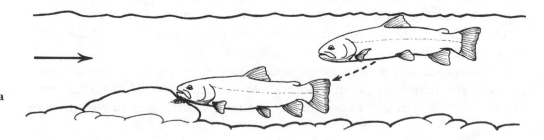

There is a trick to taking trout on dry flies in fast water. They have a "seat in the restaurant," and feed in a particular way to conserve energy.

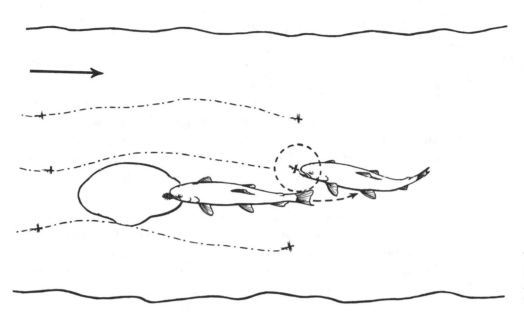

Trout cannot afford to chase small dry flies in swift water. Accuracy in placing the fly is vital to success.

the rocks will be going upstream, or there may be no current. In other words, behind rocks the current will be flowing slower, be going opposite the main current, or actually form a quiet eddy. This is true even in a fast riffle, where overhead the water is sweeping rapidly by.

This is very important if you want to understand how trout feed on dry flies in running water. Dr. Robert Bachman, some years ago at Pennsylvania State University, wrote his doctoral thesis on how native brown trout feed in a flowing stream. He determined through the use of video and film that each trout had what he called "a specific seat in a restaurant." What he meant was that each fish in the pool has its own particular feeding place. This observation can be verified by the experience of good trout fishermen. Some anglers have caught and kept a rather large fish from a specific location. Returning later to the pool, they may catch and keep another trout from the same spot. But it will not be quite as large as the first. And each succeeding trout caught would be smaller than the last one. This is proof that the biggest or strongest trout in the pool controls the most desirable feeding location. Remove that fish, and the second strongest fish will occupy that location (seat in the restaurant), and so on. I'd like to add that this often is not true in stillwaters such as lakes. But in streams that have a current I believe that this is almost always true.

This idea of a seat in the restaurant was pretty well proven by Dr. Bachman. During his study one of the largest fish in the pool, when it took up a feeding position, did so at a certain rock. There was a dark spot on that rock, clearly visible on Dr. Bachman's film. Each time this trout would feed, its nose was incredibly close to this spot. In other words, the fish didn't hide behind that rock, but it took up a carefully selected position every time.

Why?

Before I answer the question, consider that no large trout can afford to swim up through two or three feet of water and take a minute insect from the surface, then return to its former position. The trout would actually consume more energy than it received by eating the insect. But if the fish could take the insect without expending energy—in other words, not being forced to swim to the surface and return—then it could do so. And that is what I believe such trout do in flowing water.

Holding its position, the trout sees an insect floating toward it on the surface. As the insect comes into the trout's window, the fish decides whether it can take the insect or not. If the trout elects to consume the insect, it tilts its fins so that they lift its body up and back with the current. The fish actually glides to the surface. Once there, it sucks in the insect. It then tilts the fins again, and with a subtle flick of its tail the trout changes its attitude and the current forces it to dive, allowing it to plane down and back to its holding position. All of this is similar to a glider, which has no motor, yet can rise against the flow of air, maneuver, and return to port. The trout does the same thing. If you think about it for a moment, you realize that any trout that you see taking insects from the surface in flowing water always drifts up and back, with the head tilted a little to the rear. Reaching the surface, the fish sucks in the insect, then tilts downward and returns to the bottom upstream from the point where the fly was taken.

If you will agree for the moment with this idea, let's pursue it a little further to understand how trout take insects off the surface. A trout looks through a window, which is similar to a cone. Anything outside that cone that is on or above the surface, scientists tell us, the trout cannot see. Only when the fly comes into that cone of vision can the trout see it. The trout probably sees the fly enter its vision only a short distance upstream from its holding position. The fish rises if it decides to take the fly. The actual distance the fly drifts while it is under the trout's observation is short. And over this short distance the currents are going to be the same. *Thus every insect that floats to this trout is going to come along the same path.* For example, if a drifting insect is swept slightly to the right, and then back to the left before it is taken by the trout, every other insect will follow the same path. **This is important—for the trout doesn't have to know all of the currents in a pool. But it thoroughly understands exactly the currents that deliver each fly to it!**

This means that over the short distance the imitation dry fly floats on the surface while the trout is inspecting it, it must travel exactly the same path as a natural. If it does not, the fish will refuse it. Most fishermen know that a fly floating unnaturally is said to be dragging. Currents pulling against the leader are what drag the fly unnaturally. But drag is important only for that short distance that each trout sees the fly. It is vital that we use a leader that will allow the fly to float drag-free during the brief inspection period.

But there is a little more to doing the right thing to catch a trout on a dry fly. Not only must the fly float drag-free, but it also must be cast accurately. As the trout sees the fly come into its cone of vision, it has to glide up, take the fly, and return with the aid of the current. This means that it has to take the fly at a specific position on the surface. If it takes the fly too far downstream, it cannot glide back to its holding position, but must swim back to it. If the fish takes the fly too far to the right or left, then it would also have to swim again to return. This the trout isn't going to do, since it would be using more energy than it consumes. You may wonder why, after you have made a series of casts with the same fly to a trout and gotten many refusals, the trout suddenly inhales the fly. I believe that all the casts but the one that scored either were not passing through the trout's cone of vision or were just a little too far to the right or left for the fish to take it without burning up too much energy.

So, to offer a trout your dry fly imitation, you must make it travel in such a manner on the surface that the fish sees it, and it must be floating drag-free and not too far to the right or left. Thus accuracy is called for, as well as designing a leader that will deliver a drag-free float. How we do that is rather simple, if we will take the time to do so.

Dry-Fly Leaders

So long as there is some slack in the tippet (the weakest portion of the leader—attached to the fly), you will get a drag-free float. *Drag occurs when the tippet directly in front of the fly straightens.* Currents can then work on the leader and cause the fly to float unnaturally. The key to getting a drag-free float is to build a leader that falls to the surface with a slight amount of wavy slack just in front of the fly. Fortunately this is rather easy to do.

Almost any commercial leader today is rather well designed and will do the job. On smaller trout streams and those waters where the fish are not especially wary, a leader with a total length of nine feet is a good one. If you fish beaver ponds, lakes, spring creeks, or rather still waters, where the fish are wary, a longer leader is usually needed. I often use a leader of fifteen or sixteen feet under these conditions. *The key to getting a drag-free drift is the crucial slack in front of the dry fly.* Purchase a standard leader at a fly shop. Let's say, for example, that it is nine feet long, tapering

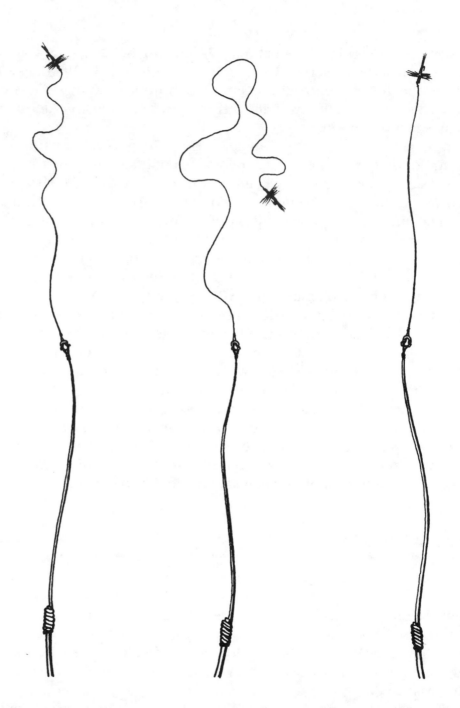

It is vitally important to make your dry fly float drag-free to entice a trout into taking it. The way to accomplish this is to make the tippet fall in soft waves, as shown. Too long a tippet will fall in waves but deliver the fly inaccurately. Too short a tippet will fall straight, resulting in drag. The text explains how to adjust the tippet quickly and easily.

to 5X. The X indicates the tippet portion of the leader. Incidentally, while it is approximate (since modern monofilament is now often stronger than older nylon), there is a rough guide for determining what X really means. To determine the pound test of a tippet, subtract the number in front of X from nine, and you'll get the approximate pound test. For example, a 5X leader will test about four pounds, and a 2X leader will test approximately seven pounds.

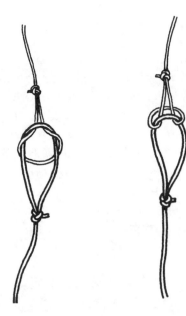

Use the loop method to make a quick-disconnect tippet. But be sure to loop properly as shown on the left—not on the right.

To get a good, drag-free float, take the nine-foot leader and remove about two feet from the tippet. This will get rid of the entire tippet, and the cut end will be slightly stronger than the tippet just removed. Make a Surgeon's Knot or, better, a Non-Slip Mono Loop (see chapter 7) in the small end of the leader, where the tippet section was removed. What you have is a seven-foot tapered leader with no tippet. You can now make a similar loop in a piece of regular 5X tippet material (if that is the size you choose) and loop it to the loop on the leader. This allows you to quick-change tippets anytime you want to.

For an example of how to build a proper leader that will give you a drag-free float, we will start with a three-foot section of the 5X material, looping it to the doctored leader. Attach a No. 12 Adams dry fly to the tippet. Now make a cast. If the fly tends to fall back on itself (which it may do with such a long, thin tippet), you need to clip the fly from the tippet and shorten it to, say, thirty inches. You may find that the fly still falls back on itself and won't straighten. Again clip off the fly and shorten the leader to about twenty-four inches. Now you may find that the leader falls in soft waves but doesn't quite straighten. *That is what you need to get a drag-free float.* Later you may see a small gray fly hatching, so you switch from the No. 12 Adams to a No. 16. The tippet that served you well with the No. 12 Adams will not work properly with this much smaller fly. The tippet will fall on the water perfectly straight, because the tippet is now too short and will deliver the energy of the cast so well that the entire leader falls straight. What you must do is unloop and discard the twenty-four-inch piece and start again with a longer section. Attaching the fly, make a series of casts and keep adjusting the leader until the tippet falls in soft waves. This does require a little more work, for a proper tippet must be matched to the fly being cast. The tippet lengths given here are for example only. Depending upon your casting skill, the tippet length will vary. You have to conduct this test to match your own skills.

Remember, any time the leader tippet falls back on itself, the tippet is either too long or too thin and cannot transmit enough energy to turn over the fly. If the tippet falls to the surface perfectly straight, then the tippet is either too short or too thick. This is the basis for determining if you have a properly constructed leader that matches the fly in use.

Extra long tippets are often required to get the best drag-free drift, but realize that with longer tippets, accuracy may suffer when presenting the fly.

This bird was killed by carelessly discarded monofilament. Never throw away old monofilament line or tippet material. Take it home for proper disposal. Birds looking for nesting material will be attracted to the mono, but if a bird becomes entangled in the line, its death is all but certain.

The above is a really simple method of building a leader to give you a drag-free float. I believe the most important factor in dry-fly fishing is that the tippet must be matched to the dry fly. Using this technique, you can master the most important principle in effective dry-fly fishing—making the fly float properly to the fish.

The major reason why I suggest using a loop at the end of the leader, to which you will loop the tippet, is simply common sense. During fishing you frequently have to renew the tippet. Without a loop you must utilize a portion of your tapered leader to tie in another tippet. With the loop-to-loop method, you simply disconnect the tippet to be discarded and loop on a new one. Using this technique you can often make one leader do for many trips.

There are many myths about what you should do when fly fishing. One of them is a formula that quickly allows you to correctly match the tippet to the fly. The formula says to divide 3 into the hook size. For example, if you are using a dry fly that is dressed on a No. 12 hook, by dividing by 3 you arrive at a tippet size of 4X. Everyone wants simple answers to complex situations, but rarely do such answers exist. Such is true in this case.

Several factors determine how the fly will travel through the air: What it weighs, the materials used, the type of hook used, how much air resistance it has, and even its general shape. The divide-by-3 formula (some people say divide by 4) takes none of this into consideration. A Catskill-style dry fly is tied so the whole fly is slenderized. The body is very sparse, and only a few turns of hackle support the pattern. But a fly such as the Humpy is bulkier and may have a body of almost twice the diameter, and it will certainly carry much more hackle. If you hold the two flies dressed on the same size hook in your hand, you quickly realize that these two flies will cast entirely differently.

Each caster throws his fly in his own style. Some develop high speed; others throw a wider loop, with little line speed. Such factors also affect how the tippet and fly will turn over and fall to the surface. The only way you can really ascertain which tippet will be right for you is to tie on the fly you will be using and cast it. Almost always you will have to make some adjustments to get those desirable waves in the tippet directly in front of the fly.

If you are fishing a stream that is new to you, and you haven't a clue where you should float your dry fly, there is an easy answer. The fast water in the riffle at the head of the pool, tumbling over rocks, creates **foam**. This foam floats through the pool you are fishing. It travels where the swifter currents flow through the pool. Look for streaks of foam that are moving through the pool and you will have found the "food highways" that trout will use when feeding. Foam that is not moving, perhaps trapped along the bank, should be ignored.

Foam can help you in another way. If you feel that your tippet has not been properly tied, you can quickly check it if there is foam on the water.

The foam, unattached to anything, is free-floating through the pool with the natural currents. Cast your fly beside a small patch of foam and observe how both drift. If the foam and the fly begin to travel different paths almost immediately, you are getting drag, which you may not be able to see. However, trout will often know the difference. The best bet is to lengthen the tippet slightly.

False Casting

Another common mistake dry-fly fishermen make occurs when they are working a feeding fish. If the fish is feeding where the surface is calm or slick (this problem doesn't occur where the water is ruffled), you must use care in false casting. The fly is offered to the fish. It drifts along, and then is picked up so you can make another offering. The fly is false-cast to dry it, then placed back on the surface. The tendency is to false-cast the fly in the direction of the feeding fish. But two mistakes occur when this is done. One, the fish may see the fly line unrolling through the air. More often, at the end of the forward cast and as the backcast is started, the abrupt change in direction will flush water from the fly. Minuscule droplets of water shower down on the surface. While they may seem inconsequential to you, they are certainly noticed by trout, which often feed on insects so small anglers have difficulty seeing them. This problem of water showering on the surface is acute when using a braided-butt leader. The hollow braid tends to accumulate water and flushes off an extra large amount as the fly is false-cast. The answer, of course, is to make a backcast and keep all forward casts out of sight (by casting off to the side) and eliminating droplets falling to the surface.

Lines for Dry Flies

The most popular line size for trout is a floating number 6. For decades it was a number 7. For many dry-fly fishing situations, anglers could perform better and catch more fish if they used a considerably lighter line. As trout become more sophistical from increased fishing pressure, I predict that size 4 or size 3 lines will be the most popular for most trout fishing. I have used a 3-weight for years when tossing dry flies and smaller underwater imitations.

The average leader for dry-fly fishing is about nine feet. On calmer waters—spring creeks and lakes and ponds, where the surface is still—leaders often may be thirteen to sixteen feet in length. The longer the leader, the more difficult it is to properly turn over and accurately present the fly to the target. If we could fish with shorter leaders, we would cast more accurately, turn the near weightless dry fly over better into the wind, enjoy the sport more, and have more fish take our dry flies.

It is important to understand why we use such long leaders. Once this is understood, then ways can be developed to get around the problem. While the leader furnishes a near invisible connection between the fly and the line, it also serves another and just as important function. What frightens a trout feeding on a dry fly is the impact of the line on the water. Rarely is it the leader's or fly's impact. Through experience fly fishermen have determined that nine-foot or longer leaders arc generally required to get the impact of the fly line far enough away from the fly to prevent alarming the fish.

Once this principle is understood, we can adapt our tackle to obtain shorter and more accurate casting leaders. The most popular fly line used when fishing dry flies is a 6-weight. The first thirty feet of most 6-weight lines weighs 160 grains. The same length of 3-weight line weighs only 100 grains—a considerable difference. When you are fishing dry flies, other

Limestone creeks like this one offer some of the most challenging trout fishing. But the trout are usually wary, so I recommend a light, 2- or 3-weight outfit for this fishing.

than in a very heavy breeze, 100 grains of 3-weight line will easily cast any dry fly.

What I'm suggesting is that you switch to a 3- or, at the most, a 4-weight line for most all your fly fishing. These lines will even work well in a moderate breeze, because they are so thin that they tend to penetrate the wind better. Obviously, if you are throwing heavy nymphs and streamers, you will need a heavier fly line.

If you switch to a 3-weight line, the leader can be shortened considerably. A tapered dry-fly leader not exceeding nine feet is very efficient when using such a light line. Unless the water is very calm, the impact of the line is so gentle that from that distance, the fish never seems to know it has fallen to the surface.

Floatants

There is a common mistake made by people who dress flies to make them float. First, on delicate dries I prefer a liquid floatant, rather than a paste. The paste types certainly float the fly well, but they also tend to clump together and mat the hackles on small flies. I prefer the paste-type floatant when I'm dressing larger flies or flies fished in swift, rough water. Typical of this type are hoppers and larger caddis, such as the Elkhair Caddis.

Dry-fly oil is a liquid that keeps all the quills separated, and I think flies dressed with it give a better impression of the actual insect. But a precaution must be taken when using these oils. Immerse the fly, take it from the bottle, false-cast it several times, and drop it on the water, and you will find that it will often result in a refusal. The reason is that the oil on the fly has not been completely dried or removed. When the imitation is dropped to the surface, the oil leaches from the fly to the water, surrounding the fly with an oily film. No fish is going to take a fly that is floating in a prism of color.

To prevent this, after the fly is removed from the oil, false-cast it several times to dry it. Then drop it to the surface and drag it through the water to flush away any surplus oil. False-cast again to dry it thoroughly, and then present it to the trout. You can make it even easier if you dress your dry flies in the off season with fly oil and allow them to dry. There is no reason you have to dress them just before use.

Special Ties

When trout are feeding in slow, clear water they are very easy to frighten. They also have more time to look at the imitation. Almost all insects drifting along on the surface do so with the body sitting in the surface film, not suspended on their legs.

When such conditions exist, two special types of flies are called for. Either Paraduns or thorax-tied flies will often cause a fish to strike when it appears to have lockjaw. (See chapter 5.) My best luck with these two patterns has been with them dressed on hooks No. 16 to 20. If you carry some of these in assorted sizes and in dun, cream, and mahogany, you can usually score on finicky trout that will constantly sip insects from the slick surface and ignore your other imitations.

Another tip that may help you select the proper imitation when using dry flies is to realize that mayflies appear in different colors at various times of the year. In winter, hatching flies are very dark, even black in color. In early spring the colors are dark gray, slowly changing as the weather warms to lighter gray, and then brown. Then, as late spring approaches, flies become tan or cream-colored, and by early to midsummer the flies are almost all gray again. Understanding this concept will let you select the proper color of mayflies to offer the trout.

Slow Down

A major mistake made by many people who see a trout rising to dry flies is to hurry. There is an urgency to get the cast out there as soon as possible. But that often results in disaster. Always remember that the first cast you make to a rising trout is the most important one. Every succeeding cast increases the chance that the fish will either be alarmed and flee or at least become aware that danger is nearby. So it's very important to first slow down and get into proper position with tackle that is as perfect as you can get it.

When a trout drifts back to take an insect on the surface, many anglers make the mistake of casting at the ring—which will be downstream from the trout's holding position. Once this is realized, understand that the deeper the trout is, the farther back will be the rise ring. A trout drifting up to take an insect in two feet of water may be holding only two or three feet in front of that ring. But a trout coming from a depth of four feet may be holding six feet forward of the ring. You should adjust your cast accordingly.

Don't worry about the fish taking a few flies and leaving—that will almost never happen. If you want a lesson in fly fishing and you can stand the strain after you locate a rising trout, try this. Note the time on your watch when you first saw the fish rising. Become a spectator. Sit down where the fish can't see you and time how long the fish continues to take insects from the surface. You may be amazed. Such feeding may continue

Not rushing, and taking the time to study the situation, selecting the right fly, and easing my way into the proper casting position allowed me to take this gorgeous rainbow. This careful approach is vital for success with big fish.

for from fifteen minutes to more than an hour. There is really no hurry to get off a cast.

The purpose of this exercise is to convince you that once you have located a rising fish, you shouldn't rush your presentation. If you have binoculars, take time to study how the fish is rising, where it's taking the insects from the surface, and where it positions itself for the next take. With binoculars you can often also determine what kind of fly is being eaten. If you have been fishing with a light tippet, and especially if you have caught several fish on it, the tippet may need replacing or adjusting before you offer the fly. You should make it a firm rule that any time you have landed a larger fish on a light tippet, you should snip off the first few inches of tippet and retie.

If the fish is rising along the far shore, usually it is best not to cast directly across the current, since the current will often push against the line and cause the leader to drag the fly. Most of the time when dry-fly or nymph fishing, I prefer to be downstream of and almost behind (just a little to one side) of the feeding trout.

Eddies

There is a very common dry-fly fishing situation in which many anglers fail. Along the bank the angler finds an indentation that forms an eddy (often called a Lazy Susan). The same situation exists where there are willows or bushes along the banks. The water here is slower on the downstream side and behind the bushes. These indentations are off a swift flow of water and create quiet water, where large trout will often hold and feed. The problem is that when a fly is dropped into such small, still pockets, the swifter outside currents grab the line or leader and drag the fly, resulting in a spooked trout or at least a refusal.

What is needed here is to gently drop the fly with a liberal part of the tippet on the surface of the pocket, but with plenty of slack in the tippet and the front of the line. This slack will allow the fly to either sit dead still in the calm water or even circulate around in the miniature eddy—just as a natural insect would—until the currents pull the leader straight.

A right-angle cast is almost always a disaster in such a situation. But there is a simple technique that will allow you to get a strike-producing drift with your dry fly. First, position is important, and if at all possible, try to get downstream and a little to one side of the small eddy or quiet pocket. You are going to make a modified roll cast. Extend your line so that you have at least three feet more line outside the tip than you need to reach the target. Deliberately make an underpowered roll cast. *Actually drive the rod tip down in front of you.* Your line begins to unroll toward the pocket, but because the direction of the rod tip as it stops is not at the target, but in front of you, the line falls so that the leader and tippet collapse and tumble in a pile in the eddy. This allows the fly to sit perfectly still or swirl naturally on the currents. You may have to throw several casts to get the exact feel of where to apply power to drop the fly and tippet in the pocket. This is one of the most effective and frequently needed casts trout fishermen will ever use.

Power (Shock) Gum

More and more, our trout are becoming educated about fishermen. We are being forced to offer very small dry flies, No. 18 through 24, to large trout. In fact, one rule you can live by is that if the fish are not taking, a smaller fly might do better. I think one reason for this is the fish can't see a small fly as well as a big one, and thus may be fooled quicker by the imitation. But the wire diameter of such tiny hooks is so fine that should the fish put up a real battle, the hook may bend open. And such small hooks have so little "bite" that they don't hold enough meat to allow you to put much rod pressure on the fish.

Another problem when fishing large trout is that what breaks the leader is a jerk on it—rarely is it a steady pull. If we can eliminate serious jerking on the fragile tippet, especially when we are connected to a trophy trout by a tiny hook, we dramatically increase our chances of landing it.

Fortunately there is a way out of these situations. There is a commercial product that resembles regular monofilament but is really more like a rubber band. It is called Power Gum or Shock Gum. It can be purchased in better fly shops. Because it has the consistency of rubber, it has to be attached with a special knot, although some shops now sell the material with monofilament on each end to aid in connecting it to your leader. This special knot is illustrated in chapter 7. For best results it is recommended that you cut your butt section within a foot of the fly line. Attach about four or five inches of Power Gum and then connect the other end to the rest of the tapered leader. This has little effect on casting, so long as it is kept short.

In practice the Power Gum acts like a shock absorber or a rubber band. It is not a complete answer, for you still have to fight the fish properly. But it does give you an edge. If a large fish is hooked on a very small fly, as the fish jumps or runs off, the elasticity of the Power Gum absorbs what would often be tippet-snapping jerks. While Power Gum or Shock Gum are not well known by the general fishing public and are used mainly by experienced trout fishermen, the material can be used in other applications. For example, anglers interested in catching very large bass and many saltwater species on fragile tippets may find that Power Gum will allow them to take fish they may otherwise consistently lose.

High-Visibility Flies

As we get older, leaders become thinner, hook eyes become smaller, and tiny dry flies seem to disappear on a long cast. In fact, some of my friends refuse to fish the Trico hatch, simply because they can't see the miniature flies. Others will know that fish are feeding on flies that should be matched with a No. 20 or smaller imitation, but will simply refuse to fish such small flies because they can't see them. Even younger people with poor vision avoid using smaller patterns even when they would be effective.

But there are some answers to this problem. One is to do what George Harvey does. George is the best trout fisherman whom I have fished with in the United States. Some years ago George insisted that wings and body coloration were vital to consistent success. Duck and other feathers were dyed to match the wing colors of hatches. A stickler for detail, he often chastised someone who didn't follow this formula.

But a few years ago all of this changed. George is now in his nineties and still fishes in warmer weather near his home in Pennsylvania. Years ago his eyesight began to fail him. His vision has always been exceptional, and for decades he had no problem seeing the tiny imitations. Now things were different. Even a fly as large as No. 18 was difficult to see. He had to do something. That something benefits all of us who are having problems seeing small dry flies on the surface.

George began tying his wings from bright, fluorescent materials. He found that under normal daylight conditions, bright pink wings were most visible. On overcast days chartreuse seemed to be more easily seen. Now when the fly fell to the surface, that bright spot of color made it easy for George to track the fly.

Did he lose strikes because the wings didn't exactly match the coloration of emerging insects? Not that he could determine—and neither could I and some other friends who began using this technique. For example, many of us enjoy using Royal Wulffs in rough water, because they float well and the white wing is easily seen. If you really want visibility, try tying some Royal Wulff flies with fluorescent wings of bright orange or chartreuse; you'll see them twice as easily—and catch more fish. I also now tie many of my parachute patterns with several strands of pearl-colored Krystal Flash at the wing. Take the Krystal Flash and continue to fold the strands until they are about ¾ inch long. Tie in as you would a conventional thorax or parachute wing. Build the fly and then clip the many folds of pearl Krystal Flash at the correct height. Because the Krystal Flash is spiraled, the Mylar reflects light no matter what direction the fly approaches. At first you won't believe how far you can see this; and it is much easier to work with than hair or feathers. Finally, it looks more like an insect's wing than any other material I have tried. Believe me, the fish don't seem to care what the wing material is—but for those of us with declining eyesight, those tiny flies now stand out like beacons in the night.

Strike Indicators

Another trick to being able to see small dry flies is easy to do. When midges and other tiny insects are hatching, a strike indicator can spell the difference between no hookups and a great day. You don't attempt to watch the dry fly. Use a commercial closed-cell foam, pinch-on strike indicator that can be purchased at almost any fly shop. This indicator is designed for drifting nymphs. But with a little modification it works just as well when fishing tiny dry flies. Generally bright pink is the most visible, although on overcast days chartreuse is easier for me to see. However, on many hard-fished waters today, a plastic floating indicator tips off wise fish so they refuse your offering.

What makes a better indicator for such fish is one from untreated wool (which still has the lanolin in it). By clipping a short section of the yarn and attaching it with a slip knot in the leader, you have a delicate, floating indicator. It usually pays to dress the wool yarn with a bit of paste fly floatant. What works even better is to combine a small piece of black and then a bright fluorescent-colored wool yarn. The black shows well when drifting over glare water, and the brighter yarn is best seen in more subdued light. Be sure to clip the wings evenly, so the indicator doesn't spin and twist your leader. This is by far my favorite of the many indicators available today. If a slip knot is used, you can remove or adjust the position of the yarn on the leader.

Another good indicator is a buoyant dry fly attached with a short length of leader material, with the nymph dangling below. The dry fly must be buoyant enough to float while suspending the nymph below.

When fishing midges, you should grease the entire leader except for a short portion in front of the fly. It is nearly impossible for almost anyone to see a tiny midge imitation sitting in the surface film. To detect the strike, watch the tippet section, which will be easy to see floating on the surface. If it moves, set the hook!

Spinner Falls

When fishing spinner falls (mayflies that have laid their eggs and fallen to the surface to die), you rarely have a problem seeing the imitation—unless it's very small. Most Trico patterns, for example, are dressed on No. 18 to 24 hooks. Such small spinner imitations, lying flat in or on the surface film, can be really difficult to see. Again, George Harvey saved the day. Spinner wings have a translucence that is difficult to imitate. George takes five to seven strands of pearl Krystal Flash and lays them at right angles to the thorax, attaching them as spinner wings. The pearl Krystal Flash is the same color as the natural's wings. It also is very light and aids in floating the imitation. But what makes it exceptional for many of us who have trouble seeing tiny flies at a distance is that Krystal Flash is a super-thin strand of twisted Mylar. Because the strand is spiraled, it reflects light when viewed from any angle. Using George's technique, I have been able to see the tiny Tricos at more than fifty feet. It has worked so well that I now incorporate the pearl Krystal Flash in many of my spinner imitations.

Try a Different Line Weight

Manufacturers now mark their fly rods for the size of fly line that best fits them. Like everything else this is simply a guide. For general fly fishing, the indicated number almost always is correct. But for much dry-fly work it is often a good idea to use a line one size lighter than the manufacturer calls for. For example, if the rod is supposed to be mated to a 6-weight line, there are times when a 5- or even a 4-weight line will do a better job.

When you are fishing on wind-free days or the surface is calm and still, any impact on the water seems to frighten the trout. Using not only a long leader but also a line one or two sizes lighter will help you get more strikes. The recommended line will load the rod nicely and deliver the fly at relatively high speed. This can mean a fairly heavy impact as the line alights on the slick surface. If you use a line a little too light, the rod is never able to load fully (although it will cast the fly well), and so the line's flight speed is slower, and it floats more delicately to the surface. For many years a few of my friends, who are excellent dry-fly fishermen, have been deliberately using a line one size too light for the rod.

The reverse situation is also true. When dry-fly, nymph, or wet-fly fishing, you rarely cast more than thirty feet. On windy days the casts are usually much shorter. Most fly lines are calibrated so that a specific line weight matches the rod when thirty feet of line is extended outside the rod tip. If you are fishing into a breeze and using only ten to fifteen feet of your line, you can't load the rod as well as if you had the full thirty feet outside the tip. Add the complications encountered in trying to turn over a leader and fly into a breeze (especially with a short line) and you have problems.

When you are forced to cast short distances into a breeze, try a line one size heavier. If you are casting a 6-weight rod, use a 7-weight line. You'll be pleasantly surprised by how much better you can cast and make the desired presentation.

Dry-Fly Leaders

In most cases when you are fishing a dry fly, a leader of nine to twelve feet is desirable. If you are fishing tiny brooks that have small pools and are overhung with foliage (I call this tunnel fishing), then a shorter leader

A short leader is often desirable on fast water like this North Carolina stream.

is called for. When conditions force you to fish on long, still ponds, where the fish are exceptionally wary, then you may need to extend the leader length considerably. I have had great success using leaders sixteen to eighteen feet long, with a tippet of four or five feet. Admittedly you can't handle such a long leader on a windy day, and accuracy is somewhat hampered. But it allows you to present a fly so very softly, and the long leader and tippet allow the fly to float drag-free for many yards. Don't worry about setting the hook on the strike; you'll have no trouble with that. On slow water the strike should not be too quick anyway.

A long, fine leader will give you a quiet presentation to trout living in a calm lake.

When fishing ultra-long, slick waters, such as the Henry's Fork, that have incredibly wary trout, anglers have developed another method of presenting the fly. By wading carefully into position upstream of the trout, they approach the fish with a minimum of disturbance. Getting off slightly to one side of the fish, they make a cast. The cast is aimed at an elevated angle, and as soon as the forward casting motion is stopped, the rod is dropped almost to the surface. This causes the line to fall to the surface up-current of the fish, but with a good bit of slack in the line and leader. The higher the cast is aimed, the more slack results. This accomplishes two things. It allows the angler to let both line and leader fall to the surface without fear of any portion descending over the fish. It also permits the fly to come to the fish before the leader. Until the leader straightens, the fly floats drag-free. This trick, while developed on the tough-fishing Henry's Fork of the Snake, is applicable to many similar waters.

For decades anglers have tried to sink their leaders when dry-fly fishing. I followed that advice, too. But if I have learned anything about fly fishing, and particularly trout fishing, it is that traditional methods are often the opposite of what we should do. I believe that this is certainly true with leaders when fishing dry flies. The major problem when presenting a dry fly to a wary trout is to let it float to the fish free of drag. On the surface of flowing water there are a few currents—but underneath are many more. What creates drag is the various currents tugging against the leader—straightening it, and pulling the fly unnaturally. Common sense then tells us that if we can fish the fly where fewer currents surge against the leader, we lessen the drag problem. I began greasing the rear half of my dry-fly leaders many years ago. This causes them to float on the surface. It amazed me how much this reduced the drag factor. A leader that is mostly below the surface has many currents acting on it. One floating on the surface film is subject to far fewer. There is another plus to this, too. A major fault of dry-fly fishermen is making the backcast before all line and leader are removed from the water. If there is any line or leader below the surface, tearing it free to make a backcast often makes a disturbance that frightens the fish. If the rear half of your dry-fly leader is greased so that it floats, the backcast can be made with a minimum of disturbance.

There is another situation where greasing almost your entire leader is advantageous. Midge pupae hang suspended in the surface film. Trout eat millions of them. A pupa that is sunk well below the surface often is ignored. Getting your imitation to hang suspended in the film is often difficult with a conventional dry-fly leader. This is especially true when fishing in flowing water, where the current tends to drown the leader and fly.

In such a situation, grease all but three or four inches of the leader in front of the fly. (Incidentally, I often make the tippet section four or five feet long when fishing midges.) The cast can now be made, and because the entire leader floats, the imitation now hangs properly in the surface film. Greasing the entire leader doesn't work. When applied all the way to the fly, the floatant often leaves a residue on the leader tippet directly in front of the fly; such a residue discourages the fish from striking.

While I'm discussing leaders, another thought occurs to me. Never straighten your leader by drawing it through a piece of rubber. Nylon monofilament is similar to a garbage bag—both are made of plastic. For example, if two men grab the ends of a bag and stretch it taut between them, with a knife you can make a lengthwise slice along the bag, and

If you make a backcast when any line is on the water, it will rip from the surface and make a disturbance. This is a major reason why many anglers fail to catch fish in calm, slick water. Be sure you have all line off the water before you make the backcast.

both men can't tear the bag. But should they hold it so that the bag is tight, and the knife nicks the bag, it will shear apart. That is exactly how monofilament reacts to a nick. Any nick in monofilament can mean a drastically weakened strand. When you fold a piece of rubber around a monofilament leader and draw it through the clenched rubber, a series of tiny nicks are placed in the monofilament. Examine the nylon after such a procedure and you will see this.

Instead, grasp the butt section in your clenched hand. Firmly gripping the leader, slowly pull it through your closed fist. This will straighten the leader, although you may have to do it two or three times. Because you are pulling it through your hand, you'll not put too much pressure on it (it hurts if you do).

Close to the Bank

A very common problem is often encountered when the angler sneaking along a stream spies a trout lying close to the bank. It may be two or three feet off the shoreline, and either lying motionless or feeding. Obviously the first thing to do is determine if the fish is resting, taking dry flies, or feeding below the surface. Once that is established, the angler can then select the imitation that should do the job.

It is at the point of presentation that the angler fails, even though a good cast is made with the proper fly. Dick Frazer, who operates Cedar Lodge on the South Island of New Zealand, says, "It is the one major mistake that most anglers make, even good ones, when they try to catch a fish lying just off the bank." I heard him constantly reminding people not to make the mistake.

This angler took this beautiful New Zealand rainbow because he did not cast between the bank and the fish.

The mistake is to cast the fly so that it lands between the shoreline and the fish. Always cast to the outside or toward the center of the river from the trout. There are several reasons for this. The first is that extreme accuracy is called for to drop a fly between the bank and the fish. A puff of wind in the wrong direction can send the leader and fly into the grass—or onto the trout. Second, frequently the water between the fish and the bank will be flowing at a slow pace, or there may even be eddies; both of these situations make it difficult to get a drag-free drift. The third reason is that if the fly is placed inaccurately well outside the fish, you haven't spooked the trout and another presentation is possible. And fourth, the fly will drift more naturally by the fish if it comes along the main current. Add all of these reasons together, and you understand why, in almost all situations, it is best to offer the fly to the outside or toward the center of the river, not between the bank and the trout.

Caddis Imitations

The caddisfly is rapidly replacing the mayfly on many trout waters. Mayflies cannot tolerate impurities in water as well as caddis do, and so caddisflies are becoming more important to trout and fishermen. There is no doubt that the most popular caddis imitation is the Elkhair Caddis, which is deadly in many situations. It is best fished in faster water. Other imitations produce better where the water is slower and the fish can have a longer, better look. Caddisflies and mayflies do not stand on their legs with their bodies high above the surface. Yet many of our dry-fly imitations do just that. The Catskill-tied fly, for example, is one that is slenderized and appears delicate. But its very light construction causes the body and wing to ride high above the surface. This is an unnatural attitude, which the trout rarely sees. That's why parachutes, Paraduns, and thorax ties are much better weapons for the angler working slower water. These imitations have the body close to or sitting on the surface. In slow, slick water the fish can make a much more careful examination of its prey, and the trout does not have to be in a hurry to take it.

Two of the best imitations of the caddis when fishing in slower water, or when the surface is very slick, are the Goddard Caddis and La-Fontaine's Dancing Caddis. These flies float with the body resting on the surface film—and appear more natural.

Ants

Wherever there are trout, there are ants of some kind. I can think of three situations this past year when fish were ignoring everything I offered them, and the ant scored. On an air-clear pool of deep water on the South Island of New Zealand, I cast four different dry flies and a nymph to a five-pound brown trout that simply ignored everything. Tying on a No. 16 ant, I made a single cast well above the fish. As the ant drifted near, the big trout slowly rose and sucked it in.

Later I fished Spruce Creek near State College, Pennsylvania. The water was slow-moving and slick. Again several types of dry flies were cast to a fish that held steady in the current. A deer-hair ant was dropped almost on the trout's nose—and instantly was accepted.

A few months later in Argentina, on the Mello River, my guide crouched on a high bank, offering instruction about where a large rainbow was feeding in less than a foot of clear, slow-moving water. Paraduns, thorax ties, and conventional dry flies, carefully cast to this steady-rising trout, were all refused. I tied on a No. 16 black ant. The first drift over the fish saw it move up in the water until its back protruded above the surface. But the trout allowed the ant to pass by. I waited maybe two full minutes (which seemed like ten) and again cast the fly eighteen inches ahead of the fish. This time the fish rose very slowly, stuck its head completely out of the water, and inhaled the fly. I struck; the fish leaped and then roared downstream. On the jump I bowed to prevent the leader from parting as the fish fell on an underwater weed bed. It propelled itself onto the grass and broke the fragile leader before I could recover. All three of these fish had ignored different types of dry flies but fell to an ant imitation.

To be perfectly correct, you don't call an ant a dry fly. It falls in the category of terrestrials, which are land-borne insects that inadvertently fall to the water, where trout greedily eat them. Terrestrials include grasshoppers, ants, beetles, leafhoppers, and similar insects. The two major differences between conventional dry flies and terrestrials are that dry flies are imitations of aquatic insects, while terrestrials imitate land-borne creatures; and that drys usually sit on the surface, while terrestrials ride in the surface film—creating an entirely different profile.

But ants are surely the best terrestrial imitations to use for consistent hookups. Ants live wherever trout live. And it is believed by a number of experienced trout fishermen I know that trout and many other freshwater species really enjoy eating ants.

Every aficionado of ants has his or her favorite pattern. Among the most popular is the McMurray Ant, which is composed of two small balsawood balls suspended on a super-thin piece of monofilament. The balsa wood is colored and then a few turns of hackle are added to make a very realistic ant. It comes in a variety of sizes and is very effective. It also floats well. Another top-choice ant is one made from closed-cell foam. It's easy and quick to make—and it does catch fish. Ants made from dubbed fur have been around for years and they work well, although they tend not to float as well as some others. My favorite ant pattern is made from deer hair, not clipped, but attached to the hook and pulled forward to make the traditional two lumps that form the ant's body. I like this ant because it falls to the water with a detectable "plop" that I think imitates the sound ants make when they tumble from a tree branch to the surface. I fish it in rather large sizes, from No. 10 through 14, rarely smaller. The times when I have been able to convince a reluctant trout into striking have been frequent when I switched to an ant.

Most floating ant patterns sit low in the surface film and are often hard to see. This is especially true when fishing under trees that shade the water, or early and late in the day. Many years ago I started painting fluorescent paint on my ants so I could see them better when fishing Maryland's Big Hunting Creek, near where I began my fishing career. I felt pretty proud of myself for being what I thought was innovative. Decades later, fishing with George Harvey and Ralph Dougherty, I discovered that they had been painting their ant bodies probably years before it occurred to me. George has even improved on the painting trick by tying, on the top of the ant body, a cut-wing fluorescent-dyed hen saddle feather, which is really visible. If you plan to paint a deer-hair or dubbed-fur ant body, you will need first to coat the surface with head cement before you can establish the bright spot of paint.

There is a special period in dry-fly fishing when the floating ant will outfish every other dry fly. Usually it's in September, but that can vary a little depending on where you are in the country. Ants can take wing and migrate. They will fly incredible distances. I know nothing about ant entomology, but I do look for and pray for that occurrence. You'll see tiny rings appearing on the surface as fish subtly suck in the ants that have fallen to the water. During intensive migrations the surface is literally covered with their bodies. Trout, and smallmouth bass, go wild. Use any floating ant imitation and you'll have some of the highest success ratios of casts to hookups that you'll ever know.

Even older than the floating ant is the sinking ant pattern. It was one of the early wet flies, recognized as a deadly weapon in the angler's arsenal. Wrapping the body, usually with brown or black thread, and then coating the thread with clear cement makes this simple pattern. I prefer to fish it up and across stream, much as you would any nymph. It is particularly effective in slow pools, where the trout can take a prolonged look at the offering. Sizes 12, 14, and 16 do best for me.

Four terrestrial patterns that are deadly for trout everywhere. Top row, left to right are a grasshopper and a deer-hair ant, one of the best ant patterns.
Bottom row, left to right are two of the same deer-hair ants. But the one on the left has a spot of fluorescent paint on its back, and the one on the right has a fluorescent feather wing. A bit of fluorescence makes tiny ant patterns much easier to see.

Grasshoppers

Of all the terrestrials, perhaps the most popular and certainly one of the most exciting to use at times is the grasshopper. God does not make big grasshoppers early in the season. So if you are going to fish hoppers when they first begin to appear, use small ones. I have never found hoppers to be very effective when tied on hooks smaller than No. 10—or larger than No. 4. My own experience has taught me that grasshoppers are most effective late in the season. I suppose that's because enough of them have been blown or hopped into the river by then that trout are beginning to recognize them.

Dirt banks that overhang the stream and usually have a lot of grass growing on them are often called cutbanks. These often lean out over the water, furnishing a "roof" that allows trout to hide underneath and watch for food that may pass by. It is such cutbanks bordering grassy fields that can deliver some of the best hopper fishing. But I believe most people fish these cutbanks wrong. They cast the hopper tight against the bank. That's okay if the fish is holding where there is no overhanging bank. But if the fish is holding underneath such a bank, often it will not see the hopper. The hopper should be fished about a foot off the bank.

Here's why. Imagine you're standing at the entrance to a garage beside your home and an airplane flies nearly directly overhead. From the doorway you can look up and clearly see the airplane. Now step back well inside the garage and you will not be able to see that airplane, which is hidden by the roof of the garage. The same thing happens to a trout. Should the fish be holding along the edge of a cutbank, it will clearly see a hopper drifting directly overhead. But if the fish is lying well back under the bank, the hopper will be like the planc—and remain unseen. However, if the imitation is cast so that it drifts a foot or so off the bank, or even underneath the overhanging bank, the trout will see it. Because a grasshopper offers a lot of protein, trout will move a considerable distance to take one, where they might ignore a small mayfly following the same path.

I have spent some time lying on the bottom of a trout stream while a friend tossed hoppers on the water. Watching them as they drifted overhead, I was struck by one thing. Every hopper I saw always had its legs protruding through the surface. While I have taken many fish on imitations of grasshoppers that had no legs, I now use patterns with legs. I just feel more confident doing it.

There are several methods recommended for fishing the hopper. Some say that you should twitch it occasionally as it drifts along. Others maintain that a typical dry-fly dead drift is best. Yet other experienced anglers say that you should deliberately retrieve line until the leader tippet is taut, and the current will then draw the hopper across the surface, leaving a tiny V.

Which one is right? I have tried all of them on occasion, and I have failed and scored with each retrieve. My best results have come with making a cast so that the hopper actually contacts the surface with a good plop. I twitch the fly two or three times within the first four feet of the drift, then allow it to dead-drift. I figure that hoppers soon get exhausted and stop struggling. This observation has come from watching many hoppers fall into the water. If my favorite retrieve isn't working, I try one of the recommended three.

Hoppers can also be used to locate big trout—and indeed, to chum them to the surface and put them in a feeding mood. Gather a bunch of hoppers and position yourself upstream from where you think a good trout may be holding. Drop a live hopper into the stream and watch it drift by the suspected location. Continue to drop them on the water on a fairly regular basis. If a fish begins to rise, feed a few more to it. Then either you or a friend can get in position to cast. Cut off the supply of live hoppers and offer the trout an imitation. Some people feel that **chumming trout**—or any fish—is unethical. I don't, and it has helped me land some dandy trout.

There is another situation when a grasshopper pattern will turn a trick. A good trout is located, perhaps sipping on something very small—or at least ignoring everything cast to it. Even though apparently exact imitations pass right by its nose, the fish refuses every offering. At such times, changing to a grasshopper can often turn the trick. And if stoneflies are working around the surface, a grasshopper can be used as a pretty fair imitation, providing it is about the same size as the stones.

Grasshoppers offer a large portion of food to trout, and when trout are taking them, you can fool even trophy fish.

Jassids

One of the most popularized of all the terrestrials is the small black jassid—a leafhopper. Charley Fox and Vince Marinaro, who introduced most American anglers to terrestrial fishing, wrote quite a bit about this insect. Like the Griffith's Gnat, it often will fool finicky trout sipping on some small insects that I can't see or identify. In fact, next to carrying a few ants and hoppers in your terrestrial box, this would be my third choice.

The jassid is usually tied with a jungle cock nail feather dressed on a No. 18 or 20 hook. The bright jungle cock feather makes it easy to see. It was this feather that gave me the idea of painting the backs of my ants with a bright paint. Since jungle cock is now difficult to obtain, you can make jassids out of many small feathers. Select a pair of very short, small feathers. Coat them with head cement and glue them together. Add a minute bit of dubbed fur to the hook shank, plus two or three spirals of a good, tiny dry-fly hackle, and then lay the wing flat on top of the hook.

Griffith's Gnat

One great dry fly that has helped me take hard-to-catch trout is the Griffith's Gnat. I usually tie this on a No. 18, 20, or 22 hook. If you can wind hackle on such small hooks, it is the simplest fly you can tie. Place the hook in the vise, select from a dry-fly neck the smallest hackle, and simply make three or four turns along the hook shank. That's it! Some tiers will wrap a tiny peacock-herl strand on the shank and then spiral the hackle over it—both styles work well.

This fly looks like nothing to a fisherman—but must look very good to trout. When trout are eating midges, midge pupae, the pupae of small flies, or when any very tiny flies are on or in the surface film, the Griffith's Gnat is a good choice. I have often used it, for example, when I have exhausted my supply of properly tied imitations during a Trico hatch. I generally tie it with a grizzly hackle, but I find that at times a light brown, a ginger, or even a dark brown works, too. Gary Borger tipped me off about how the Griffith's Gnat can work when emergers are coming to the surface. "Clip off the hackle on the bottom, and it is one of the best emergers you can use," Gary told me. I saw some emergers working one day in Montana. Having no such patterns with me, with my nail clippers I trimmed off the hackles on the underside of the Gnat, and it took three fish very quickly.

I guess that the ant and the Griffith's Gnat are the San Juan Worms of dry-fly fishing. As the credit card company advertises, "Don't leave home without them."

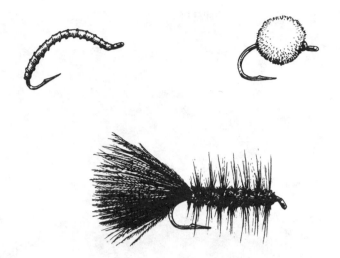

These three underwater patterns will take trout (and many other fish) anywhere in the world: the San Juan Worm, the Egg Fly, and the Woolly Bugger. These flies are so effective that some anglers consider them unsporting, and on certain waters there are attempts to forbid their use.

Nymphs and Wet Flies for Trout

First, let me say that there are three underwater trout flies that I would take anywhere that I wanted to be sure to catch fish. They are so effective that some anglers feel they are unsportsmanlike. There certainly is no denying that they are among the most effective underwater flies ever used on trout. The three flies are the San Juan Worm, the Egg Fly, and the Woolly Bugger.

That said, it is certainly true that most people prefer dry-fly fishing for trout. First, it's certainly more satisfying to see a good fish poke its head out of the water and take your offering. Second, it's perhaps the easiest method of fly fishing for trout. Because the line, leader, and fly are all above the surface, the angler easily can see what is being done right and wrong—and make corrections.

But perhaps 90 percent of what a trout eats is consumed underneath the surface. Drowned insects and nymphs (aquatic insects that live most of their lives underwater) form the bulk of their diet. And while few anglers are acutely aware of it, drag on a drifting nymph is even more destructive than drag on a dry fly. The trout, who feed underwater nearly all the time, are more concerned with a nymph that is being dragged unnaturally than they are with a dry fly that doesn't float properly. Attention to this fact is important in nymph and wet-fly fishing. While some dry-fly purists scorn those who fish with anything else, if you want to catch many more trout than you do now, then learning to be a good wet-fly and nymph fisherman will certainly be a positive step.

Nymph fishermen are as divided in their approved techniques and methods as dry-fly anglers—maybe more so. I have also found that some

Where it's possible to see the trout, you can often detect when it has taken your nymph by seeing the white inside of its mouth. The slight white shown inside this trout's mouth means it's time to set the hook.

anglers oppose the use of indicators to detect when the trout accepts the imitation you are drifting. Indicators can be any small object that is attached to the leader or line, easily seen, that the angler watches for an indication of a strike. Indicators can be closed-cell foam, dry flies, small floats, greased yarn, and a number of other materials, all easy to cast.

Usually those who object to using indicators learned to fish successfully through years of experimenting and concentration—and generally they learned well before anyone knew much about indicators. It is my opinion that most of the old-timers who object do so because they resent the fact that newcomers to the sport did not spend the time on the water learning to do it the hard way—as they did. Whether or not you use an indicator is, I believe, a personal thing. If you don't like them, don't use them. But if others are getting a great deal of fun from using indicators, then I urge them to continue to do so.

If you are new to nymphing, you will also run into a lot of flak about whether you should use nymphs that are weighted or unweighted. One school claims that unweighted nymphs float more realistically in the water column, better deceiving the trout. These anglers feel that unweighted nymphs are more buoyant and are more easily affected by the underwater currents—as they should be. If the nymph is so buoyant that it won't sink to the proper depth, they feel that adding split shot to the leader, or tying in short strands of leader material and suspending the required number of split shot from them, works much better. This method takes the nymph down to the fish's level but allows the unweighted pattern to flow much more naturally with the current.

Another group claims that rather than adding a lot of weight to the leader, which definitely complicates casting, they prefer to place it on the hook body before they build the pattern. In this manner, casting is much easier and the flies get down quickly. Anglers who use this method will build the same size patterns with different sink rates. So that they know which flies sink extra fast, fairly fast, or slowly, they will color-code the heads by using different tints of tying thread. Thus my fastest-sinking nymphs have a black head; brown indicates medium-fast-sinking nymphs. I use light tan for those flies that sink slowly. Because the thread used to tie off the head is usually a small portion of the total fly, I find that the different-colored threads have no effect on whether or not the fish takes the fly.

My own personal feeling is that, as in many other cases where strong opinions exist, there are merits to using both weighted and unweighted nymphs. When fishing in fast, tumbling water, where visibility is not great, I prefer nymphs that are already weighted. Casting is so much easier—and more accurate. The trout's visibility is limited by conditions, and the nymphs are sweeping by quickly. To survive, the trout has to make a hasty decision and grab what it thinks may be food that's passing by. Since the water is fast, you need to get the nymph down fast. An unweighted pattern that depends upon added split shot (often some distance from the fly) frequently descends too slowly to the target area, at least for me. In such a situation I feel that a nymph body that has quite a bit of lead on it will dive fast and will catch me more fish.

Another situation where I think that weighted nymphs excel is when fishing in clear, deep pools, where the trout are lying far down in the water column. Here visibility for the trout is superb. In such a situation I find that the highly noticeable split shot hanging near an unweighted nymph often spoils the presentation as it drifts toward the fish. This was driven home to me several times in the air-clear waters of New Zealand. Instead, a weighted nymph that is able to get down to the desired depth, devoid of anything but the fragile leader it is attached to, is much better.

A common fault when fishing nymphs is to false-cast a number of times. This serves to air-dry the fly. Since nymphs are usually made from fur or synthetics resembling fur, air-drying the pattern makes it sink slowly when deposited in the water. Try to keep false casting to a minimum. Since most fishing is conducted at short distances, roll casting keeps the fly wet and is much more desirable. For most anglers, a roll cast is actually a more accurate cast than the conventional one. It also lessens the chance of the fish seeing the fly line in the air, while keeping the fly wet, so that it will sink quickly. Since the nymph is turned over and gently dropped to the water on the roll cast, the entry is also softer than with a conventional aerial cast. Some of the best nymphing I know is in limestone streams in the winter. These streams come out of the ground at a temperature usually in the forties. Fish feed throughout the year in such watersheds, and some of the very best fishing I've had—for example, on the LeTort in Carlisle, Pennsylvania—has been when the ground is snow-covered.

But if you fish in very cold weather where water will freeze in the guides (and on the fly), roll casting often helps. First, roll casting does not

Trout often feed well on warm winter days. If you are fishing a nymph or scud pattern, it is best to use a roll cast to help keep the fly and the rod guides from icing up.

require bringing much line back through the guides. Thus less ice accumulates there. And since the fly remains wet for all but the very brief time when it is lifted from the water and rolled forward, it doesn't pick up ice.

The tuck cast is also useful when fishing nymphs. This cast must be made with weighted flies—dry flies and similar unweighted patterns don't work. A number of books illustrate this cast. The idea behind the tuck cast is to make a presentation so that the fly sinks deeper in the water column. The cast is made when fishing by standing downstream from the target. The fly is directed twelve to fifteen feet above the water. Extra speed is applied on the forward cast, and even a double haul can be used. The idea is to generate too much speed for the cast. This causes the fly to travel forward very rapidly. The key to making this cast is to overpower a high forward cast. And once the cast ends, the rod should remain

A tuck cast helped me take this trout.

stationary. What occurs is that the fly travels forward at great speed so that at the end of the cast, it bends the rod tip slightly forward. The tip recoils and flips the fly back underneath the leader and sometimes even the line. It is important not to move the rod after the power stroke is completed. Pulling back after the cast will partially straighten the leader.

The cast appears to be a disaster as it falls to the water with considerable slack in the forward end of the line and leader. The nymph enters the water downstream from this slack and begins to sink, while the slack leader and line are drifting downstream. By the time the leader and line are rather straight, the fly has sunk much deeper than it could have with a normal cast. The tuck cast can also be used with streamer flies to get them deeper in the water column, too. It is a vital tool in the nymph fisherman's arsenal.

There are a few nymphs that seem to work just about everywhere and most of the time. Obviously you may have to vary the size, and you might have to either weight them or get them down deeper in the water column. But the following nymphs should always be in a serious trout fisherman's fly box. A Gold-Ribbed Hare's Ear is in my judgment the best all-around nymph pattern. In a new place I often try it first, and if the size and sink rate are okay, the fly generally produces. Dave's Red Squirrel Tail Nymph is another top choice. A Zug Bug has fish appeal that few nymphs possess. One of the oldest is the Pheasant Tail Nymph, and the Gray Muskrat Nymph is another hot item. In many places a Yellow Stonefly Nymph (sometimes called a Golden Stonefly) will turn the trick. And Gary LaFontaine's Sparkle Caddis Pupa is a must. A personal favorite on waters from California to Maine is the Prince Nymph. Just in the past year I have been using John Barr's Copper John. This is a dressed-up Brassie fly and I now believe it is one of the finest nymph patterns I have ever used. I never fail to have some with me.

There is another kind of nymph that is rapidly gaining acceptance. The concept is an old one. George E. Skues wrote about it in his book, *Nymph Fishing for Chalk Stream Trout.* Some very good American anglers began fishing with it in the early 1970s, but many fly fishermen have ignored it. It is called the floating nymph. John Goddard, who I feel is the best trout fisherman I have ever fished with, is a staunch advocate of this imitation and had developed several patterns for this fishing. It looks like a standard nymph pattern tied on an extra-fine hook—but with one difference. At the thorax on top of the hook shank, some device is tied in to make the nymph float in the surface film. This is usually a small ball of polypropylene or dubbing fur, or it can be a minuscule round plastic ball captured in a tiny bit of nylon stocking.

Trout don't want to work any harder than they have to in order to get their food. That's one reason that the floating nymph can be so effective. Aquatic insects leave the bottom and swim to the surface, where they float along, cracking the outer skin and pushing up their wings to dry. Once the wings are dry, the insect leaves the surface. During the wing-drying stage, the insect is totally helpless as it floats along. Trout realize this and simply suck in this easy-to-get, drifting food. Often, even though a fine hatch of mayflies may be on the surface, wiser and larger fish will take just the floating nymphs, ignoring the mayflies that would have to be chased to be captured.

Standard dry-fly outfits are fine for such fishing. But the floating nymphs should be dressed on fine-wire hooks to aid them in staying on the surface or in the film. Also, casts should be short—a long one is twenty feet. It's difficult to see such a small fly (usually dressed on hooks from No. 12 through 18) at a greater distance. Dress the fly with a good oil floatant—I feel that paste floatants sometimes gunk up on the pattern and may spoil its natural appearance. And I prefer a little longer-than-normal dry-fly tippet for this work. Don't try to make a hard cast—do it as gently as possible. The soft cast, coupled with the longer-than-normal light tippet, allows the fly to come to the surface ever so gently. These floating nymphs, when banged down on the water, often penetrate the surface film and begin sinking—something you don't want. The fish usually suck in these insects much as a trout would take a dry fly in slow water. This calls for a slow, delicate strike. Just lift the rod easily when you feel you have a take. In an emergency, when I did not have any floating nymphs with me, I have picked out an unweighted nymph, dressed it in dry fly oil, and used it. It doesn't float as well as the nymph tied for the purpose, but it has saved the day for me on several occasions.

Lakes have no flowing current. But they are often "nymph factories," producing excellent fishing and big, hefty trout that simply gobble up the enormous amount of food produced there. Since there is no current to move your offering, you must supply any motion. Don't be in a hurry to get started fishing—take time to observe. If you see trout that are working noisily near the surface, that is where you want to fish your fly. For such angling, a floating line and long leader are called for. If the fish are gently tailing or moving slowly, the retrieve should be slow. But if the fish appear to be chasing their prey, then a faster retrieve is desirable.

Most of the time the nymphs that trout are taking are close to the bottom, or they are along weedlines (the outer edges of the weeds). The trout may also be feeding just above the tops of the underwater weed beds. For such work a sinking fly line is best. In a clear lake the monofilament lines often will produce better than colored ones. Unlike rivers, where you have a pretty fair idea how deep your line and fly are traveling, deeper lakes make it difficult to judge how far down your offering is. And when trout are feeding at a specific depth (as they often do in lakes), you need to know where your fly is and how to get back to the strike zone on each cast. Fortunately that's easy to do. Your line and fly will sink at a given rate. Make your cast, and do a countdown. As soon as the fly hits the water, start counting: "One thousand one, one thousand two," etc. After a certain count, begin your retrieve. Let's assume that you want to fish just above an underwater weed bed. If on a count of one thousand twelve you snag the weeds, back off a count or two. This method is amazingly accurate. To verify how accurately you can fish a certain depth, test this technique in a swimming pool, where you can see your countdown. The countdown technique is good not only for fishing a lake for trout, but in any area of fly fishing where you want to control the fishing depth of your fly, in fresh or salt water.

When fishing in lakes, you will find that mayfly and caddisfly nymphs are usually abundant. Generally I find that in lakes, No. 14 through 18 are the best, although I always carry a few flies that are slightly larger and smaller.

One of the largest sources of protein in a lake for trout is the damselfly. These are large nymphs, and when they are hatching and moving to the surface, trout will sometimes feed exclusively on them. There are a host of damselfly patterns, and most of them will work. If you fish a lake regularly, be sure you always have a few imitations of the damselfly with you.

In many lakes and small ponds trout will sometimes cruise the shoreline searching for food. Frequently they will travel in a rather defined pattern. If you find this situation, hide along the shoreline behind some brush and watch. Don't be in a hurry. Locate one or more cruising trout and figure out their swimming pattern. Once that is accomplished, plan your strategy. If the fish seems to swim past a certain light-colored spot on the bottom, cast your fly to that spot well after the trout has gone. Allow the fly to sink to the bottom. Wait! When the trout returns and is a few feet from the fly, make a slow, gentle retrieve. This is the most natural of presentations. The trout will usually see the nymph and streak in for an attack.

There is a technique employed by a few fly fishermen when fishing nymphs that I do not regard as fly fishing. But if it's what you enjoy, then go for it. Fly casting, to my mind at least, is that style of angling where the line delivers the lure. Spinning, bait fishing, and plug casting require that the lure or sinker provide the weight that pulls the line from the reel to the target. There is a major difference between the two.

In order to get nymphs down deep and fast, some anglers are employing a long length of monofilament spinning line, which is attached to either a level size 2 fly line or a conventional fly line. Either the weight tied in the heavy nymph or a lead split shot attached to the line near the fly is used during false casting to "pull" enough line through the guides to get to the target. In my view this is spin casting with a fly rod. There is no doubt that the method is effective and can be used with nymphs either for trout, or for steelheading at relatively short distances.

Knowing when a trout will take a nymph is often difficult. If you can see the fish, the chore is easier. Make your presentation and watch the fish—not the fly, which will be nearly impossible to see. If the trout moves up or to one side, tilts down slightly, rolls the body, or shows you the white inside of the mouth, strike! Almost certainly the trout took either your nymph or one close to it.

Most of the time we can't see the fish, and knowing when to strike takes years of training. I suppose I fished ten years with nymphs before I felt I knew when the fish was mouthing my offering. For many years I have averaged more than two days weekly fishing around the world. Most people don't have that kind of time to perfect their nymph strike techniques. For such anglers an indicator is a godsend.

Strike Indicators

The indicator is essentially a tiny bobber. It floats either on or just below the surface and is highly visible to the angler—and is usually ignored by the trout. If the indicator changes drift direction, stops, or is pulled under, it means a trout has grabbed your nymph and it's time to strike. Young and completely inexperienced anglers have been able to fish rather effectively on their first trip with the use of an indicator. Guides on rivers such as the Big Horn, where nymphing is often the most popular method, use the indicator to get many novice anglers their first trout. Some experts who spent years learning to fish without an indicator resent how easy it is for a first-timer to catch trout on nymphs. They vocally object to its use. But even if you plan to fish without an indicator, I suggest trying one when you first dabble in nymph fishing. They will help you recognize much quicker that you are getting strikes. If you later choose not to use an indicator, the training you received with it will be invaluable.

Indicators have one basic characteristic: they are buoyant. They are made from a host of materials. One of the most convenient to use, and very effective, is the commercial "stick-on" closed-cell foam pad. You purchase a rectangular piece of foam, with contact glue backing. Small dumbbell-shaped pads are pre-punched in the rectangle, and you simply lift one of the dumbbells from the pad. It is pressed around the leader at the desired point. What you now have is a light, easy-to-cast bobber that is secured to the leader. It has the advantage of soft impact and is easy to see. The disadvantage is that it has a one-time use. It can be removed only by destroying it as it's pulled from the leader. It is also not as durable as some other indicators. Also, the foam dumbbell pads can be made smaller with either a scissors or a nail clipper, so indicator size is adjustable.

Another type is a tiny ball with a hole through the center. Your leader is inserted in the hole and the ball positioned on the leader. To keep it at this point, a toothpick is inserted between the hole and the leader to capture it, and then the excess of the toothpick is broken off and discarded. This type of float has the disadvantage of hitting the water with a fairly loud splash. It has the following advantages: It's easy for the angler to see, it's nearly indestructible, and because the toothpick can be removed, the ball can be repositioned on the leader.

Paul Bruun used a weighted nymph to fool this nice trout.

Another clever indicator is a small tube of closed-cell foam. A heated wire is pushed through the center to sear a smooth hole. A piece of leader material is pulled through the hole, and a small piece of yarn is attached so that it protrudes from the top of the foam tube. When the fish takes, the polypropylene yarn comes to a vertical position. The advantage to this is that it is perhaps the most visible of all indicators, and the yarn alert even makes the strike more noticeable. It does land with quite a splash, however.

There is another indicator you can make yourself. It is made from gift yarn, which is polypropylene yarn, and it can be purchased in gift shops and other places where handicraft materials are sold. It is approximately ½ inch in diameter. Buy either the fluorescent green or, better, salmon pink. Split the yarn into two halves, for the original diameter is far too large. To help the yarn float better, place one end in a vise and use Dave's Bug Float or one of the other silicone paste fly floatants, rubbing it vigorously into the yarn. When the yarn is saturated with the silicone, cut it into four- or five-inch lengths. These are stored in a small Ziploc bag. The bag takes up little space in a fly jacket. When you want to use an indicator, remove a section and tie it to your leader with a slip knot. Pull the knot tight and the yarn stays pretty much where you place it. It is important to trim the yarn ends short (I leave about ½ inch), and the ends must be even. If the ends are not even, the yarn will cause the leader tippet to spin and twist. There are several advantages to this indicator. First, it is easy to store and carry. It has the distinct advantage of your being able to wind it inside the guides, if that becomes necessary. It is highly visible, and it casts almost as if there were no indicator on the leader. The disadvantage is that it doesn't float quite as high as some of the closed-cell units, and it must be clipped off when you are finished—thus destroying it.

There are numerous commercial indicators now on the market and all work. However, where the trout are fished over constantly, they soon recognize large and bright indicators. For such fish, nothing has been more effective for me than sheep's wool containing natural lanolin (the wool has not been washed). Attach a short length with a slip knot to the leader, and then clip the ends evenly. Rub in a small amount of silicone fly dressing, and the yarn indicator looks like a small pair of mayfly wings. If you combine black and a bright color, you can see the indicator in either glare or shaded waters.

When you are fishing nymphs, it's vital to understand that the nymph should float as naturally in the current as possible. Since trout feed far more on nymphs than on dry flies, you can see that a natural drift is important in deceiving the trout. Generally anglers will cast the nymph up and across stream. The nymph is allowed to sink and hopefully drift back in a natural manner to the trout. But currents tugging on the line and leader soon ruin any natural drift. What an indicator can do for you is increase the natural drift time. Because the indicator floats almost vertically above the nymph, it reduces the amount of pull that currents exert on the line and leader. By throwing a cast so that the indicator is upstream of the fly, you ensure that the fly, hanging down from the indicator, will almost always float for a longer distance in a natural manner.

Streamers for Trout

Perhaps the first trout taken by most anglers was caught on a streamer fly. It imitates one of the trout's most preferred foods—baitfish. And it appears not to require much expertise to use it effectively. Just cast it out and strip the line back—and that's the way most people fish streamers. Streamer fishing can be very deadly, but it also requires some definite techniques if you are to get full measure from these patterns. No other type of fly will do a better job in deceiving large fish into taking your offerings. Generally, large trout don't want small insects. When hungry, they want some "groceries"—and larger streamers fill that bill very nicely. Streamers are best used when insect hatches are not peaking. During hatches, the trout are often so concentrated on them that they ignore other offerings. Another great time to use streamers is when light conditions are poor. That's when larger trout will frequently come out and prowl for food.

There are two basic types of streamer flies: imitations and exciter patterns. Both work well, but for trout, good imitations almost always will outscore the exciter types. Exciter streamers are usually brightly colored flies that may contain some reflective Mylar or similar material. The idea here is not to offer the trout something that looks like a food source, but to present an appealing "something" that they will hit. Imitative patterns are those that actually try to duplicate minnows that trout are feeding on. Incidentally, a good guideline for what color patterns to use is to fish with flies that have the basic coloration of the bottom. That is, if the lake, river, or stream bottom is light tan, then light tan streamers will usually be the most effective. In Alaska streams, for example, often the gravel bottom is olive or light olive. The basic food supply for the big rainbows (other than when salmon are spawning) is the sculpin. Olive-colored sculpins will usually outfish any other color of the same pattern.

A major mistake made by the majority of anglers who fish streamers is to activate the fly by flipping the rod tip up and down. This creates two problems. First, the up-and-down rod motion creates a tremendous amount of slack. Fish often hit as a fly pauses on the retrieve. If you flip the rod up then drop it, the fly zips forward, then pauses. Slack occurs in the line. Should the fish strike, there is a good chance of failing to hook it. Another good reason for not using the rod to activate the fly is that the fly overreacts. Minnows swim about in short darting motions, or in slow steady movements. They don't leap several feet through the water column. If you want to make an interesting observation, go to a swimming pool. Cast your streamer well out into the pool and let it sink deep. While watching the fly, lower your rod and make your normal flip up and down with the tip. You may be amazed at how far the fly leaps through the water with even a minimal amount of rod movement. Such great forward jumps of the fly are most unnatural.

To obtain the most natural swimming motions, the rod tip should be pointed at the fly (placing the tip in the water an inch or two will ensure a tighter line between you and fly), and the line hand should strip the line to activate the fly.

There are several streamer retrieving techniques. The most basic is when you are fishing across a stream of fair to large size. Cast the fly very slightly downstream and across the current as far as you wish. As soon as the fly drops below the surface, you can activate it by varying the strips made with the line hand. But my favorite method when fishing a streamer this way is slightly different. Keep the rod tip pointed at the fly and follow it as the fly drifts downstream. This prevents a deep sag in the line. The deeper the belly or sag in the line, the faster the fly will swim, (like a crack-the-whip motion) and the quicker slack will accumulate—slack that may cause you to miss a strike. As the rod follows the downstream drift of the fly, rock the rod tip up and down only a few inches. If the tip is moved no more than six inches in an up-and-down motion, the fly darts about in short spurts. Only a tiny bit of slack develops in the line when this technique is used. The line hand controls slack by constantly taking a few inches out as it occurs. This method has served me well for decades.

You'll get more strikes if you can present the streamer so that the fish gets a full look at it, instead of the fish looking at the end (much as you would look at a knife if the point were directed toward you). It's much better to offer the fly so that it drifts sideways to the fish. Decades ago, a wise fly fisherman became famous for what he called the **greased-line method**. Basically what he did was retrieve the streamer so that the fish viewed its full profile. This has become a standard technique when fishing for Atlantic salmon and steelhead. But strangely, trout fishermen have ignored this very successful method of retrieving a streamer fly.

To accomplish this trick is rather simple once you understand the problem. What usually occurs is that a cast is made across the current. As the fly is moved downstream, the water pushes a deep belly in the line. This causes the fly to turn and head downstream. This, of course, presents the fly traveling head-on toward the fish. The trick is not to allow that deep bend in the line from the current—then the fly will float sideways to the fish.

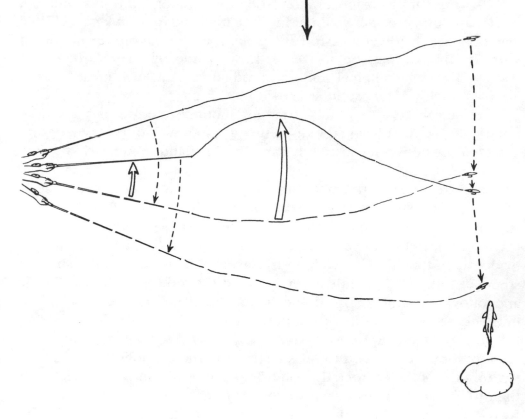

Mending line upstream when the current forms a bow, as shown here, gives the fish a full-profile view of your offering. Sometimes you may have to mend several times to get the proper drift.

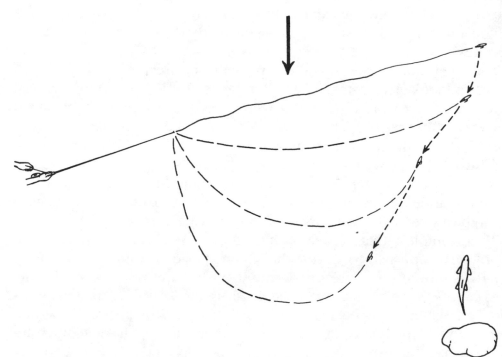

Failure to mend line upstream causes a deep bow or sag in the line. This will make the fly swim too fast and offer the fish only a slim profile of the fly.

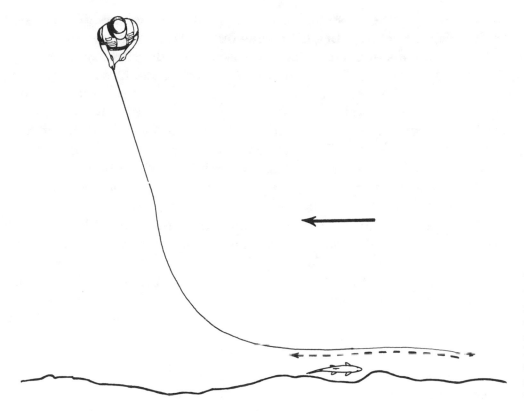

Throwing the fly straight toward the streambank and retrieving will give the fish only a brief end view of your offering. Instead, a curve cast like this one allows the fly to sweep along the shoreline for some distance, increasing your chances of a strike.

After the cast is made and as soon as a downstream bow begins to appear in the line, the rod tip is lifted upward and rolled upstream. This lifts the line and forms an upstream mend. This technique is repeated as often as is needed as the fly drifts through the water. The greased-line trick is one that will surely take more trout (and bass) in larger rivers.

Another technique that I use frequently on small streams or when fishing along cutbanks is to make a strong right-angle **curve cast**. For example, a stream is running north to south; you are standing on the west side and casting to the east bank. With a conventional method, the fly is thrown across and downstream. Then a retrieve is begun. But this often presents the fly for only a brief moment along the shoreline (where the fish are probably holding), and then the fly moves out toward midstream. During this type of presentation the fly is being viewed from the end, instead of from the side. Instead, cast directly across the stream. Use a side cast, but when you come forward, overpower the cast as much as you can (even using a double haul). This results in the streamer fly going toward the bank, but the overpowering of the cast causes the rod tip to flip into a deep curve, with the streamer well upstream and along the bank. Now you can retrieve the fly so that it swims parallel to the bank for a considerable distance before it begins moving out into the main stream.

This same hook or curve cast can be used to deadly effect when fishing from a drift boat. Big fish will often lie in a pocket of still water behind a rock or on the downstream side of a group of willows or other obstruction. They dart out into the fast water, grab their prey, and move back into the quiet holding water. As you drift by, to get the fly behind the willow into the quiet water would mean you would have to throw a right- or left-hand curve. But if you practice the side cast just described, you'll find you'll be able to investigate with your streamer a lot of good holding water you may have been ignoring.

There is another great method for fishing trout that are holding in small to medium-size pools. Use a floating line and a long leader, at least ten feet—twelve feet is often better. I prefer a weighted streamer that doesn't snag easily on the bottom for this. A small Clouser Minnow is ideal for this because it goes down fast and the hook point rides up. The cast is made up to the head of the pool and the fly allowed to fall to the bottom. Then the fly is stripped back in a rush. One or two quick pulls are made. The fly lifts off the bottom, leaps forward, and then dives back to the stream floor. The process is repeated. I've seen reluctant trout that appear almost to be dozing come alive, spin on their fins, and swoop in and grab a streamer when I've used this retrieve. This is not a surefire technique, but it is one that sometimes will work when nothing else does.

Another special trick for certain conditions works wondrously well. I tie streamers on bendback-style hooks. This causes the hook point to ride up and be hidden by the wing. Tied properly and fished correctly, it is virtually weedless. There are occasions when fish are cruising just above underwater weed beds, such as in many western lakes. Generally they are cruising in search of either dragonfly nymphs or small emerging nymphs. But throw a bendback-style streamer fly in, allow it to sink to the top of the weeds, and you have a much more attractive fly for bigger trout. They see this swimming in among the weeds and just above them (it will rarely snag the weeds, if you retrieve slowly), and they will swoop in and grab it.

Where the stream flows swiftly, and there is a good pocket that may hold a nice trout, you can use a spider dry fly or a streamer to "tease" the fish into hitting. Station yourself directly upstream from the hot spot, and far enough away so as not to alert the trout. Make your cast so that the fly lands even with and to the right side of the hot spot. Now flip the rod to the left. This will cause a line bow to form to the left. The fast water, pushing against the line and leader, will make the fly swim to the left, and almost at right angles to the spot. When the line straightens and the fly swims as far left as it will go, flip the rod and line to the right. The fly will reverse itself and swim back to the right. By using this tech-

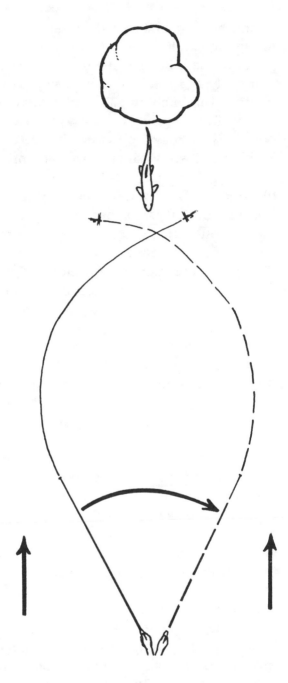

Try this trick to tease a fish holding in the current. If you flip the rod back and forth, the current flow will cause the fly to zigzag in front of the fish, often drawing a strike.

nique, and repeating the flipping to the left and right, you can make a fly swim back and forth in front of a fish and sometimes tease it into striking. The method works very well with both streamers and spiders. If you are using a spider dry fly (or skater), I suggest greasing the front portion of the line and all but the leader tippet to prevent the fly from occasionally drowning.

Another great trick with streamer flies is to be ready to begin retrieving immediately upon impact with the water—something so many people don't do when casting to a hot spot. Imagine that you are a trout and you are lying in ambush. Something plops in the water overhead and you look up. Tumbling unrealistically down is a bunch of feathers attached to a hook. But if the angler throws the fly to the target area and the retrieve begins as soon as the fly hits the water, the trout will hear the plop and look up, and see what appears to be prey darting away! Much better.

Sculpins are a major food source for trout. Sculpins do not have a swim bladder. That means any time they stop swimming, they will sink to the bottom. For that reason most sculpin patterns should be fished close to or on the bottom. Many sculpin flies are dressed with a long-shank hook that has an exposed point. Such flies will often snag on the bottom when fished as recommended. I prefer sculpin flies that are weighted (so that they will sink to the stream floor) and tied so that the hook rides inverted, or that carry a weed guard. Sculpins are most active very early and late in the day, or when light levels are low, such as on rainy days and very overcast ones. These are good times to fish this pattern.

Regardless of which streamer patterns you use, some should be dressed with little or no weight, some with a little weight, and some with enough weight so that they will sink quickly. By carrying patterns that can be fished at different depths, you will be able to work a greater portion of the water column.

Leader length is often a problem when fishing streamers. Years of fishing for trout have convinced me that underwater, they are not very leader shy, unless the water is extremely clear. Obviously, you can't tie a fifteen-pound-test leader to a small fly. The reason, of course, is that using such a heavy leader is like welding a stiff, monofilament rod to the fly. This ruins its action. If you would ever lie on a stream floor and watch all of the debris, air bubbles, and other flotsam that drifts on the current, you would realize that a trout sees all sorts of stuff passing by. I believe that for this reason, where the current is fairly swift, trout seem to disregard leaders to a great degree. When fishing streamers in such current, a short leader of less than thirty-six inches is recommended, and I often use leaders less than a foot in length when fishing a sinking line. The short leader will help get the fly down quicker—and keep it where the fish are holding. However, on clear, long, still pools, and in clearwater lakes, I find that a long, thin leader is a definite asset. Here the fish have great visibility and will be turned off by too short a leader. Incidentally, this is one reason why I think that split shot dangling from the leader, or pinched on it near the fly, will turn off trout in such waters when you are fishing nymphs.

There are some basic streamers that all trout fishermen should have in their arsenal. Fortunately you don't need many, but they should be carried in several sizes and in varying weights. Here are my recommended streamers, and not in order of preference, since I think you should carry all four: Zonker, Clouser Minnow, Sculpin, and Woolly Bugger. Actually, the Woolly Bugger is not really a streamer—but can be fished as one. I would always carry Zonkers (which I dress on streamer-length hooks in sizes 4 to 10) in black, chartreuse, olive, and all white. Clouser Minnows for trout seem to be best if they are dressed on No. 6 through 10 regular-shank hooks. The two most effective color combinations for trout, at least for me, have been a yellow belly with either a brown or olive top wing. When streamers in these colors work along the bottom, I think trout take them for either crayfish or sculpins. I prefer sculpin patterns that are tied on long-shank hooks in sizes 4, 6, and 8, and in only two colors—either olive or medium brown.

Woolly Buggers are exceptionally versatile flies. I tie them in sizes from No. 2 all the way to a small No. 12. Color combinations are usually black, tan, or dark brown. However, my favorite, and for me the most effective, is a Woolly Bugger with a black marabou tail and a body of six to ten peacock-herl strands twisted along with a very thin piece of copper or gold wire for added strength and then wound the length of the hook shank. A grizzly hackle is then palmered over the herl. In the water this herl body looks really attractive to both the trout and to me.

Night Fishing for Trout

While few people do it, night fishing for big brown trout is decidedly the best way to take a real trophy. On many hard-fished waters the really large brown trout feed only after dark. That means your only chance of catching one is to fish then. I must confess that night fishing is not nearly as attractive to me as daytime fishing. Fishing for me is more than catching fish. What makes the sport so interesting is the companionship of others, seeing all of nature around you, and yes, watching a fish take your fly. But there's no denying that if you want to catch a very large brown trout, fishing during the nighttime will offer you the very best chance to score. Because of that I have learned to fish at night and have taken some very big browns.

Offered here are a few tips on fishing big browns at night. If you fish smaller streams, those that average less than eighty feet wide, it's best to locate the fish first. This is easy to do. With the aid of a wading staff, walk the banks at night with a powerful flashlight, scanning the bottom with the light. If you see a fish, immediately remove the light. Wait a full minute or two, and then swing the light over the area to see if the fish is still there. If so, remove the light immediately. If you hold the light on the fish, it will often spook and leave the area. In smaller streams the use of a

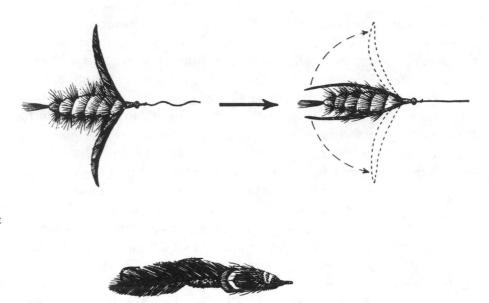

You need special flies and techniques to take big brown trout at night. Two of the best flies for night fishing are George Harvey's Night Fly (top) and the large Muddler Minnow, tied with a stinger hook at the rear.

powerful flashlight at night is the fastest way to learn where big trout are feeding. Once the fish's location has been determined, move quietly upstream from it. Get in position and cast your night fly (which will be discussed in a moment).

In larger rivers flashlights sometimes work, but often the water is too deep. Very often the larger brown trout will come to the head of a pool and lie along a quiet area directly adjacent to fast water. They will hold along this seam and will take anything that moves. One of the best places to search with your fly for huge brown trout at night is in the tailrace area below a dam. At night the water flow is often reduced, and the fish will hold along the outside bends (where the deeper water is), and then make frequent cruises in along the edges and gravel bars, searching for crayfish, sculpins, and other large morsels. These big browns are looking for a substantial meal. This tailrace fishing is especially effective during October, November, and December, when the big browns often move from downriver to near the base of the dam as the spawning urge strikes them.

In smaller streams, where a big brown may be from three to ten pounds, flies such as George Harvey's Night Fly are excellent. You can find an example of this in George's book, *Techniques of Fly Fishing and Fly Tying*. This fly is constructed in the shape of a football and is usually dressed on a No. 4 or 2 hook. But what makes it very different is a pair of wings that stick out from the sides, much like a pair of oars on an ancient galley ship. The body shape and the outrigger-type wings create maximum resistance in the water on the retrieve. This causes vibrations, which the night-feeding brown trout can quickly sense and locate. The fly is cast down and across stream, and by hand-twisting the line on the retrieve, you very slowly bring it back. When you are night-fishing smaller streams, a retrieve rate of perhaps eight inches every ten or fifteen seconds is advisable.

On the larger rivers and in lakes, where you may encounter very big browns—often more than ten pounds, and as much as twenty pounds—a different type of fly is employed. Here a fly that is four to six inches long is used. The fly is constructed with a weighted hook, and the hook rides inverted, or point up. This allows the fly to be crawled along the bottom and not snag. A rear stinger hook, about No. 6, is attached to the main hook (usually a No. 1/0 to 3/0) with twenty-pound monofilament. This stinger gets many of the fish that short-strike the fly. The pattern is constructed much like a giant sculpin. The head is a large, trimmed deer-hair head that will push through the water much as a boxing glove would. The fly is cast out and allowed to sink all the way to the bottom. Then, in slow strips of no more than six to ten inches, the fly is retrieved. An effort is made to keep the fly in contact with the bottom whenever possible. Both of the suggested methods work very well on night trout, and if you are after a trophy brown, this is decidedly the best method to catch one.

Bass

One of the interesting facets of fly fishing is that when you try for a new species, you may use the same basic tackle, but many factors are different. The various species live in dissimilar environments, and they frequently have characteristics and habits totally different from other kinds of fish. The way they hide, feed, strike, and even fight may be totally dissimilar. And that calls for a variety of tackle, fly patterns, and techniques. To be a well-rounded fly fisherman, you need to be able to adapt to the requirements for different species.

The methods used for trout are sometimes effective as well for both species of bass (largemouth and smallmouth). But there are major differences, too. Trout (unless they are very large) feed mainly on insects, and except for dry flies and terrestrials, they take most of their food underwater. Bass, when they are less than twelve inches, also are very much like trout—feeding a great deal on insects and nymphs. But larger bass of both species can frequently be encouraged to feed on top—and in many situations it is the best way to take the larger bass. Excepting dry-fly fishing for trout, perhaps the advent of surface fly fishing was started when anglers began to entice bass into taking deer-hair and cork popping bugs. Bass also prefer much larger lures. And unlike trout, both species of bass can easily be beguiled into hitting exciter-type patterns. These are

Smallmouth bass favor rocky areas, but largemouths like this one prefer weeds. This bass came from Currituck Sound, North Carolina.

patterns in outlandish colors that resemble nothing any angler has ever seen in the water.

There are some fundamental differences when fishing for smallmouth or largemouth bass. Smallmouth bass, as a general rule, prefer smaller, sleeker patterns than do largemouths. Of course, this is a generalization, but it holds true in most situations. Smallmouths also seem to strike flies that are retrieved slightly faster than for largemouths—which most of the time tend to go for a slower-moving fly. Realistic imitations often score better with smallmouths than with largemouth bass.

Cover requirements for the two species are different. Largemouths will live in water with higher summer temperatures. They seem to be comfortable and will continue feeding when water temperatures are in the high eighties. But smallmouths seem most active when summer temperatures are more often in the seventies and rarely reach the high eighties. Smallmouths tend to feed better throughout the winter, although both species will feed until water temperatures reach about 35 degrees. Largemouths can tolerate a bottom that has more silt and mud. Smallmouths gravitate to areas where there is considerable rock rubble or at least a gravelly bottom. Largemouths prefer to lurk in shadowy ambush places such as around old stumps, sunken logs, and similar cover. Smallmouths will most often be seen near rocks, which they use for current breaks, ambush, and sanctuary.

Some of the best smallmouth bass fishing in the United States is in rivers, both the big limestone ones of the East and great western rivers such as the John Day in Oregon and the Snake in Idaho. Many people think of western rivers as basically trout waters—but there are a number of superb smallmouth rivers in the West. Smallmouths gravitate to rocky areas in all waters, and in rivers it is the best place to seek them. The shape of the rock in the river can also be vital to the angler. If the rock slants upstream or protrudes vertically, there is a slack current immediately in front of the rock, and the fish will hold there. They can see anything coming to them and still not fight the current. But a rock that slants downstream will not hold fish on the upcurrent side. Instead, the bass will hold behind the rock in the quiet water. Rocks are often the key to locating smallmouths, and recognizing the shape of the rocks, especially in rivers, is often the answer to drawing strikes.

Popping Bugs

One of the major reasons so many of us enjoy bass fishing is we can catch them on surface flies, called popping bugs. These are generally made from balsa wood, cork, or high-floating molded plastics. I have been actively fishing poppers for more than forty years—and if I had a favorite type of freshwater fishing, it would be with a popping bug, on a good, big river, for smallmouth bass. I learned many of my fly-casting techniques using bugs for smallmouths and spent a good deal of my early fly-fishing career chasing nothing else. The early bugs I used had splayed feathers for a tail. These flopping feathers in flight often underwrapped the hook, spoiling the presentation. Added to that were one or more hackles

Here is an old photo of me with one of the first smallmouth bass I took on a popping bug. I got my start in fly fishing by chasing smallmouths on the large limestone rivers of the mid-Atlantic region.

wound around the hook between the tail and the body. These radiating hackle fibers, combined with the splayed feather tails, created a very wind-resistant bug that was difficult to cast. Even worse, when one fell to the water, all of that feather dressing impeded the action of the bug. To make it worse still, the hook was a short-shank model that had the point nestled underneath the body of the bug. To be hooked, the bass had to grab the entire bug, and the angler hoped that the small clearance be-

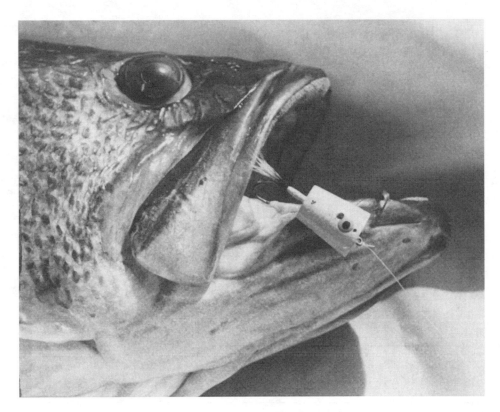

This 9-pound Georgia largemouth fell for a Lefty's Bug, one of my favorite poppers.

tween bug body and hook point offered enough purchase to hold the fish (see chapter 5).

Over the years I began to develop my own popping bug for bass, which is now known as Lefty's Bug. The large, air-resistant tail, which often fouled on the cast, was eliminated. In its place is a short tail, generally of squirrel tail, that is lashed to the hook shank from the back of the bug body to the end of the straight portion of the hook. It extends just beyond the bend of the hook. This tail is tied very short so that it can never foul on the cast. You don't need a long tail on a bug, but one is necessary, for it acts much like the tail on a kite—giving the bug body better flight characteristics. There are no radiating hackles to impede its flight. The bug is sleek and casts very easily. Incidentally, in smaller sizes it is a deadly bluegill bug, too.

The hook's location on the bug body is important. Many commercial popping bugs for bass have the hook eye located well up in the face of the fly, sometimes even in the center of the face. While this may help the bug create more surface noise, it makes it much more difficult to lift the bug from the water. That's especially true if the bug is some distance from the angler. Lefty's Bug, and I think any well-designed popping bug, will have the hook eye located at the base of the body. It allows you to make all the noise needed to attract a fish, but it also holds the bug in the best position to lift it from the surface.

A longer-shank hook should be used. Short-shank hooks tend to make the bug sit flat on the water, with the point near the surface and hidden under the bug's body. Longer-shank hooks tend to hang well below and away from the body. The fish actually contacts the hook first on the strike. The longer hook also tilts the bug body so that it pops better and lifts more easily from the surface for a backcast. I believe, for all popping-bug fishing except where you are fishing on lakes for largemouths, that a design similar to Lefty's Bug will result in an easier cast and take more fish.

When you are fishing on lakes or ponds, where there is no current, and largemouth bass are the target, a slightly different bug is often effective. Under such conditions the bug is not going to go anywhere, and the bass has plenty of time to look over its prey before it strikes. While in many situations I prefer a fast-moving popping bug, on lakes and ponds often the best retrieve is a very slow one. A good largemouth popping bug fished on a lake or pond may have a lot of dressing. All of it is to get more motion and movement in the bug while it sits on such still water. For that reason anglers dress largemouth poppers with lots of feathers, and a decided attraction is a series of rubber bands that extend outward from the body of the bug.

The bug is cast into a likely spot and popped once or twice. Then it's allowed to sit motionless. Some people say that lighting up a cigarette and smoking it, and not popping more than a half dozen times until the cigarette is finished, is about the correct pace. After the bug is popped, the feathers undulate for a short time and the rubber bands work back and forth. Then the bug is allowed to sit still. Hopefully a bass is underneath, trying to decide if it wants to strike.

Norm Bartlett is a good friend of mine and a very innovative fly rodder. Norm took a very old largemouth popping-bug pattern and improved it into what I consider to be by far the best pond and lake popping bug I've ever used (see chapter 5). This was the Gerbubble Bug, invented early in this century by Tom Loving for fishing on Chesapeake Bay's tidal rivers for largemouths. The original Gerbubble Bug was sort of rectangular, and protruding at right angles from the sides of the body were feathers. It was a terrific bug. Norm substituted marabou feathers for standard saddle hackles. Instead of thin hackle fibers sticking out from the sides, the body (and the tail) now held the ultra-soft marabou feathers. When this fly landed on the water, these fluffy feathers began moving with the tiniest activation by the angler. Norm's Gerbubble Bug has three or four times more action while the bass is examining it from underneath. This may the very finest of all largemouth popping bugs.

There is another popping-bug design that for some purposes serves better than any other. This is the Pencil Popper. I think that Jerry Jarosik developed it, and it is a sleek, round tube, tapering at one end. The bug is made from balsa wood and the end is tapered in a pencil sharpener—hence the name Pencil Popper. Properly made, it often carries a stiff weed guard immediately in front of the hook point. Because of its slender shape, it better resembles a baitfish than any other type of bug. For that reason, when I want to imitate a baitfish struggling on the surface, I will use the Pencil Popper. It also is a better bug to fish in thick weeds, such as where lily pads cover the surface. Lily pads have a frustrating habit of snagging most popping bugs—even those with weed guards. But the face diameter of a Pencil Popper is often less than half as wide as that of a conventional bug. This sleekness, combined with a good weed guard, allows you to swim it through much more vegetation than you could a conventional bug.

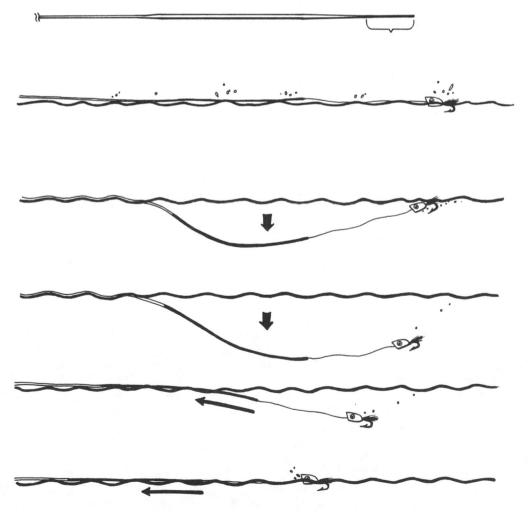

Here is an effective and fascinating way to tease bass with a popping bug and a sink-tip line, with the sinking portion shortened to five feet, and a leader of about six or seven feet. Make a cast and allow the sink-tip to drag the bug underwater. If you start to retrieve, the bug will swim underwater, but the retrieve also makes the line loft upward. Eventually the line and the bug will surface. Stop retrieving and the bug will sink again, and you can repeat the whole process.

There is a neat trick when working popping bugs where you employ a sinking line and a long leader—at least ten feet in length. If you make a cast, and as soon as the popper strikes the surface, you begin your retrieve, you can bring the bug back in a normal manner. So long as you continue to strip line, the sinking fly line stays very close to the surface, and the bug pops as if you were using a floating line. But if you allow the sinking line to sink deep in the water column, it will slowly drag the popper below the surface. Once the bug has descended well below the surface, begin retrieving the sinking line. This will pull on the bug and cause

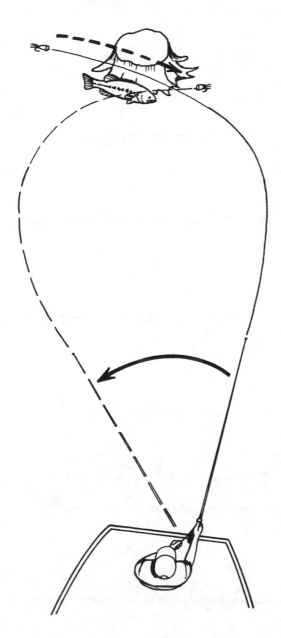

Flipping the rod back and forth is a great way to tease a bass holding in front of a stump or other obstruction.

it to dive toward the bottom. Then stop stripping line, and the buoyancy of the bug will cause it to swim vertically toward the surface. Repeat the operation and the bug will dive, and as soon as you stop retrieving, the bug will again move toward the surface. By using the strip-and-stop retrieve, you can cause the bug to move forward but also to swim up and down in the water column. Sometimes a wary bass, watching this bug's antics, just can't help but strike it.

Another great trick for inducing a fish to strike is a **teasing method**. If a bass is lying in front of a stump, a rock, or other cover and seems reluctant to strike, you can often tease it into hitting. Toss the popping bug to the right side of the stump or obstruction. Retrieve about six or eight feet. Stop, and then flip the rod tip in a rolling motion to the left. This will cause the line to bow to the left in a curve in front of the stump. By slowly retrieving, you can now make the bug move to the left of the stump. Stop retrieving. Now flip the rod to the right, forming a curve to the right, and repeat the retrieve. Using this method, you can cause a popping bug to pop and swim back and forth in front of the bass, without ever bringing the lure toward you. It is often a deadly technique.

It has been my experience that the fly fishermen who prefer **deer-hair bass bugs** are almost always fly tiers. That's understandable, since they are so much fun to make—and they certainly can be dressed in pretty colors. But they have two major disadvantages, at least for me. The deer hair is air-resistant, and it soaks up water. Deer-hair bass bugs never cast as nicely as cork and balsa wood bugs. And the longer they are fished, the more water the deer hair soaks up. After a few fish are caught, often the bug floats poorly and takes on water. The added water carried within the bug makes it much more difficult to cast. In almost all situations I prefer popping bugs made from either balsa wood or cork; this is a personal choice. But if you enjoy deer-hair bugs, have fun with them!

There is one place where a deer-hair popping bug is supreme. In many lakes the bass have little cover, or poor ambush spots. Bass also love shade, and in many clearwater lakes, shade is at a premium. But on lakes where many people live along the shorelines, there are boat docks. Boat docks, as almost any lake fisherman knows, are hot spots for bass. They furnish an ambush location—and that all-important shade.

But once people begin walking to and fro on the docks, and motorboats roar into action, the bass will frequently quit the docks for quieter waters. That means that the best bass fishing around boat docks usually occurs early in the morning or late in the evening, when there is reduced people and/or boat traffic. A good technique is to slip quietly up in your boat but stay a fair distance away from the dock. In the stillness you will want to be as quiet as possible. One favorite technique for enticing the bass into striking is to drop a popper on the boat dock and then "plop" it

Early fall is a great time to fish fast-moving poppers for smallmouth bass, like this 5-pounder from the Susquehanna River.

onto the surface. It's an effort to convince the bass that something has just fallen from the dock. But balsa-wood and cork popping bugs often come down with such a solid "thunk" that the noise alerts the bass. This is where a deer-hair bug with a weed guard is the ticket. Deer-hair bugs arrive on the dock without a sound. They can then be dragged off the dock and into the water without alarming the bass.

Smallmouth bugs differ slightly from largemouth types. Smallmouth prefer a smaller bug, and they seem to strike better if the bug moves much faster. This is particularly true if you fish smallmouths in moving water, such as large rivers. The retrieve method is definitely different. The majority of largemouth bass fishing occurs in lakes, sloughs, tanks, and farm ponds. Here the largemouth prefers to view the bug before striking. But smallmouth bass in rivers have a different problem. If a bug is cast upstream of a good location and is allowed to drift, sometimes without moving for a minute or more, the current may take it silently overhead of the bass—and it may be unnoticed.

On a fast-moving river the bug has two advantages. A constantly manipulated popper is going to attract attention and will never drift overhead of a smallmouth without it being aware of the bug. Put yourself in the smallmouth's position. As it lies behind a rock, it sees a parade of things drifting by on the current. If whatever goes by is unmoving or inert, it lacks appeal. Suddenly here comes something that appears small, helpless, and struggling. The instincts take over and the bass rises quickly to strike before the creature can be taken away on the current. The other advantage of a fast-moving bug is that it can cover so much more water. In a large river, where the bottom is unseen, the more water your popping bug can cover, the more fish you offer it to, and the better your chances for a hookup. In fact, in many bass fishing situations I try to have the bug (or streamer) hit the water moving toward me. This is especially true in shallow water or when the fly or bug lands near an ambush spot. The bass's reaction when this strikes the water and begins moving is to catch it before it escapes.

One of the best methods of fishing for smallmouth on large rivers is to use a floating shooting head and combine it with a popping bug. I prefer a shooting line that is about thirty-five feet long (you have to be a slightly bet-

Larry Kreh demonstrates that long casts are often productive for fishing large rivers for bass.

ter than average caster to use this long a line), and I make it from double ta-pers that are one size larger than the rod calls for. Thus an 8-weight rod will handle a thirty-five-foot number 9 floating shooting-head line. I suggest using regular commercial shooting line in about size .030 to .038, which is thin and looks like a number 3 level line. With such an outfit a good caster can cast effortlessly to ninety or a hundred feet, and retrieve the bug to within about thirty-five feet, before picking up and sending it out over the water again. This same method can be used to fish streamers, too.

Bass Patterns

Among the streamers there is one fly that is supreme for smallmouths, and it has certainly performed well with largemouths. In fact, if I were limited to one underwater streamer for all my fishing, it would be the Clouser Minnow (see chapter 5). For smallmouths my favorite Clouser Minnow pattern, when I want to imitate baitfish, is to dress the fly with a white or yellow bucktail underwing and a top wing of gray. Approxi-mately four to eight strands of pearl Krystal Flash are tied in between the white and chartreuse bucktail.

Another color combination that has been very successful for me with both smallmouth and largemouth bass is a white belly of deer hair and a

A nice smallmouth bass and an assortment of flies that appeal to these great gamefish.

chartreuse deer-hair upper wing, with the same number of pearl Mylar strands in the center between the wings. I prefer a 1/50-, 1/32- or 1/24-ounce pair of lead eyes to get the fly down. Bob Clouser, who invented the pattern, has several other color combinations that also work well. He has a fly shop at 101 Ulrich Street, Middletown, PA 17057, and you can contact him to get them. If you tie flies, I suggest that you buy several of his favorite patterns and use them as samples to tie from.

The fly is fished two ways. It is cast across and very slightly downstream and allowed to sink and dead-drift. Since the hook point rides up, it rarely snags. The most popular method is to cast, let the fly descend below the surface, and then strip in a normal fashion, activating the fly by recovering line with the line hand.

If I were to list a half dozen fly patterns for largemouth bass, and another half dozen for smallmouths, one pattern that would be among the first three mentioned would be the Red-and-White Hackle streamer (see chapter 5). This is a very old fly, developed in the last century. The fly is as simple to make as any you'll ever tie. A regular shank hook (usually No. 2 to 1/0) is positioned in the vise, and six or eight white saddle or neck hackles are tied at the rear of the shank in splayed manner (like a pair of frog's legs). The fly can be tied as short as two and a half inches or as long as seven inches. Feathers should extend about two and a half inches behind the hook. Then the front of the hook shank has red hackle palmered to the hook eye. That's it! If you would like the fly to sink deeply, then add a conehead at the front of the fly.

I have tried many other color combinations with this pattern; some looked terrific to me but were only mildly accepted by bass. The fly is fished by throwing it in a likely spot and then slow-stripping to bring it back in a swimming motion. The feathery rear frog's legs kick and swim in an enticing motion, and the palmered hackle bends and flexes as the fly sweeps forward, then pauses. An unweighted Red-and-White Hackle fly can be dropped almost on the nose of a bass, for its water entry is incredibly soft. It also remains almost suspended in the water, so that you can swim it in front of a bass and slowly tease it along—something few other fly patterns can do and many bass find irresistible.

Bass in Ponds

Farm ponds are one of the best places to seek trophy largemouth bass. Many ponds are hard-fished when first constructed, but gradually the owners lose interest, and fishing pressure is reduced or even stops. Over time the few bass left in the pond grow larger. Then someone comes along, throws in a fly, lure, or bait, and hangs into a real trophy.

There's no better place than a farm pond to get a youngster started in fly fishing.

Farm ponds are often fertile and grow a fine crop of bluegills, frogs, insects, and other food that largemouth bass feed on. These can be great fish factories. This vast food supply grows some mighty fine bass. A number of farm ponds are also off the main roads, and even off the back roads. Many are out of sight of the public, and so they are only fished by the few who know about them.

There are some special techniques that when learned can help you catch many more bass from farm ponds. An understanding of how a farm pond is designed is helpful in understanding how to fish it. Most ponds are shallow on one end, deeper at the other end. Both areas can be effectively fished—at different times of the day and according to the season. And many ponds have a standpipe at one end—almost always located at the deepest spot in the pond. The standpipe is a device that allows water to flow through it when the pond level gets too high. This means that the pipe itself furnishes some structure for bass to hide near and also to use as an ambush location. It is one of the best places in a pond to fish a fly— usually deep down. Any overhanging trees along the banks are great spots to find bass, since they furnish shade and insects fall from them. Always swim your fly near any trees that grow along a farm pond bank. A super-hot spot is any place where there is rock rubble along a shoreline. Most farm pond banks are of dirt, which furnishes little cover for crayfish, frogs, and other aquatic creatures. Boat docks create both shade and an ambush location. In midsummer the standpipe and the boat dock can be two of the best places for a fly fisherman to investigate.

There is a proper way to work a farm pond with a fly rod. Most ponds have fences nearby; high grass and other obstructions litter the banks. All

WRONG: Irv Swope demonstrates how not to fish a farm pond or lakeshore. A backcast thrown over the ground is bound to hit a tree or some other obstruction.

of these can snag your backcast. If you proceed around the pond in the wrong direction, you will be throwing your fly line back into these obstructions. Let's say you are walking with the pond on your left and you are right-handed. That means the backcast will be made toward the obstructions. But if you turn and walk with the water on the same side as the hand you cast with, you can keep your backcast over the water, reducing your chances of fouling the backcast.

RIGHT: Throwing his backcast over the water, Irv has a much better chance of success.

A brochure for farmers put out years ago by the federal government was a key to teaching me how to fish farm ponds. Farmers plagued with too many bluegill in their ponds wanted to get rid of many of them. This brochure, developed by fishery scientists, told them how to do it by spreading a chemical in the water that killed these small but prolific fish. Since the chemical could be harmful to both bass and bluegill, a special technique was used to prevent killing the bass.

The scientists said you should spread the chemical on windy days, when the water was rippled slightly. The scientists also said that the bass feed in the shallows during the very early morning and late evening, and that most of the time they spend their daylight hours in the depths. The bluegill had just the opposite habits. They preferred to remain in the depths until the sun was well up, and then they moved to the shallows, remaining there during the bright portion of the day. Maybe that is why they are often called sunfish. The scientists suggested not placing the chemicals in the water along the banks until several hours after dawn. During the day the wind-rippled water would dissipate the chemicals, so that they would not harm the bass.

What this told me is that you should fish for bass along the shorelines early and late in the day—and in the deeper parts of the pond during midday. Of course, it also told me where to fish for the bluegill, too.

Farm ponds take on a water temperature nearly equal to the air temperature during midsummer in the midportion of the United States. While some bass will feed when water temperatures are in the upper eighties, most of the larger bass do not. But these bass have to eat, and they will do so when the pond's summer temperature is at its lowest during a twenty-four-hour period. That is usually from midnight to dawn.

I have never had great success with smallmouth bass when fishing at night. This would include the use of fly, spin, and plug tackle. But largemouths are a different breed. Some of the biggest largemouth bass I have caught in farm ponds were taken on hot July or August nights. Two types of flies were effective. One was the popping bug. It needs to be worked slowly, with a minimum amount of noise. Loud popping sounds never drew many strikes for me. The other factor important in getting large numbers of strikes is that the bug has to be popped frequently. The reason may be that a constant sound source is easier for bass to locate. The other fly that I did very well with was the Red-and-White Hackle fly. This ancient bass pattern, with its hackle radiating out from the hook and a wagging tail, creates a lot of underwater vibration, even at a slow speed, which the bass are easily able to find.

For many anglers, bonefish offer the ultimate challenge in fly fishing. They are more nervous than a cat in a dog pound, and when hooked they make high-speed runs that few gamefish can match.

Bonefish and Permit

Several special fishing techniques will help you catch more bonefish. If you don't hire a guide, and you seek your own bonefish, you know that cold weather can put them off the flats. The worst times to fish the flats are during and just after a cold spell. That is especially true if the flats are light in color. The bottom reflects the heat back into the atmosphere. But where there are grass-covered flats or where the bottom is dark in color, the water will be several degrees warmer. At such times these are good flats to fish. An even better place is where there is a basin or bay with a dark bottom. Such bodies of water frequently will drain through small outlets on a falling tide. This concentrates the warmer water. The bonefish will often feed in these warm water flows.

Another excellent place to fish for bonefish is where, on a falling tide, the flat is drained through a portion of the flat that is slightly deeper. These deeper portions are indentations that drain the last of the water from the flat into a nearby channel. One of the best places to find these is at Christmas Island. These are some of the finest wading flats in the world. If you can locate these drainage areas, you can often stand for the last half of the falling tide in one place and throw your flies to bonefish that are using these slightly deeper ditches to escape from the flat to deeper water.

When you are wading for bonefish, the type of shoes worn is important to comfort. For many years we simply slipped on a pair of old sneakers and stepped into the water. Any old-timer can tell you that it could sometimes be a painful experience, as the shoes filled with mud and small, sharp stones or shells. In 1983 I went to Christmas Island and began wading in diving shoes. They were much better, but the soles were not made for walking, and before my next trip my shoe repairman glued heavy neoprene soles on them—much better. Today many models of flats wading shoes are available. Remember, flats boots that are light in color are much cooler than darker ones. Most have thick, comfortable soles on them. Those with a sole of heavy, absorbent felt, while comfortable, pick up grit and dirt while you are wading. Unless these are scrubbed well and air-dried when you return home, they will pick up odors. Actually, there is almost no chance to slip on a saltwater flat, so the felt sole isn't needed. One other tip—I find that after several trips the zippers will become difficult to move and sometimes even get stuck. The treatment that works for me is this: Wash the wading boots with warm, soapy water and rinse well as soon as possible upon returning home. When they are thoroughly dry, rub a bar of soap into the zipper teeth on both tracks. A candle works just as well, and the wax remains longer on the zipper teeth. With either of these applications the zipper will usually work well for many trips.

There is a method I use when wearing the boots that prevents almost any grit or mud from getting inside. It requires the wearing of long pants, which I very much suggest. There are three reasons for wearing long pants. They help prevent sunburn to the legs. Some flats have minute shells imbedded in the muck, and if you wade these flats with bare legs, these tiny shells get into the skin and feel like itching powder. This itching can last several days. Long pants will reduce that itching to a minimum. The main reason for wearing them is to keep out grit and dirt. There is a proper procedure for putting on the diving boots. Put on your long pants, then the boots. Do not put the pants inside the boots! Fold the pant legs around the boots and then place a pair of gravel guards around the boots and over the folded pants. Close the gravel guards. The gravel guard, clamped firmly around the boot, will not allow any grit to force its way upward and into the top of the boot. The pants, because they are positioned outside the boot, cause any debris that enters the top to flow down and out the bottom of the pant legs.

When fishing permit on the flats, you should usually try to fish them during spring tide weeks, when there is more water on the flats. To maneuver and feed well, permit need more water than do bonefish. Few permit will feed on a flat that has less than two feet of water—although I once saw a permit on its side, swimming like a flounder after a crab in the Marquesas Keys, west of Key West.

Permit tend to move faster than bonefish, so you usually have less time to make your cast. That means you need to be ready to throw your fly when you see one. Permit are very hard to see, simply because most of their body is silvery in color. There is a thin black line along the back and along the outside edge of the tail. Many times what you will see is this indistinct Y coursing through the water.

For many years we caught few permit with fly tackle. Those taken were usually caught while fishing around wrecks. But with new flies and different techniques, many permit are now being taken. Del Brown, as of this writing, has taken nearly five hundred permit on fly, far more than any other angler. He says, "The main criterion for taking a permit on a fly is that you fish for them a lot and throw flies to many of them." That is certainly true.

Del's advice is worth listening to: He feels that most of the time you should throw the fly no more than three feet in front of a permit and allow it to sink quickly.

The natural crab, threatened by a permit, dives as fast as it can for the bottom, hopefully to hide from the predatory fish. The crab doesn't slowly go to the bottom; it goes as fast as it can. Therefore, **crab imitations** that sink in a horizontal position, or slowly, are not as effective as those crabs that are weighted at the forward end and dive—just like a natural crab—instead of settling like a saucer through the water. Remember, if the crab pattern has its weight evenly distributed over the bottom, that will cause it to settle slower. Del uses his famous Merkin Fly, and he tapers the front end so that it will dive faster.

A natural crab won't root around on the bottom while a permit is around. That would create a puff of mud that might give its location away. Instead it sits motionless on the bottom, hoping that the permit won't see it. The crab lies motionless on the flat's floor as the permit streaks toward it. The permit knows that the crab will be motionless, so it's expecting that.

Only if a permit looks over the imitation and obviously is moving away do experienced permit anglers move the fly—and then only a tiny bit. The fish will notice any subtle movement on the part of the crab fly. Crabs know this and refuse to move when a permit is close by. Therefore, lack of fly movement once the offering is dropped to the sea floor is critical.

Permit have the ability to suck in a crab, crush it, and rapidly spit out the shell. The fly fisherman has to watch the fly and the fish. The fly line should be gently taut between the angler's hand and the imitation crab. If any pressure is felt on the line (the permit may be sucking in the fly), use a strip strike to set the hook.

The only exception to the above, so far as an exact imitation is concerned, is when I use a Clouser Minnow, dressed with ⅟₃₆- or ⅟₂₄-ounce lead eyes. This fly has been fairly effective on permit and big bonefish. It is dressed on a No. I/O hook. The bottom of the wing is of white bucktail, then eight to ten strands of pearl Krystal Flash are tied on, and the top half of the wing is a similar number of chartreuse-colored bucktail strands. It is tied rather sparsely. Throw the fly well in front of a cruising permit. As soon as it is seen, allow it to sink quickly to the bottom. Let it lie still; if the permit refuses it, make only the tiniest movements to the fly. That should be done only if you feel the permit has lost interest. I've seen permit circle a fly and appear to be moving away, then suddenly dart down and grab it.

Occasionally, there are times when a floating crab pattern works well on bonefish and permit. Crabs are often plucked off the surface by both of these fish. Where the tide is moving fairly fast, especially in a channel, a floating crab will often do a better job than one on the bottom. That is why you should carry different crab patterns dressed so they float, sink fairly rapidly, or sink very quickly.

The size of a crab pattern need not be large. Permit eagerly eat crabs that are the size of a quarter or smaller. I never use a fly larger than this. This is especially true when fishing for bonefish. For bonefish, one the size of your thumbnail is ideal, and for permit you never need one more than twice that size. The best floating crabs I have used are the rug yarn types, where strands of acrylic rug yarn are tied at right angles to the hook shank and then trimmed to shape. For legs, rubber bands knotted at the ends work well. The fly is thrown in front of the fish and given very little movement.

When you are forced to fish in thick turtle grass for bonefish, a Bend Back style of fly is preferred (see chapter 5). Better hookups occur if Bend Back flies are dressed on 2X or 3X long hook shanks rather than on normal shanks. While experienced anglers caution that the hook should be bent only slightly, I bend them farther when tying flies to be fished in this dense grass. Since the fly is usually moving in among the strands of turtle grass, the fish doesn't notice that the fly's wing is slightly separated from the hook shank. Also, I will use buoyant wing materials such as bucktail when possible. In stands of turtle grass the bead-chain and lead-eye flies, such as Clouser Minnows and Crazy Charleys, frequently entangle in the grass, so you should avoid using them at this time.

When cruising bonefish, the distance the fly is placed in front of the fish is governed by fishing conditions. Obviously a No. 2 fly dressed in the same pattern as a No. 8 will have to be dropped farther ahead and with more caution. The size and weight of the fly are critical to how far ahead it must be positioned on the cast. The materials the fly is made from are

Nearly all bonefish flies are fished on the bottom. For this reason almost all are tied with the wing reversed, so that the hook point rides upright.

also an important factor. An epoxy fly, or a crab that has the belly plastered with epoxy or similar hard materials, crashes atop the water with a loud splash. On the other hand, a fluffy fly enters the water with a fairly soft impact.

The most popular size hook to dress flies on for bonefish is No. 4, standard length. The following suggestions on how far ahead of the bonefish you should place the fly are offered with the assumption that you are using a No. 4 hook and the fly is neither one that crashes hard to the surface nor parachutes to the surface. Examples of flies that you might use for the following suggested distances are the Crazy Charley with bead-chain eyes, the Gotcha, and the Clouser Minnow.

On wind-rippled water the fly can often be placed four to five feet in front of the fish. In water more than two feet deep, unless conditions are very calm, the same cast usually works well. But when fish are in water less than eighteen inches deep, the fly must be thrown farther ahead. If conditions are very calm, along with extra shallow water, a fly that is offered at least twelve feet ahead is suggested.

When fish are tailing (they will have the head down and tail projecting above the surface), the fly can be placed much closer. I frequently will drop the fly within two feet of the fish. But the direction in which you retrieve the fly past the bonefish is important. Consider that the bonefish is doing one of two things. The fish is wriggling and rooting in the bottom.

It is poised over a spot that it feels holds food, and with a sudden sucking motion the bonefish inhales part of the bottom and any prey that may be hidden there. Either way the fish creates a puff of mud around the prey. Because bonefish consider themselves prey (and they are, to barracudas and sharks), they always try to keep their heads pointed into the tide when dislodging food. The current sweeps the mud away from their eyes and gives them maximum vision while on the bottom. Rarely does a bonefish create a muddy disturbance from a downcurrent position. Such an action would clothe its head in murky water, making it vulnerable to a predator.

If this is understood, the angler notes the current direction after seeing the fish rooting and tailing. A cast is then made upcurrent and slightly to the far side of the fish. Then the fly is slow-stripped in short spurts through the puff of mud. Since the fish is actively seeking prey, it will usually not notice the fly's impact close by. Since it is in a feeding mood, it will usually hit the fly immediately.

When fishing for bones (especially in the Bahamas and along the coasts of Mexico and Belize), bonefish will often mud. That is, they will collectively root in the bottom for food. I have seen muds so large that they would cover ten football fields in some of the open basins and bays in the Bahamas. What is very effective for fly fishermen is to locate a mud smaller than this. Many times when a tide falls, the fish will collect in a deep pool that is surrounded by dry flats, or nearly dry ones. The fish will then mud in the bottom. At such times a fly that sinks quickly, such as a Clouser Minnow or Crazy Charley (both with lead eyes), and is worked through the active part of the mud, will draw a strike on nearly every cast. Since vision is reduced for the fish in the mud, fighting a bonefish doesn't usually disturb the others. You also should fish where the bones are actively feeding. The brightest-colored mud will indicate that. Note the current direction and then cast at the upcurrent edge of the brightest mud. The school will frequently be progressing slowly over the bottom, so you will want to continue to cast where the mud is the brightest. Because it is not very challenging, I prefer not to fish in such muds.

There is another, more subtle type of mud that usually indicates larger bonefish. As you are moving over a flat in a boat, you may note what appears to be a faint and small, thin cloud of mud. It seems to be dissipating in the tidal flow. Look around; see if you can locate another such cloud, but one a little denser. Chances are you can. Have the boat move in that direction, and perhaps you will see another cloud even more dense—and finally, locate a big bonefish. What happens is that larger bonefish frequently cruise alone or with only one or two other bonefish. They will tilt down over a suspected prey hidden in the sand. They disturb the light sand or mud covering the bottom to expose the prey. This creates that small cloud of mud that you see. The darker the mud cloud, the fresher it is, and the closer you are to the bonefish. Many trophy bonefish have been located using this trick.

The bonefish's habit of making these depressions in the sand is also helpful in determining if a flat might have actively feeding bonefish on it. The depressions closely resemble a minor volcano after it has blown its top. If the depression is fresh, it will be obvious to you. If it was made several days to more than a week ago, surrounding bottom sand or mud will begin to sift over the edges, something that is easily discernible. When you pole a flat, look for such blowholes. If they are fresh, then you can assume that fish are actively feeding here. If you see no bonefish, it may be

Irv Swope shows that there is a great deal of satisfaction in fly fishing on small streams.

that you are there on the wrong tidal phase. Try to return later when the tide is different.

You may have encountered the situation where you are familiar with certain flats where you have had consistent luck for a long time. Then you go there at the right time on several occasions and see few bonefish. The flats appear the same, and there has been no major environmental occurrence. The water seems as clear as ever, and there's been no additional fishing pressure. What happened to make them abandon the flat? Scientists have determined that bonefish graze flats, just as cattle or sheep graze a field. If they crop the grass too low, then the cattle and sheep feed in another area. The same thing happens to bonefish. There is only so much food on a flat, and when the bonefish have harvested a good bit of it, it becomes uneconomical from an energy standpoint for them to continue seeking food there. Thus they will head to nearby flats and allow this one to recover, just as a farmer allows certain fields to lie uncultivated.

Fly Fishing Small Streams

Scattered around the middle portion of the United States (from Indiana and Ohio through Pennsylvania, New Jersey, and south into Alabama and east to the Atlantic Ocean) are hundreds of smaller creeks and streams. These are waterways that are too small to be considered rivers. They are warmwater streams, not suitable for trout, although in the upper ends of many, trout do thrive.

The most common fish that anglers seek in these watersheds are small- and largemouth bass, sunfish of various species, rock bass (sometimes called redeyes), and fallfish. Occasionally pickerel will also be found in some of the more northern creeks.

Such creeks are usually too small for boats, although many can be fished with canoes. The anglers paddle (often dragging over the shallows) to the best fishing areas. Where mill dams or natural dams impede the flow, there will often be pools too deep to wade, which can be effectively fished from a canoe. But most of these streams are best fished by wading. All you need is a pair of old sneakers, although wading shoes designed for the purpose are much better. I prefer light summer pants, since wading is usually performed during the warmer summer months.

Only a few flies are needed, and I stick them in a small block of plastic foam hung around my neck, or I carry one small box loaded with the right patterns. The ideal fly rod is a 5- or 6-weight, and a floating line is all you'll need. The leader should be about nine feet, tapering to a tippet of four or six pounds.

One of the most effective flies is a tiny popping bug dressed on a No. 8 or 10 hook. Keep the offering sparse—no need for rubber bands and heavily adorned hackled bugs. Color seems to be unimportant. I actually prefer yellow, because I can see it so well. You will be fishing many shaded areas where the bright spot of yellow helps you see better.

Other flies that are deadly are small Clouser Minnows, dressed on No. 6 or 8 hooks. Those dressed with medium brown or medium olive are especially effective when worked along the bottom. I believe that the fish think they are either crayfish or sculpins. Small sculpins dressed on No. 6 or 8 hooks are also deadly. Little Zonkers in white, chartreuse, yellow, black, or olive work very well. Woolly Buggers are also a good bet. Along with these you should carry a few bluegill flies. Any wet flies will work, but one of the best is simply a No. 8 or 10 regular-shank hook wound with chenille and a wrap or two of grouse hackle at the front.

These streams are great training grounds for the fly fisherman who wants to learn many of the fundamentals of angling. You are fishing small, clear streams, where visibility is high and you can see fish. You are soon aware that the fish can also see you. Many things you do are quickly observed to be correct or foolish. If you see a smallmouth bass taking something off the surface and you wade through the pool at a rapid pace, you

The water below a dam is often a hot spot for smallmouth bass and other species.

instantly recognize that the bass felt the vibrations as the waves pushed against it, and the fish flees. Slow wading is the ticket.

You also quickly learn that the larger fish in most pools, when feeding, will be located at the tail of the pool, or at the head. Both of these areas have a stronger flow and concentrate the water, thus giving the fish easier access to any food being carried by the currents. It doesn't take long to learn, too, that you need to approach the lower end of a pool with stealth, and that a careful cast in the tail of the pool will catch you a fish. But making a cast well up into the pool may spook all fish lying between you and where your fly landed. Frightened by the line falling on the surface inches above them, these fleeing fish alert all other fish upstream from them in the pool.

Shade is useful and you quickly understand this. It's so much better to stand in the shade and close to the bank and cast into a small, clear pool than it is to position yourself out in bright sunlight. And bass, especially, prefer to hang out in shaded areas.

I learned a good lesson early in my small-stream fishing career. A friend and I fished a small stream where I had been doing very well on sunfish and smallmouth bass. I elected to go upstream from the bridge, while my friend, an excellent fly rodder, would fish downstream. We agreed to meet at a certain time for lunch. Then we planned to fish another nearby portion of the stream that afternoon.

Fish were in a taking mood, and I was kept busy landing small and medium-size sunfish and a number of smallmouths. The best one was a fourteen-inch bass that hit a small popping bug as it dropped near a log lying in the shade along a steep bank.

When I returned to the car for lunch, my friend was late. He finally arrived with a glum look on his face. He had caught almost nothing. Neither of us could understand it. It was hard to believe that fish upstream of the bridge were hitting so well and those below were so turned off. After lunch we drove to another section of the same stream. This time I fished down and my friend fished upstream. The situation was reversed. He did well, while I did poorly. From that experience we learned that there is a right and wrong way to fish these streams, if you are wading.

Apparently what happens when you wade downstream is that the debris, silt, and mud alert fish that someone is coming. We have confirmed this on many trips since that time, and we don't doubt for a minute that wading downstream will result in catching fewer fish.

These streams are training grounds for polishing many fly-fishing techniques. One of the most difficult techniques to master is knowing when a trout will accept your artificial nymph. There is a very brief and barely perceptible pause in the drifting line when the fish has the fly inside its mouth. You have only a very brief time to set the hook before the trout expels it. These pauses in the line's drift are often difficult to detect when you are a novice. But work with nymphs or wet flies, allowing them to drift in small-stream pools, as you would in a trout river. While bluegill will often hit the fly much stronger and give you a more perceptible pause in the line, they also take many flies very gently. I can think of no place better than a small stream filled with sunfish and small bass to learn quickly about seeing the pause in the drifting line when a fish inhales an underwater fly.

INDEX

Note: Boldface page numbers indicate an illustration.

Bimini Twist, 25, 148-51, **150–51**
Binoculars, 62, 76-77, **77,** 172
Birds, as indicators of fish location,
    62-63
Bitten, Dennis, 103
Bivisible dry fly, 103
Black Ghost (streamer), 110
Black-Nose Dace (streamer), 110
Blanton, Dan, 98, 114
Bluefish, 61, 91, 138
Bluegill, **24,** 108-09, 118, 213, 222,
    225, 234
Blue marlin, 108
Boat docks, fishing for bass from, **72,**
    73, 217-18, **223**
Boats
    color of, 70
    fighting fish from, **136**
    fishing shoreline from, 116
    noise of, 78, 217
    and small streams, 233
Body strikes, 128, 130
Bonefish, **226,** 226-233
    approaching, 78, **80,** 81
    casting range for, 11, 229-30
    casting to, **53,** 84, 91, 229-30
    catching, 118, 159
    fishing in turtle grass for, 229
    flies for, 230, **230**
    grazing behavior of, 74, 229-31,
      233
    hook size for, 230
    locating, 51, **52–53,** 56, 59, **59,**
      229-232
    and muds, 60, 231-32
    presentation to, 84, 89, 229-30
    wading for, 78, 226-27
Bonito, 63, 96
Borger, Gary, 188
Bowing (to a fish), 134
Boxfish, 56
Brassie fly, 194
Brown, Del, 228
Brown trout, 51, 77, 113, 143, 161, 184,
    night fishing for, 207-09
Bruun, Paul, **198**
Bubbles, as indicator of fish location,
    58-59
Bulkiness, of fly, 97
Burke, Dr. Edgar, 102
Butt guide, 21-23, 130-31

C

Caddis dry fly, 99, **100,** 106-07, 170,
    183, 196
Casa Mar, Costa Rica, 114
Casting, *see* Fly Casting
Catskill-tied flies, **100,** 100-101, **101,**
    167, 183
Caucci, Al, 102
Cerelli, Amy, **68–69**
Channel bass, 61
Christmas Island, 55, 226-27
Chumming, 187
Cigar-shaped grip, 21-22, **22**
Cleats, metal, 73
Climbing casts, 38-40
"Clock face method" of casting, 1,
    27-28
Clothing, color of, 69-70
Clouser, Bob, 113, 221
Clouser Minnow
    bass and, 113, 220
    bonefish and, 113, 229-31
    design of, **112,** 112-15
    for fishing small streams, 234
    permit and, 113, 229
    trout and, 113, 204, 207
Cobia, 56, 61, 96, 128, 140
Color
    of clothing and equipment, 69-70
    of flies, 97, 171, 175, 207, 217,
      220-21, 234
    as indicator of fish location, 51, 61,
      200, 226, 228
Comfort lift, **138**
Comparadun dry fly, 102
Conventional Dry Flies, 99-105, 184
Conventional Nail Knot, 9, 144-46,
    146, 157, **157**
Copper John Nymph, 194
Cork-type drag washers, 14-15
Cortland Braided Mono Running Line,
    7
Cortland Line Company, 4, 8
Crab imitations, 228-29
Crappie, 109
Crazy Charleys, 229-31
Creature imitations, 95, 117-19
Currents
    approach and, 74, **75–76,** 82, **82,**
      162-63, 231